Advance Praise for *Head First Programming*

"*Head First Programming* does a great job teaching programming using an iterative process. Add a little, explain a little, make the program a little better. This is how programming works in the real world and *Head First Programming* makes use of that in a teaching forum. I recommend this book to anyone who wants to start dabbling in programming but doesn't know where to start. I'd also recommend this book to anyone not necessarily new to programming, but curious about Python. It's a great intro to programming in general and programming Python specifically."

— Jeremy Jones, Coauthor of *Python for Unix and Linux System Administration*

"David Griffiths and Paul Barry have crafted the latest gem in the Head First series. Do you use a computer, but are tired of always using someone else's software? Is there something you wish your computer would do but wasn't programmed for? In *Head First Programming*, you'll learn how to write code and make your computer do things your way."

— Bill Mietelski, Software Engineer

"*Head First Programming* provides a unique approach to a complex subject. The early chapters make excellent use of metaphors to introduce basic programming concepts used as a foundation for the rest of the book. This book has everything, from web development to graphical user interfaces and game programming."

— Doug Hellmann, Senior Software Engineer, Racemi

"A good introduction to programming using one of the best languages around, *Head First Programming* uses a unique combination of visuals, puzzles, and exercises to teach programming in a way that is approachable and fun."

— Ted Leung, Principal Software Engineer, Sun Microsystems

Praise for other *Head First* books

"Kathy and Bert's *Head First Java* transforms the printed page into the closest thing to a GUI you've ever seen. In a wry, hip manner, the authors make learning Java an engaging 'what're they gonna do next?' experience."

— **Warren Keuffel, Software Development Magazine**

"Beyond the engaging style that drags you forward from know-nothing into exalted Java warrior status, *Head First Java* covers a huge amount of practical matters that other texts leave as the dreaded 'exercise for the reader....' It's clever, wry, hip and practical—there aren't a lot of textbooks that can make that claim and live up to it while also teaching you about object serialization and network launch protocols."

— **Dr. Dan Russell, Director of User Sciences and Experience Research IBM Almaden Research Center (and teaches Artificial Intelligence at Stanford University)**

"It's fast, irreverent, fun, and engaging. Be careful—you might actually learn something!"

— **Ken Arnold, former Senior Engineer at Sun Microsystems Coauthor (with James Gosling, creator of Java), *The Java Programming Language***

"I feel like a thousand pounds of books have just been lifted off of my head."

— **Ward Cunningham, inventor of the Wiki and founder of the Hillside Group**

"Just the right tone for the geeked-out, casual-cool guru coder in all of us. The right reference for practical development strategies—gets my brain going without having to slog through a bunch of tired, stale professor-speak."

— **Travis Kalanick, Founder of Scour and Red Swoosh Member of the MIT TR100**

"There are books you buy, books you keep, books you keep on your desk, and thanks to O'Reilly and the Head First crew, there is the penultimate category, Head First books. They're the ones that are dog-eared, mangled, and carried everywhere. Head First SQL is at the top of my stack. Heck, even the PDF I have for review is tattered and torn."

— **Bill Sawyer, ATG Curriculum Manager, Oracle**

"This book's admirable clarity, humor and substantial doses of clever make it the sort of book that helps even non-programmers think well about problem-solving."

— **Cory Doctorow, co-editor of Boing Boing Author, *Down and Out in the Magic Kingdom* and *Someone Comes to Town, Someone Leaves Town***

"I received the book yesterday and started to read it... and I couldn't stop. This is definitely très 'cool.' It is fun, but they cover a lot of ground and they are right to the point. I'm really impressed."

— **Erich Gamma, IBM Distinguished Engineer, and co-author of *Design Patterns***

"One of the funniest and smartest books on software design I've ever read."

— **Aaron LaBerge, VP Technology, ESPN.com**

"What used to be a long trial and error learning process has now been reduced neatly into an engaging paperback."

— **Mike Davidson, CEO, Newsvine, Inc.**

"Elegant design is at the core of every chapter here, each concept conveyed with equal doses of pragmatism and wit."

— **Ken Goldstein, Executive Vice President, Disney Online**

"I ♥ *Head First HTML with CSS & XHTML*—it teaches you everything you need to learn in a 'fun coated' format."

— **Sally Applin, UI Designer and Artist**

"Usually when reading through a book or article on design patterns, I'd have to occasionally stick myself in the eye with something just to make sure I was paying attention. Not with this book. Odd as it may sound, this book makes learning about design patterns fun.

"While other books on design patterns are saying 'Buehler… Buehler… Buehler…' this book is on the float belting out 'Shake it up, baby!'"

— **Eric Wuehler**

"I literally love this book. In fact, I kissed this book in front of my wife."

— **Satish Kumar**

Other related books from O'Reilly

Learning Python

Programming Python

Python Cookbook

Other books in O'Reilly's _Head First_ series

Head First Java™

Head First Object-Oriented Analysis and Design (OOA&D)

Head First HTML with CSS and XHTML

Head First Design Patterns

Head First Data Analysis

Head First Servlets and JSP

Head First EJB

Head First PMP

Head First SQL

Head First Software Development

Head First JavaScript

Head First Ajax

Head First Physics

Head First Statistics

Head First Rails

Head First PHP & MySQL

Head First Algebra

Head First Web Design

Head First **Programming**

Wouldn't it be dreamy if there were an introductory programming book that didn't make you wish you were anywhere other than stuck in front of your computer writing code? I guess it's just a fantasy...

Paul Barry
David Griffiths

Beijing • Cambridge • Farnham • Köln • Sebastopol • Taipei • Tokyo

Head First Programming

by Paul Barry and David Griffiths

Published by O'Reilly Media, Inc., 1005 Gravenstein Highway North, Sebastopol, CA 95472.

O'Reilly Media books may be purchased for educational, business, or sales promotional use. Online editions are also available for most titles (*safari.oreilly.com*). For more information, contact our corporate/institutional sales department: (800) 998-9938 or *corporate@oreilly.com*.

Series Creators:	Kathy Sierra, Bert Bates
Series Editor:	Brett D. McLaughlin
Editor:	Brian Sawyer
Cover Designers:	Steve Fehler
Production Editor:	Scott DeLugan
Proofreader:	Colleen Toporek
Indexer:	Angela Howard
Page Viewers:	David: Dawn; Paul: Deirdre, Joseph, Aaron, and Aideen

Printing History:

November 2009: First Edition.

Dawn (without whom the book would never have been finished)

Aideen (future singer/songwriter)

Deirdre (super mom)

Paul

Aaron and Joseph (real-life surfer dudes)

No surfers or snakes were harmed in the making of this book.

 This book uses RepKover,™ a durable and flexible lay-flat binding.

ISBN: 978-0-596-80237-0

We dedicate this book to the first person who looked at a computer and then asked the question, "I wonder how I make it do *this*... ?"

And to those that made programming complex enough that people need a book like ours to learn it.

David: To Dawn. The smartest person I know.

Paul: This one's dedicated to my father, Jim Barry, who, 25 years ago—when I needed a push—pushed me toward computing. That was a good push.

Authors of Head First Programming

Paul Barry

David Griffiths

Paul Barry recently worked out that he has been programming for close to a quarter century, a fact that came as a bit of a shock. In that time, Paul has programmed in lots of different programming languages, lived and worked in two countries on two continents, got married, had three kids (well... his wife Deirdre actually *had them*, but Paul did play his part), completed a B.Sc. and M.Sc. in Computing, written two other books, written a bunch of technical articles for *Linux Journal*, and managed *not* to lose his hair... a situation that, sadly, may in fact be changing.

When Paul first saw *Head First HTML with CSS & XHTML*, he loved it so much he knew immediately that the Head First approach would be a great way to teach programming. He is only too delighted, together with David, to create this book in an attempt to prove his hunch correct.

Paul's day job is working as a lecturer at The Institute of Technology, Carlow in Ireland. As part of the Department of Computing & Networking, Paul gets to spend his day exploring, learning, and teaching cool programming technologies, which is his idea of fun (and further proof that Paul probably needs to get out more). Paul hopes his students think the stuff he teaches is fun, too.

David Griffiths began programming at age 12, when he saw a documentary on the work of Seymour Papert. At age 15, he wrote an implementation of Papert's computer language LOGO. After studying Pure Mathematics at University, he began writing code for computers and magazine articles for humans. He's worked as an agile coach, a developer, and a garage attendant, but not in that order. He can write code in over 10 languages and prose in just one, and when not writing, coding, or coaching, he spends much of his spare time travelling with his lovely wife—and fellow *Head First* author—Dawn.

Before writing *Head First Programming*, he wrote another book called *Head First Rails*, which is an excellent read and would make a thoughtful gift for any close friend or family member.

You can follow him on Twitter at:

```
http://twitter.com/dgriffiths
```

Table of Contents (Summary)

	Intro	xxiii
1	Starting to Code: *Finding Your Way*	1
2	Textual Data: *Every String Has Its Place*	37
3	Functions: *Let's Get Organized*	77
4	Data Files and Arrays: *Sort It Out*	113
5	Hashes and Databases: *Putting Data in Its Place*	145
6	Modular Programming: *Keeping Things Straight*	177
7	Building a Graphical User Interface: *Going All Gooey*	215
8	GUIs and Data: *Data Entry Widgets*	257
8½	Exceptions and Message Boxes: *Get the Message?*	293
9	Graphical Interface Elements: *Selecting the Right Tool*	313
10	Custom Widgets and Classes: *With an Object in Mind*	349
i	Leftovers: The *Top Ten Things (We Didn't Cover)*	385

Table of Contents (the real thing)

Intro

Your brain on Programming. Here *you* are trying to *learn* something, while here your *brain* is doing you a favor by making sure the learning doesn't *stick*. Your brain's thinking, "Better leave room for more important things, like which wild animals to avoid and whether naked snowboarding is a bad idea." So how *do* you trick your brain into thinking that your life depends on knowing Programming?

Who is this book for?	xxiv
We know what you're thinking	xxv
Metacognition	xxvii
Bend your brain into submission	xxix
Read me	xxx
The technical review team	xxxii
Acknowledgments	xxxiii

1

starting to code

Finding your way

Writing programs gives you the power to control your PC.

Almost everyone knows how to *use* a computer, but few people take the next step and learn how to *control* it. If you use other people's software, you will always be limited by what other people think you want to do. Write your own programs and the only limit will be your own imagination. Programming will make you more creative, it will make you think more precisely, and it will teach you to analyze and solve problems logically.

Do you want to be programmed or be the programmer?

Programming lets you do more	2
So how do you run your code?	5
Create a new program file	6
Prepare and run your code	7
A program is more than a list of commands	12
Codeville: Your program is like a network of roads	13
Branches are code intersections	14
if/else branches	15
The Python code needs interconnecting paths	20
Python uses indents to connect paths	21
Loops let you run the same piece of code over and over again	28
Python's while loop	29
Your Programming Toolbox	35

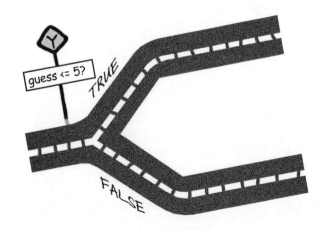

textual data

Every string has its place

2

Imagine trying to communicate without words.

All programs process data, and one of the most important types of data is **text**. In this chapter, you'll work through the basics of **textual data**. You'll automatically **search** text and get back **exactly what you're looking for**. Along the way, you'll pick up key programming concepts such as **methods** and how you can use them to **bend your data to your will**. And finally, you'll instantly **power up your programs** with the help of **library code**.

Your new gig at Starbuzz Coffee	38
Here's the current Starbuzz code	39
The cost is embedded in the HTML	41
A string is a series of characters	41
Find characters inside the text	42
But how do you get at more than one character?	43
The String Exposed	48
Beans'R'Us is rewarding loyal customers	50
Searching is complex	52
Python data is smart	54
Strings and numbers are different	64
The program has overloaded the Beans'R'Us Server	67
Time... if only you had more of it	68
You're already using library code	69
Order is restored	74
Your Programming Toolbox	75

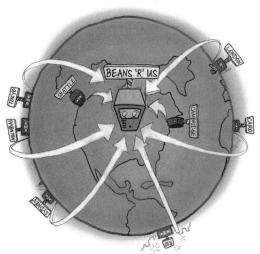

functions

Let's get organized

3

As programs grow, the code often becomes more complex.

And complex code can be hard to read, and even harder to maintain. One way of managing this complexity is to create **functions**. Functions are **snippets of code** that you use as needed from within your program. They allow you to **separate out common actions**, and this means that they make your code **easier to read** and **easier to maintain**. In this chapter, you'll discover how a little function knowledge can **make your coding life a whole lot easier**.

Starbuzz is out of beans!	78
What does the new program need to do?	79
Don't duplicate your code...	81
Reuse code with functions	82
Always get things in the right order	84
Return data with the return command	87
Use the Web, Luke	93
The function always sends the same message	94
Use parameters to avoid duplicating functions	96
Someone decided to mess with your code	102
The rest of the program can't see the password variable	104
When you call a function, the computer creates a fresh list of variables	105
When you leave a function, its variables get thrown away	106
Starbuzz is fully stocked!	110
Your Programming Toolbox	111

STARBUZZ
CORP
" BE INSPIRED
GET TOTALLY WIRED"

data files and arrays

Sort it out

4

As your programs develop, so do your data handling needs.

And when you have lots of data to work with, using an individual variable for each piece of data gets really old, really quickly. So programmers employ some rather awesome containers (known as **data structures**) to help them work with lots of data. More times than not, all that data comes from a file stored on a hard disk. So, how can you work with data in your files? Turns out it's a breeze.

> Hey, dude, it's Chapter 4... time for a break - let's catch some waves.

Surf's up in Codeville	114
Find the highest score in the results file	115
Iterate through the file with the open, for, close pattern	116
The file contains more than numbers...	120
Split each line as you read it	121
The split() method cuts the string	122
But you need more than one top score	126
Keeping track of 3 scores makes the code more complex	127
An ordered list makes code much simpler	128
Sorting is easier in memory	129
You can't use a separate variable for each line of data	130
An array lets you manage a whole train of data	131
Python gives you arrays with lists	132
Sort the array before displaying the results	136
Sort the scores from highest to lowest	139
And the winner is...?	142
You somehow forgot the surfer names	143
Your Programming Toolbox	144

hashes and databases

Putting data in its place

Arrays aren't the only show in town when it comes to data.

Programming languages come with other data-arranging goodies too, and our chosen tool, Python, is no exception. In this chapter, you'll **associate** values with names using a data structure commonly called the **hash** (better known as *dictionary* to Python-folk). And when it comes to working with **stored data**, you'll read data from an *external database system* as well as from regular text-based files. All the world's awash with data, so turn the page and start applying your ever-expanding programming skills to some cool data-processing tasks.

Who won the surfing contest?	146
Associate the name with the score	150
Associate a key with a value using a hash	153
Iterate hash data with for	154
The data isn't sorted	158
When data gets complex	160
Return a data structure from a function	164
Here's your new board!	168
Meanwhile, down at the studio...	169
The code remains the same; it's the function that changes	170
TVN's data is on the money!	174
Your Programming Toolbox	175

modular programming

Keeping things straight

6

The code that you write will make its way into many programs.

And, although **sharing** is good, you need to be *careful*. One programmer might take your code and use it in an **unexpected** way, while another might change it without even letting you know. You might want to use one function in all your programs and, over time, that function's code might **change** to suit your needs. Smart programmers take advantage of *modular programming techniques* to keep their workload manageable.

Head First Health Club is upgrading some systems	178
The program needs to create a transaction file	179
Use strings to format strings	180
The Format String Exposed	186
A late night email ruins your day	187
$50,000... for a donut?!	188
Only the sales from your program were rejected	189
The new bank uses a new format	190
Your coffee bar program still uses the old format	191
Don't just update your copy	192
So how do you create a module...?	193
The transaction file is working great, too	199
The health club has a new requirement	200
The Starbuzz code	205
The two discount functions have the same name	206
Fully Qualified Names (FQNs) prevent your programs from getting confused	207
The discounts get the customers flooding in	213
Your Programming Toolbox	214

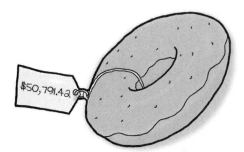

$50,791.42

7

building a graphical user interface

Going all gooey

Your coding skills are great and getting better all the time.

It's just a shame your programs are not that *nice* to look at. Displaying prompts and messages on a text-based console is all well and good, but it's so 1970s, isn't it? Add some green text on a black background and your retro look will be complete. There has to be *a better way* to communicate with your users than the console, and there is: using a **graphical user interface** or **GUI** (pronounced "gooey"). Sounds cool, but complex, and it can be. But, don't fret; learning a trick or two will have your code all graphical in no time. Let's get all gooey (sorry, GUI) in this chapter.

Head First TVN now produces game shows	216
pygame is cross platform	220
pygame Exposed	229
0... 2... 1... 9... blast off!	230
tkinter gives you the event loop for free	234
tkinter is packed with options	235
The GUI works, but doesn't do anything	238
Connect code to your button events	239
The GUI program's now ready for a screentest	244
But TVN is still not happy	246
Label it	249
Your Programming Toolbox	255

guis and data

Data entry widgets

GUIs don't just process events. They also handle data.

Almost all GUI applications need to read user data, and choosing the right widgets can change your interface from *data entry hell* to *user heaven*. Widgets can accept plain text, or just present a menu of options. There are lots of different widgets out there, which means there are lots of choices, too. And, of course, making the right choice can make all the difference. It's time to take your GUI program to the **next level**.

Head-Ex needs a new delivery system	258
They've already designed the interface	259
Read data from the GUI	260
The Entry and Text widgets let you enter text data into your GUI	261
Read and write data to text fields	262
Large Text fields are harder to handle	263
One of the Head-Ex deliveries went astray	270
Users can enter anything in the fields	271
Radio buttons force users to choose a valid depot	272
Creating radio buttons in tkinter	273
The radio buttons should work together	275
The radio buttons can share a model	276
The system tells the other widgets when the model changes	277
So how do you use models in tkinter?	278
Head-Ex's business is expanding	282
There are too many depots on the GUI	283
An OptionMenu lets you have as many options as needed	284
The model stays the same	285
Things are going great at Head-Ex	291
Your Programming Toolbox	292

Look, I don't care what you guys do, I'm gonna stay selected.

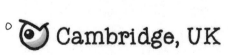 Cambridge, MA

Yeah, me too.

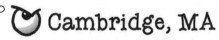 Cambridge, UK

Huh, and me.

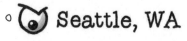 Seattle, WA

8½

exceptions and message boxes

Get the message?

Sometimes things just go wrong. You just need to handle it.

There will always be things beyond your control. Networks will fail. Files will disappear. Smart coders learn how to deal with those kinds of **errors** and make their programs **recover** gracefully. The best software keeps the user informed about the bad things that happen and what should be done to recover. By learning how to use **exceptions** and **message boxes**, you can take your software to the next level of reliability and quality.

What's that smell?	294
Someone changed the file permissions	295
When it couldn't write to the file, the program threw an exception	296
Catch the exception	297
Watch for exceptions with try/except	298
There's an issue with the exception handler	302
A message box demands attention	303
Creating message boxes in Python	304
Your Programming Toolbox	311

graphical interface elements
Selecting the right tool

9

It's easy to make your programs more effective for your users.

And when it comes to GUI applications, there's a world of difference between a *working* interface and one that's both **useful** and **effective**. Selecting the right tool for the right job is a skill that comes with experience, and the best way to get that experience is to use the tools available to you. In this chapter, you'll continue to expand your GUI application building skills. There's a bunch of truly useful widgets waiting to be experienced. So, turn the page and let's get going.

Time to mix it up	314
The music just kept on playing...	318
Not all events are generated by button clicks	319
Capturing the protocol event isn't enough	326
Two buttons, or not two buttons? That is the question...	328
The checkbox is an on/off, flip/flop toggle	331
Working with checkboxes in tkinter	332
Pump up the volume!	336
Model a slider on a scale	337
Use pygame to set the volume	339
Use tkinter for everything else	340
The DJ is over the moon!	347
Your Programming Toolbox	348

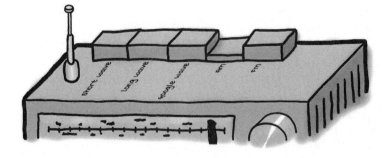

10

custom widgets and classes

With an object in mind

Requirements can be complex, but programs don't have to be.

By using object orientation, you can give your programs **great power** without writing lots of extra code. Keep reading, and you'll create **custom widgets** that do exactly what *you* want and give you the power to take **your programming skills to the next level**.

The DJ wants to play more than one track	350
Create code for each track as a function	351
The new function contains other functions	356
Your new function needs to create widgets and event handlers	357
The DJ is confused	362
Group widgets together	363
A frame widget contains other widgets	364
A class is a machine for creating objects	366
A class has methods that define behavior	367
But how does an object call a method?	369
The SoundPanel class looks a lot like the create_gui() function	370
class = methods + data	372
The Class Exposed	373
The DJ has an entire directory of tracks	378
It's party time!	382
Your Programming Toolbox	383
Leaving town...	384
It's been great having you here in Codeville!	384

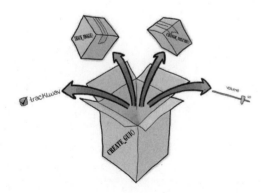

leftovers

The Top Ten Things (we didn't cover)

You've come a long way.

But learning how to program is an activity that never stops. The more you code, the more you'll need to **learn new ways to do certain things**. You'll need to master **new tools** and **new techniques**, too. There's just not enough room in this book to show you everything you might possibly need to know. So, here's our list of the top ten things we didn't cover that you might want to learn more about next.

#1: Doing things "The Python Way"	386
#2: Using Python 2	387
#3: Other programming languages	388
#4: Automated testing techniques	389
#5: Debugging	390
#6: Command-line execution	391
#7: Ooops... we could've covered more OOP	392
#8: Algorithms	393
#9: Advanced programming topics	394
#10: Other IDEs, shells and text editors	395

how to use this book

Intro

In this section we answer the burning question:
"So why DID they put that in a programming book?"

Who is this book for?

If you can answer "yes" to all of these:

1 Do you wish you had the know-how to control your computer and make it do new things?

2 Do you want to learn how to program, so you can create the next big thing in software, make a small fortune, and ← retire to your own private island?

OK, maybe that one's a little far-fetched. But, you gotta start somewhere, right?

3 Do you prefer actually doing things and applying the stuff you learn over listening to someone in a lecture rattle on for hours on end?

this book is for you.

Who should probably back away from this book?

If you can answer "yes" to any of these:

1 Are you a seasoned programmer? Do you already know how to program?

2 Are you looking for a quick introduction or reference book to Python?

3 Would you rather have your toenails pulled out by 15 screaming monkeys than learn something new? Do you believe a programming book should cover *everything* and if it bores the reader to tears in the process then so much the better?

this book is **not** for you.

[Note from marketing: this book is for anyone with a credit card... we'll accept a check, too.]

We know what you're thinking

"How can *this* be a serious Programming book?"

"What's with all the graphics?"

"Can I actually *learn* it this way?"

We know what your *brain* is thinking

Your brain craves novelty. It's always searching, scanning, *waiting* for something unusual. It was built that way, and it helps you stay alive.

So what does your brain do with all the routine, ordinary, normal things you encounter? Everything it *can* to stop them from interfering with the brain's *real* job—recording things that *matter*. It doesn't bother saving the boring things; they never make it past the "this is obviously not important" filter.

How does your brain *know* what's important? Suppose you're out for a day hike and a tiger jumps in front of you, what happens inside your head and body?

Neurons fire. Emotions crank up. *Chemicals surge*.

And that's how your brain knows...

This must be important! Don't forget it!

But imagine you're at home, or in a library. It's a safe, warm, tiger-free zone. You're studying. Getting ready for an exam. Or trying to learn some tough technical topic your boss thinks will take a week, ten days at the most.

Just one problem. Your brain's trying to do you a big favor. It's trying to make sure that this *obviously* non-important content doesn't clutter up scarce resources. Resources that are better spent storing the really *big* things. Like tigers. Like the danger of fire. Like how you should never have posted those "party" photos on your Facebook page. And there's no simple way to tell your brain, "Hey brain, thank you very much, but no matter how dull this book is, and how little I'm registering on the emotional Richter scale right now, I really *do* want you to keep this stuff around."

Your brain thinks THIS is important.

Great. Only 464 more dull, dry, boring pages.

Your brain thinks THIS isn't worth saving.

We think of a "Head First" reader as a learner.

So what does it take to *learn* something? First, you have to *get* it, then make sure you don't *forget* it. It's not about pushing facts into your head. Based on the latest research in cognitive science, neurobiology, and educational psychology, *learning* takes a lot more than text on a page. We know what turns your brain on.

Some of the Head First learning principles:

Make it visual. Images are far more memorable than words alone, and make learning much more effective (up to 89% improvement in recall and transfer studies). It also makes things more understandable. **Put the words within or near the graphics** they relate to, rather than on the bottom or on another page, and learners will be up to *twice* as likely to solve problems related to the content.

Use a conversational and personalized style. In recent studies, students performed up to 40% better on post-learning tests if the content spoke directly to the reader, using a first-person, conversational style rather than taking a formal tone. Tell stories instead of lecturing. Use casual language. Don't take yourself too seriously. Which would *you* pay more attention to: a stimulating dinner party companion, or a lecture?

Get the learner to think more deeply. In other words, unless you actively flex your neurons, nothing much happens in your head. A reader has to be motivated, engaged, curious, and inspired to solve problems, draw conclusions, and generate new knowledge. And for that, you need challenges, exercises, and thought-provoking questions, and activities that involve both sides of the brain and multiple senses.

Get—and keep—the reader's attention. We've all had the "I really want to learn this but I can't stay awake past page one" experience. Your brain pays attention to things that are out of the ordinary, interesting, strange, eye-catching, unexpected. Learning a new, tough, technical topic doesn't have to be boring. Your brain will learn much more quickly if it's not.

Touch their emotions. We now know that your ability to remember something is largely dependent on its emotional content. You remember what you care about. You remember when you *feel* something. No, we're not talking heart-wrenching stories about a boy and his dog. We're talking emotions like surprise, curiosity, fun, "what the...?" , and the feeling of "I Rule!" that comes when you solve a puzzle, learn something everybody else thinks is hard, or realize you know something that "I'm more technical than thou" Bob from engineering *doesn't*.

Metacognition: thinking about thinking

If you really want to learn, and you want to learn more quickly and more deeply, pay attention to how you pay attention. Think about how you think. Learn how you learn.

Most of us did not take courses on metacognition or learning theory when we were growing up. We were *expected* to learn, but rarely *taught* to learn.

I wonder how I can trick my brain into remembering this stuff...

But we assume that if you're holding this book, you really want to learn how to program And you probably don't want to spend a lot of time. If you want to use what you read in this book, you need to *remember* what you read. And for that, you've got to *understand* it. To get the most from this book, or *any* book or learning experience, take responsibility for your brain. Your brain on *this* content.

The trick is to get your brain to see the new material you're learning as Really Important. Crucial to your well-being. As important as a tiger. Otherwise, you're in for a constant battle, with your brain doing its best to keep the new content from sticking.

So just how *DO* you get your brain to treat programming like it was a hungry tiger?

There's the slow, tedious way, or the faster, more effective way. The slow way is about sheer repetition. You obviously know that you *are* able to learn and remember even the dullest of topics if you keep pounding the same thing into your brain. With enough repetition, your brain says, "This doesn't *feel* important to him, but he keeps looking at the same thing *over* and *over* and *over*, so I suppose it must be."

The faster way is to do **anything that increases brain activity,** especially different *types* of brain activity. The things on the previous page are a big part of the solution, and they're all things that have been proven to help your brain work in your favor. For example, studies show that putting words *within* the pictures they describe (as opposed to somewhere else in the page, like a caption or in the body text) causes your brain to try to makes sense of how the words and picture relate, and this causes more neurons to fire. More neurons firing = more chances for your brain to *get* that this is something worth paying attention to, and possibly recording.

A conversational style helps because people tend to pay more attention when they perceive that they're in a conversation, since they're expected to follow along and hold up their end. The amazing thing is, your brain doesn't necessarily *care* that the "conversation" is between you and a book! On the other hand, if the writing style is formal and dry, your brain perceives it the same way you experience being lectured to while sitting in a roomful of passive attendees. No need to stay awake.

But pictures and conversational style are just the beginning...

Here's what WE did:

We used **pictures**, because your brain is tuned for visuals, not text. As far as your brain's concerned, a picture really *is* worth a thousand words. And when text and pictures work together, we embedded the text *in* the pictures because your brain works more effectively when the text is *within* the thing the text refers to, as opposed to in a caption or buried in the text somewhere.

We used **redundancy**, saying the same thing in *different* ways and with different media types, and *multiple senses*, to increase the chance that the content gets coded into more than one area of your brain.

We used concepts and pictures in **unexpected** ways because your brain is tuned for novelty, and we used pictures and ideas with at least *some* **emotional** *content*, because your brain is tuned to pay attention to the biochemistry of emotions. That which causes you to *feel* something is more likely to be remembered, even if that feeling is nothing more than a little **humor**, **surprise**, or **interest.**

We used a personalized, **conversational style**, because your brain is tuned to pay more attention when it believes you're in a conversation than if it thinks you're passively listening to a presentation. Your brain does this even when you're *reading*.

We included more than 80 **activities**, because your brain is tuned to learn and remember more when you **do** things than when you *read* about things. And we made the exercises challenging-yet-do-able, because that's what most people prefer.

We used **multiple learning styles**, because *you* might prefer step-by-step procedures, while someone else wants to understand the big picture first, and someone else just wants to see an example. But regardless of your own learning preference, *everyone* benefits from seeing the same content represented in multiple ways.

We include content for **both sides of your brain**, because the more of your brain you engage, the more likely you are to learn and remember, and the longer you can stay focused. Since working one side of the brain often means giving the other side a chance to rest, you can be more productive at learning for a longer period of time.

And we included **stories** and exercises that present **more than one point of view,** because your brain is tuned to learn more deeply when it's forced to make evaluations and judgments.

We included **challenges**, with exercises, and by asking **questions** that don't always have a straight answer, because your brain is tuned to learn and remember when it has to *work* at something. Think about it—you can't get your *body* in shape just by *watching* people at the gym. But we did our best to make sure that when you're working hard, it's on the *right* things. That **you're not spending one extra dendrite** processing a hard-to-understand example, or parsing difficult, jargon-laden, or overly terse text.

We used **people**. In stories, examples, pictures, etc., because, well, because *you're* a person. And your brain pays more attention to *people* than it does to *things*.

Cut this out and stick it on your refrigerator.

Here's what YOU can do to bend your brain into submission

So, we did our part. The rest is up to you. These tips are a starting point; listen to your brain and figure out what works for you and what doesn't. Try new things.

1 **Slow down. The more you understand, the less you have to memorize.**

Don't just *read*. Stop and think. When the book asks you a question, don't just skip to the answer. Imagine that someone really *is* asking the question. The more deeply you force your brain to think, the better chance you have of learning and remembering.

2 **Do the exercises. Write your own notes.**

We put them in, but if we did them for you, that would be like having someone else do your workouts for you. And don't just *look* at the exercises. **Use a pencil.** There's plenty of evidence that physical activity *while* learning can increase the learning.

3 **Read the "There are No Dumb Questions"**

That means all of them. They're not optional sidebars, *they're part of the core content!* Don't skip them.

4 **Make this the last thing you read before bed. Or at least the last challenging thing.**

Part of the learning (especially the transfer to long-term memory) happens *after* you put the book down. Your brain needs time on its own, to do more processing. If you put in something new during that processing time, some of what you just learned will be lost.

5 **Talk about it. Out loud.**

Speaking activates a different part of the brain. If you're trying to understand something, or increase your chance of remembering it later, say it out loud. Better still, try to explain it out loud to someone else. You'll learn more quickly, and you might uncover ideas you hadn't known were there when you were reading about it.

6 **Drink water. Lots of it.**

Your brain works best in a nice bath of fluid. Dehydration (which can happen before you ever feel thirsty) decreases cognitive function.

7 **Listen to your brain.**

Pay attention to whether your brain is getting overloaded. If you find yourself starting to skim the surface or forget what you just read, it's time for a break. Once you go past a certain point, you won't learn faster by trying to shove more in, and you might even hurt the process.

8 **Feel something.**

Your brain needs to know that this *matters*. Get involved with the stories. Make up your own captions for the photos. Groaning over a bad joke is *still* better than feeling nothing at all.

9 **Write a lot of code!**

There's only one way to learn to program: **writing a lot of code**. And that's what you're going to do throughout this book. Coding is a skill, and the only way to get good at it is to practice. We're going to give you a lot of practice: every chapter has exercises that pose a problem for you to solve. Don't just skip over them—a lot of the learning happens when you solve the exercises. We included a solution to each exercise—don't be afraid to **peek at the solution** if you get stuck! (It's easy to get snagged on something small.) But try to solve the problem before you look at the solution. And definitely get it working before you move on to the next part of the book.

Read Me

This is a learning experience, not a reference book. We deliberately stripped out everything that might get in the way of learning whatever it is we're working on at that point in the book. And the first time through, you need to begin at the beginning, because the book makes assumptions about what you've already seen and learned.

This is not Head First Python.

We use release 3 of the Python programming language throughout this book, but this fact alone does not make this book *Head First Python*. We chose Python because it's a great programming language to start with and it's also a great programming language to grow with. In fact, Python might be the only programming language you'll ever need to learn and use (although your employer might think otherwise). Of course, you have to start with something, and we can think of no better programming language to use than Python when first learning how to program. That said, this book isn't designed to teach you Python; it's designed to teach you *programming*, so most of the things we show you are designed to *hightlight the programming concept*, not the Python feature.

You need to install Python 3 on your computer.

To run the programs in this book, you need to download and install Python 3 on your computer. This isn't as hard as it sounds. Pop on over to the Python download site and select the option that fits best with the computer you are using. Just be sure to select release 3 of Python, *not* release 2: ***http://www.python.org/download***.

We begin by teaching some basic programming concepts, then we start putting programming to work for you right away.

We cover the fundamentals of programming in Chapter 1. That way, by the time you make it all the way to Chapter 2, you are creating programs that actually do something real, useful, and—gulp!—fun. We are guessing you'll be amazed by how much you can do with less than a dozen lines of code in Chapter 2. The rest of the book then builds on your programming skills turning you from *programming newbie* to *coding ninja master* in no time.

The activities are NOT optional.

The exercises and activities are not add-ons; they're part of the core content of the book. Some of them are to help with memory, some are for understanding, and some will help you apply what you've learned. ***Don't skip the exercises.***

The redundancy is intentional and important.

One distinct difference in a Head First book is that we want you to *really* get it. And we want you to finish the book remembering what you've learned. Most reference books don't have retention and recall as a goal, but this book is about *learning*, so you'll see some of the same concepts come up more than once.

The examples are as lean as possible.

Our readers tell us that it's frustrating to wade through 200 lines of an example looking for the two lines they need to understand. Most examples in this book are shown within the smallest possible context, so that the part you're trying to learn is clear and simple. Don't expect all of the examples to be robust, or even complete—they are written specifically for learning, and aren't always fully-functional.

We've placed a lot of the code examples on the Web so you can copy and paste them as needed. You'll find them at two locations:

http://www.headfirstlabs.com/books/hfprog/ and

http://programming.itcarlow.ie

The Brain Power exercises don't have answers.

For some of them, there is no right answer, and for others, part of the learning experience of the Brain Power activities is for you to decide if and when your answers are right. In some of the Brain Power exercises, you will find hints to point you in the right direction.

The technical review team

Doug Hellman

Ted Leung

Jeremy Jones

Bill Mietelski

Technical Reviewers:

Doug Hellmann is a Senior Software Engineer at Racemi and former Editor in Chief for *Python Magazine*. He has been programming in Python since version 1.4 and prior to Python worked mostly with C on a variety of Unix and non-Unix platforms. He has worked on projects ranging from mapping to medical news publishing, with a little banking thrown in for good measure. Doug spends his spare time working on several open source projects; reading science fiction, history, and biographies; and writing the Python Module of the Week blog series.

Jeremy Jones is the coauthor of *Python for Unix and Linux System Administration* and has been actively using Python since 2001. He has been a developer, system administrator, quality assurance engineer, and tech support analyst. They all have their rewards and challenges, but his most challenging and rewarding job has been husband and father.

Ted Leung has been programming in Python since 2002 and is currently a Principal Software Engineer at Sun Microsystems. He has a Bachelor of Science degree in Mathematics from the Massachusetts Institute of Technology and a Master's of Science degree in computer science from Brown University. Ted's weblog is available at http://www.sauria.com/blog

Bill Mietelski has been an Information Technology geek for over 20 years. He's currently a Software Engineer at a leading national academic medical center in the Chicagoland area, working on statistical research studies. When he's not at the office or tied to a computer, you'll find him at a golf course chasing a little white ball.

Acknowledgments

Our editor:

Brian Sawyer was *Head First Programming*'s editor. When not editing books, Brian likes to run marathons "for fun." It transpires that this was the perfect training for working on the marathon that producing this book turned into. At times, Brian worked us very hard, and, consequently, we have a much better book.

Brian Sawyer

The O'Reilly team:

Brett McLaughlin, the Series Editor, kept an eye on what we were up to and on more than once occasion came to our rescue we when we found ourselves in trouble. **Karen Shaner** provided administrative support and very capably coordinated our techical review process.

Friends and colleagues:

David and Paul are especially grateful to **Lou Barr** for first thinking that the two of them might like to work together on this book, suggesting they do, and then working hard to get the idea approved at O'Reilly. Thanks, Lou!

David: My thanks to **Kathy Sierra** and **Bert Bates** for this extraordinary series of books. And to **Andy Parker** and **Joe Broughton** and **Carl Jacques** and **Simon Jones** and the many other friends who have heard so little from me whilst I was busy scribbling away.

Paul: My thanks to **Nigel Whyte**, Head of Department, Computing and Networking at The Institute of Technology, Carlow for supporting my involvement in yet another writing project. Also at work, **Dr. Christophe Meudec** reviewed the early chapters and offered some very welcome words of encouragement, together with suggestions as how to make things just that little bit better. **Joseph Kehoe** also reviewed the early material and liked what he saw.

Family:

David: I owe a very particular thank you to my wife, the author of *Head First Statistics*, **Dawn Griffiths**. For her wit, humor, patience, and ability to turn vague ideas into real chapters.

Paul: Thanks are due to my father, **Jim Barry**, who reviewed the early, draft material and (once again) pointed out where my writing could be improved and clarified. Regretfully, my home life suffered as working on this book grew to consume all of my free time. **Deirdre**, **Joseph**, **Aaron**, and **Aideen** had to bear the grunts and groans, huffs and puffs, and more than a few roars as the pressure reached boiling point on more than one occasion. I sometimes wonder how they put up with me, but somehow they do, and I'm very grateful for their ongoing love and support.

The without-whom list:

Our technical review team did an excellent job of keeping us straight and making sure what we covered was spot on.

Finally, we both owe a huge debt of gratitude to David's wife, **Dawn**, who not only looks after David, but also got involved in the production of this book at a time when things looked like we'd never finish. Without Dawn's help, this book would never have been done on time. Dawn is the *Head First Programming* guardian angel.

Safari® Books Online

 When you see a Safari® icon on the cover of your favorite technology book that means the book is available online through the O'Reilly Network Safari Bookshelf.

Safari offers a solution that's better than e-books. It's a virtual library that lets you easily search thousands of top tech books, cut and paste code samples, download chapters, and find quick answers when you need the most accurate, current information. Try it for free at http://safari.oreilly.com.

1 starting to code

Finding your way

I wish "sweet cheeks" here would finish with the polishing. I've got to re-bore the cam shaft and reprogram the EMS for Saturday's drift race.

Writing programs gives you the power to control your PC.

Almost everyone knows how to *use* a computer, but few people take the next step and learn how to *control* it. If you use other people's software, you will always be limited by what other people think you want to do. Write your own programs and the only limit will be your own imagination. Programming will make you more creative, it will make you think more precisely, and it will teach you to analyze and solve problems logically.

Do you want to be programmed or be the programmer?

Programming lets you do more

You've got problems to solve and work to do, but your existing software doesn't quite cut it. Even with all those programs on your computer, you still need to do something different, something specific to **you**.

If only I could program Twitter...

How do I get my website to do what I want?

Whaddaya mean, that's not the way the website was programmed?!?

Man, I'm sooooo fed up with the "same old, same old" games.

You want to do more with your computer. You want to *take control*.

Learning to program gives you the power to *create* and *solve*. Learning to program puts **you** in charge.

But, how does programming work?

Let's look at a simple game written in Python.

Sharpen your pencil

This code is a guessing-game program. Study it carefully, and opposite each line of code in the program, write down what you think the code does. If you're not sure what a particular line of code does, *don't worry*, but try to guess anyway. One line has already been entered to get you started:

```
print("Welcome!")

g = input("Guess the number: ")

guess = int(g)

if guess == 5:

    print("You win!")

else:

    print("You lose!")

print("Game over!")
```

....

....

Convert the input to a number.

....

....

....

....

....

This code is written in release 3 of the Python programming language, which is used throughout this book.

Sharpen your pencil Solution

This code is a guessing-game program. You were to write down what you think the code does.

Don't worry if your answers are different from ours. If they are similar, then everything is OK.

```
print("Welcome!")

g = input("Guess the number: ")

guess = int(g)

if guess == 5:

    print("You win!")

else:

    print("You lose!")

print("Game over!")
```

Display a welcome message.

Ask the user to input a guess.

Convert the input to a number.

Was the guessed number equal to 5?

Tell the user "You win!"

Otherwise...

...tell the user "You lose!"

End the program.

But what are g and <u>guess</u>?

You might be wondering what g and guess are in the code. They are called **variables** and they're used to keep track of data in the computer's memory.

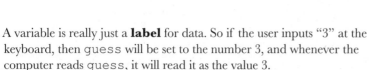

A variable

The value entered will be known as "g".

```
g = input("Guess the number: ")
```

```
guess = int(g)
```

A variable

This creates a number-version of the g-value and calls it "guess".

Watch it!

Be careful with = signs in code.

Programming languages use = signs for different purposes. In most languages (including Python), a double equals (==) is a test for equality. It means, "are these two things equal?" In contrast, a single equal (=) is an instruction (known as assignment) that means "set the value to."

A variable is really just a **label** for data. So if the user inputs "3" at the keyboard, then guess will be set to the number 3, and whenever the computer reads guess, it will read it as the value 3.

So how do you run your code?

There are **two** things that you will need to run the guessing-game program: an **editor** and an **interpreter**.

The editor saves the code you write into a file on your hard disk. The code (sometimes called the **source code**) is just text, and it can be written and read by humans.

The editor will save the source code into a file.

The source code

But computers can't process text meant for humans, at least not very well. That's why we need a tool to translate the human-friendly source code into the binary 1s and 0s that computers do understand. That's what an interpreter does. In this book, an interpreter called **Python** is used.

Hmmm... looks like a guessing game...

The Python interpreter

The interpreter translates the text of the source code into language that the computer can understand.

So we need an editor and a Python interpreter. Fortunately, Python 3 comes with a built-in application called **IDLE**, which does both jobs and more. IDLE enables you to write and edit Python code, it translates this code into binary form, and finally, it runs the Python 3 program. Because of this, IDLE is known as an **Integrated Development Environment**.

Let's see these steps in action.

Create a new program file

When you first start IDLE, it displays a window called the **Python Shell**.
Select the New Window option from the Python Shell File menu,
which creates a new edit window for you. Input your program code as text
into this edit window and you'll be on your way.

This is IDLE's Python Shell.

This is an IDLE edit window.

The New Window menu option creates an edit window.

The Python program is color-coded within IDLE's edit window. This color-coding is referred to as "syntax highlighting." Be sure to enter the code in EXACTLY as it appears here. Don't forget those ":" characters.

```python
print("Welcome!")
g = input("Guess the number: ")
guess = int(g)
if guess == 5:
    print("You win!")
else:
    print("You lose!")
print("Game over!")
```

Do this!

Go ahead and open a new IDLE edit
window and type in the code from page 3.

This is how IDLE looks on our computer. Things
might look a little different on yours. Don't
worry: the IDLE menu system and IDLE's
behavior should be the same, regardless of which
operating system you're using.

Prepare and run your code

The next step is to *prepare* your program code for execution. To do this, select File → Save from the menu to save your program code to a file. Choose an appropriate name for your program.

If you choose File → Save from the menu, you can save your code in a file.

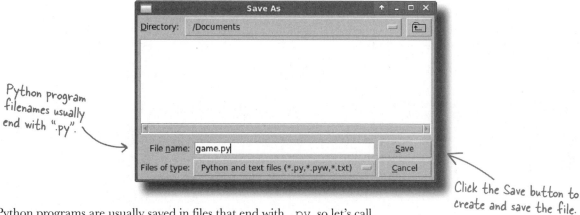

Python program filenames usually end with ".py".

Python programs are usually saved in files that end with .py, so let's call this program game.py.

Click the Save button to create and save the file.

It doesn't really matter to IDLE which directory you save the file in. Some coders like to create special directories for each new programming project. But for now, just save the code in some directory that's easy to remember.

Now, let's see what happens when we run the program.

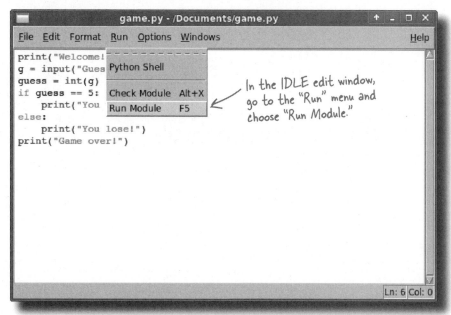

In the IDLE edit window, go to the "Run" menu and choose "Run Module."

TEST DRIVE

To run the program, you need to make sure that the edit window for the game.py program code is selected. Each time you run (or rerun) the program, you need to click on the IDLE edit window and choose the Run Module option from the Run menu. The word ***module*** is a name that IDLE uses to refer to your program code.

Here's what happens when you run the code:

> When you run your code within IDLE, any messages appear within the Python Shell, not within the edit window. IDLE automatically makes the shell the currently selected window the instant your program runs.

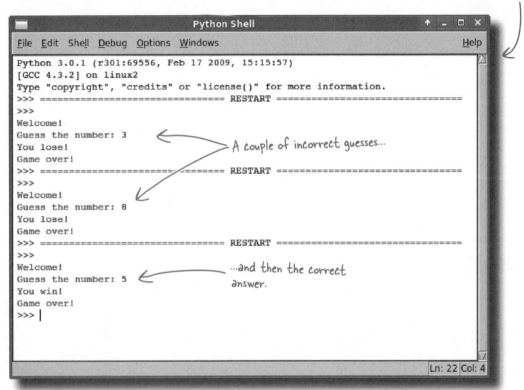

```
Python Shell                                          ↑ _ □ ✕
File  Edit  Shell  Debug  Options  Windows                    Help
Python 3.0.1 (r301:69556, Feb 17 2009, 15:15:57)
[GCC 4.3.2] on linux2
Type "copyright", "credits" or "license()" for more information.
>>> ============================== RESTART ==============================
>>>
Welcome!
Guess the number: 3
You lose!          ← A couple of incorrect guesses...
Game over!
>>> ============================== RESTART ==============================
>>>
Welcome!
Guess the number: 8
You lose!
Game over!
>>> ============================== RESTART ==============================
>>>
Welcome!
Guess the number: 5   ← ...and then the correct answer.
You win!
Game over!
>>> |
                                                      Ln: 22 Col: 4
```

Congratulations! The program works.

Each time you run the code, it displays a "Welcome!" message, accepts input from the keyboard, and then tells us whether or not we guessed the right answer. That means the program is accepting **input**, it's **processing** the data, and then it generates **output**.

there are no
Dumb Questions

Q: I've never heard of Python. Is it popular?

A: Python is used in lots of cool places. Google, Industrial Light & Magic, YouTube, and NASA (to name a few) all use Python. We think they know what they're doing.

Q: So, when I'm done with this book I'll throw Python away and use something else, like C# or Java?

A: Only if you want to. Python might be the only programming language you'll ever need. But, yes, if you want to learn another programming language, you can take everything you learn about programming in this book and apply it to any other language with the minimum of effort.

Q: But a buddy of mine told me I should learn Java or C#. Why are you not using either of these programming languages in this book?

A: Both Java and C# are great programming technologies, but they can be difficult to learn, especially when you are just starting out. This is not the case with Python. And, anyway, this is a book that's designed to teach you how to program, and using Python as your first programming language will help us to do just that.

Q: There seems to be many different versions of Python. Which should I use?

A: There are two main releases of Python: 2 and 3. This book is based on release 3 of the language. Python 3 is the future of the language; any new features are guaranteed to be added to release 3 of the language, not release 2. Of course, like all releases, Python 3 remains a free download, which makes it a no-brainer when decidiing if you can afford to use it.

Q: Will Python run on my phone, just like Java?

A: That really depends on your phone. Python is designed to run on lots of different technologies and operating systems. Running your own code on your own phone is a very specific requirement, and Java has that pretty well covered at the moment. As a programming technology, Java was initially designed to run on very small devices, so it is no big surprise that it is a strong and popular choice when it comes to telephony.

Q: Why is the Python IDE called IDLE?

A: It's partly because it sounds like IDE, but we suspect that it has more to do with Eric Idle, one of the founding members of the Monty Python's Flying Circus comedy group.

Q: Come again?!? Monty Python's Flying what?

A: Circus. Yes, we know: sounds silly, doesn't it? And, believe us, it is. It's funny, too. The creator of Python, Guido van Rossum, is a big Monthy Python fan and reportedly watched the show's reruns while he designed Python. You'll find lots of references to Monty Python folklore in the Python community. Dead parrots are a particular favorite.

Q: What does int(g) mean?

A: It tells Python to interpret the user's input as a number rather than a letter. Within programming languages, the number 5 is different than the letter '5'.

Q: So what if we'd left it out?

A: The computer would have treated the input entered by the user of the program as a letter. If you ask the computer if a letter is equal to a number, it gets confused and tells you it isn't.

Q: Why's that?

A: Because if the computer thinks that two pieces of information are of different "types," it assumes that there's no way they can be equal.

Q: So what if I had *not* typed a number when I was asked for a guess? What if I'd just entered my name or something?

A: The code would have crashed with an error. In fact, Python will complain that the program crashed with a "ValueError" (more on these error messages later in the book).

One of your users

I don't get it. How am I supposed to guess the winning number? All the program tells me is that my guess is right or wrong. Come on, give me some help here!

The program needs to do more.

At the moment, the guessing game tells the user whether his guess is right or wrong, but nothing more than that. It might be more helpful if the program displayed more informative messages, such as whether the guess is **higher** or **lower** than the correct answer. That would help the user to hone in on the right answer the next time the program is run.

We can do this by changing the code. But in what way?

We need this program to display messages that are more informative.

```
game.py - /Documents/game.py
File  Edit  Format  Run  Options  Windows            Help

print("Welcome!")
g = input("Guess the number: ")
guess = int(g)
if guess == 5:
    print("You win!")
else:
    print("You lose!")
print("Game over!")

                                            Ln: 9 Col: 0
```

Sharpen your pencil

You need to decide what messages should be displayed to the user. Below is a table showing some typical values the user might enter. What do you think the message should say?

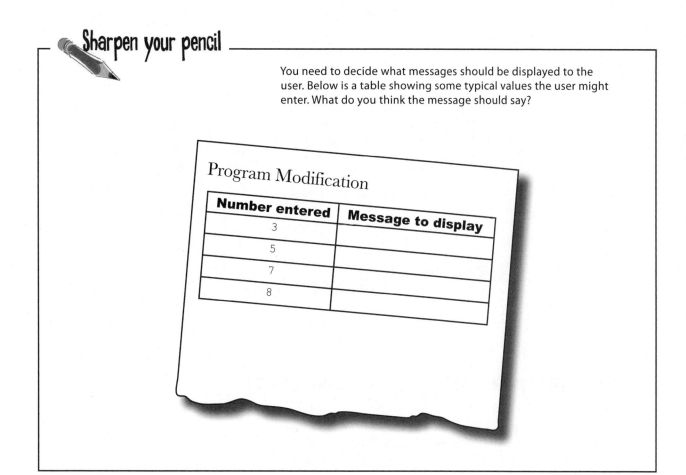

Program Modification

Number entered	Message to display
3	
5	
7	
8	

BRAIN POWER

Think about the original code. You will need to use more than just `print()` commands to provide more informative feedback. What else will you need?

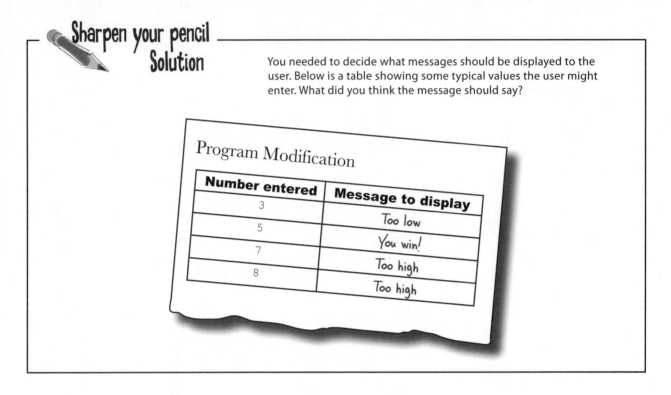

Sharpen your pencil Solution

You needed to decide what messages should be displayed to the user. Below is a table showing some typical values the user might enter. What did you think the message should say?

Program Modification

Number entered	Message to display
3	Too low
5	You win!
7	Too high
8	Too high

A program is more than a list of commands

You *could* create a program that was simply a **list** of commands. But you almost never will. This is because a simple list of commands can only be run in one direction. It's just like driving down a straight piece of road: there's really only one way of doing it.

print(), input(), and int() are examples of commands that you've already seen.

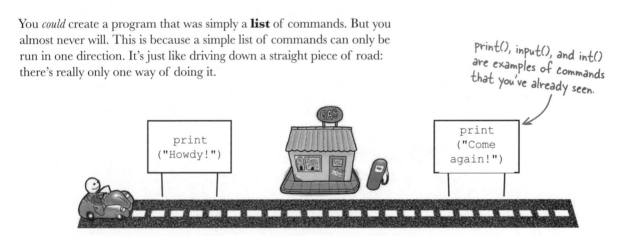

But programs need to be much smarter than that.

Codeville: Your program is like a network of roads

Programs need to do different things under different circumstances. In the game, the code displays "You win!" if the user guesses the number correctly, and "You lose!" if not. This means that all programs, even really simple programs, typically have multiple **paths** through them.

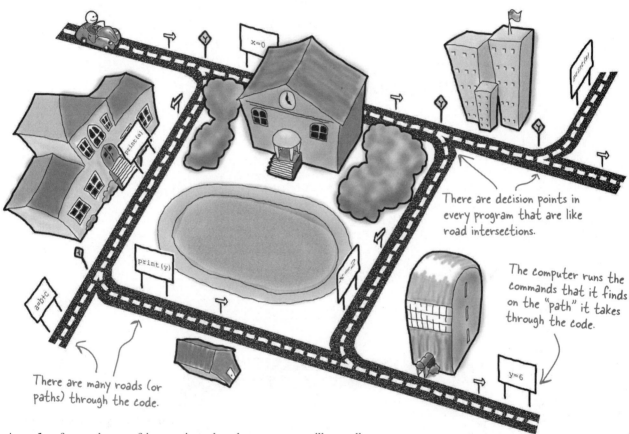

There are decision points in every program that are like road intersections.

The computer runs the commands that it finds on the "path" it takes through the code.

There are many roads (or paths) through the code.

A **path** refers to the set of instructions that the computer will actually follow (or execute). Your code is like a street network, with lots of sections of code connected together just like the streets in a city. When you drive through a city, you make decisions as to which streets you drive down by turning left or right at different intersections. It's the same for a program. It also needs to make decisions from time to time as to which path to take, but for your code, it is not like driving along a road, *it's executing a particular path.*

Let's look in more detail at how a program decides which path to take.

Branches are code intersections

Driving down a street is easy. You need to make a decision only when you get to an intersection. It's the same for your program. When a program has a list of commands, it can blindly execute them one after another. But sometimes, your program needs to make a decision. Does it run *this* piece of code or *that* piece of code?

These decision points are called **branches**, and they are the road intersections in your code.

Branches are like road intersections.

Your program makes a decision using a **branch condition**. A branch condition has the value **true** or **false**. If the branch condition is true, it runs the code on the true branch. And if the branch condition is false, it runs the code on the false branch.

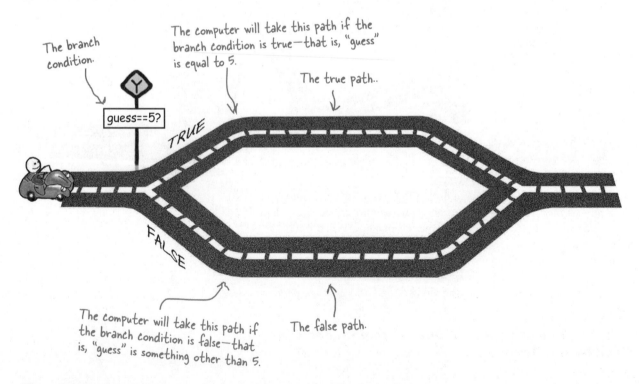

The branch condition.

The computer will take this path if the branch condition is true—that is, "guess" is equal to 5.

The true path..

guess==5?

TRUE

FALSE

The computer will take this path if the branch condition is false—that is, "guess" is something other than 5.

The false path.

if/else branches

We've already seen a branch in the Python game program:

```
if guess == 5:
    print("You win!")
else:
    print("You lose!")
print("Game over!")
```

Python, like many languages, has if/else branches. In our example, the branch condition is the `if guess == 5` piece of code. This is a **test for equality** and it will result in the value **true** or **false**.

The code on the true path is indented, and given after the **if** line. The code on the false path is indented, and given after the **else** line:

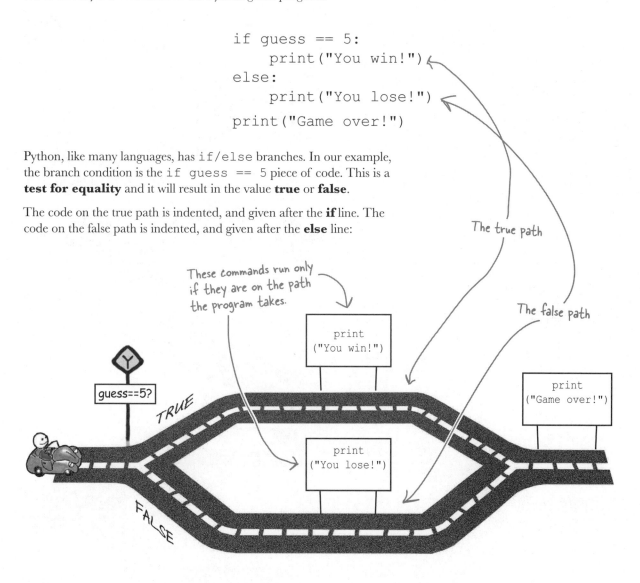

These commands run only if they are on the path the program takes.

The true path

The false path

You need to amend the game program to give more informative messages to the user.

But what will the paths in the program look like?

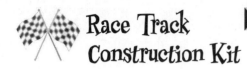

Race Track Construction Kit

The countdown's started on the Codeville Grand Prix. The cars have arrived, they're warming their tires on the grid, and the race is about to start. Can you assemble the track so that it displays the right feedback message? Note that you might not need all the pieces of track.

Number entered	Feedback message
3	Too low
5	You win!
7	Too high
8	Too high

The race start line is → fixed here.

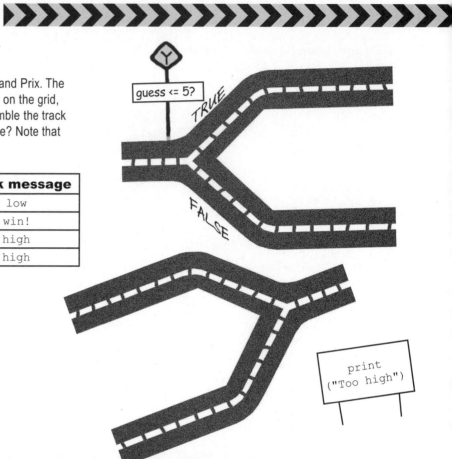

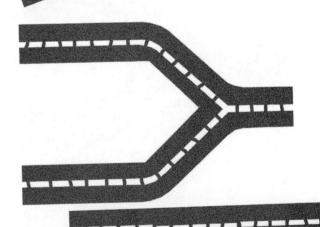

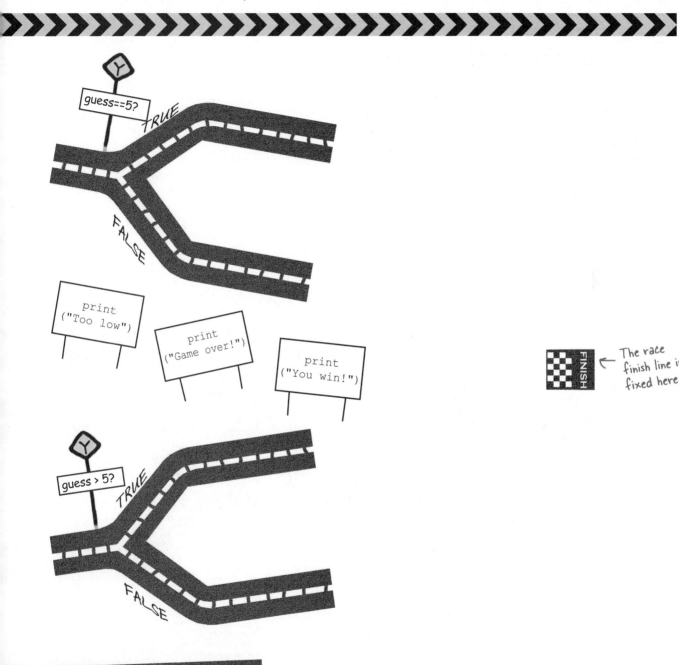

print
("Too low")

print
("Game over!")

print
("You win!")

guess==5?

TRUE

FALSE

guess > 5?

TRUE

FALSE

The race
finish line is
fixed here.

finish line

Race Track
Construction Kit Solution

The countdown's started on the Codeville Grand Prix. The cars have arrived, they're warming their tires on the grid, and the race is about to start. Were you able to assemble the track so that it displays the right feedback message?

Number entered	Feedback message
3	Too low
5	You win!
7	Too high
8	Too high

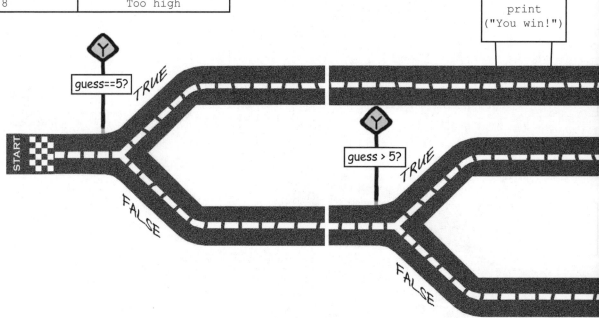

18   *Chapter 1*

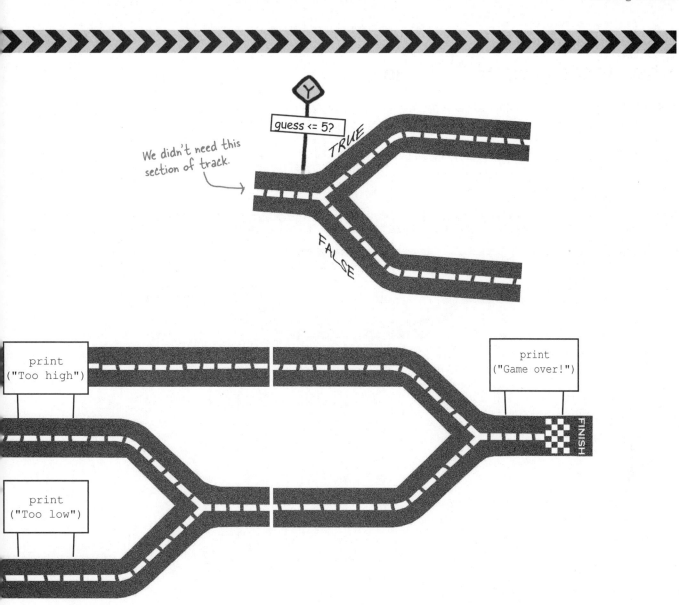

The Python code needs interconnecting paths

The solution's mapped out, and now we know that the program code will need to have paths that match this:

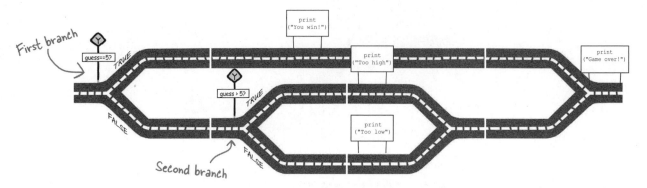

But isn't there a problem here? In the design there are many *interconnecting* paths, but so far, we have only written code that contains just **one** branch:

```python
if guess == 5:
    print("You win!")
else:
    print("You lose!")
```

In the new code, we will need to *connect two branches together*. We need the second branch to appear on the **false path** of the first.

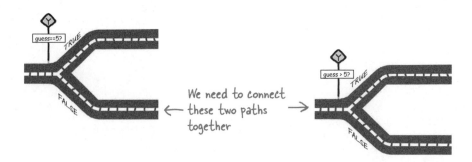

So how do you connect branches together in Python?

Python uses indents to connect paths

The code inside the `if` and `else` statements is **indented**. This isn't just to make the code pretty. In Python, **indents matter**. Let's consider a different piece of example code: something that will decide if you can drive downtown. Python uses indents to connect a sequence of commands together to form paths.

The INDENTs tell Python that the commands are in the same path

```
if fuel > 3:
    print("It's OK")
    print("You can drive downtown.")
else:
    print("Sorry")
    print("You don't have enough fuel")
print("What's next?")
```

This is the TRUE path.

This is the FALSE path.

This command is not on the FALSE path because it is not indented. So it will always run.

So how do you connect branches together? You simply indent the second branch in by **one more level**.

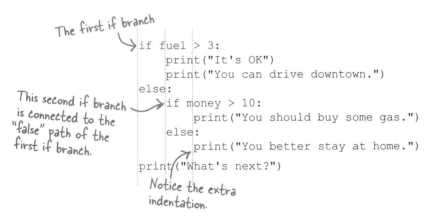

The first if branch

```
if fuel > 3:
    print("It's OK")
    print("You can drive downtown.")
else:
    if money > 10:
        print("You should buy some gas.")
    else:
        print("You better stay at home.")
print("What's next?")
```

This second if branch is connected to the "false" path of the first if branch.

Notice the extra indentation.

> **Indents matter in Python.**
>
> *Be careful how you indent code in Python; if you don't indent your code correctly, your code might do something wildly different from what you expect.*

Watch it!

You should now have enough information to go fix the code, but before we do that, let's take a look at how *IDLE* helps you **indent code.**

IDLE ...at a glance

You'll be using **IDLE** to enter all of the Python code in this book, so it's worth taking a little time to familiarize yourself with a few of its features.

Even though IDLE looks like a simple editor, it's actually **packed full** of smarts that will make Python programming much easier and faster for you. It's worth spending some time exploring IDLE's menus and help system, but for now here's a few *handy hints* to help you feel at home.

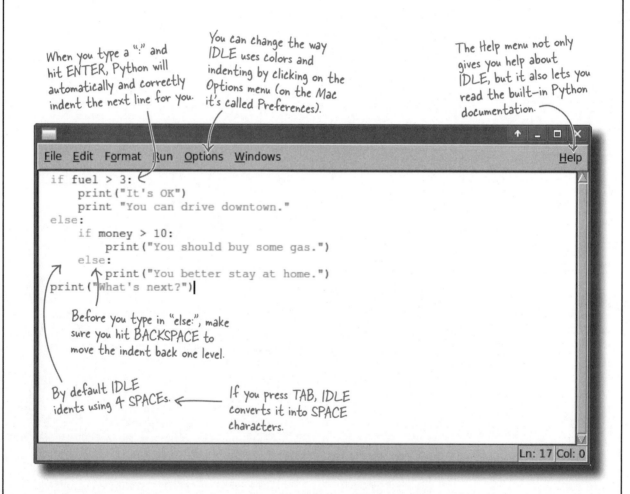

When you type a ":" and hit ENTER, Python will automatically and correctly indent the next line for you.

You can change the way IDLE uses colors and indenting by clicking on the Options menu (on the Mac it's called Preferences).

The Help menu not only gives you help about IDLE, but it also lets you read the built-in Python documentation.

```
if fuel > 3:
    print("It's OK")
    print "You can drive downtown."
else:
    if money > 10:
        print("You should buy some gas.")
    else:
        print("You better stay at home.")
print("What's next?")
```

File   Edit   Format   Run   Options   Windows   Help

Ln: 17 Col: 0

Before you type in "else:", make sure you hit BACKSPACE to move the indent back one level.

By default IDLE idents using 4 SPACEs.

If you press TAB, IDLE converts it into SPACE characters.

Pōōl Puzzle

Your **task** is to take the Python code fragments from the pool and place them into the blank lines in the game. You may **not** use the same code fragment more than once, and you won't need to use all the code fragments. Your **goal** is to complete the guessing game program.

Hint: Don't forget to indent.

```
print("Welcome!")
g = input("Guess the number: ")
guess = int(g)
```

....
....
....
....
....
....
....

Note: each code fragment from the pool can be used only once!

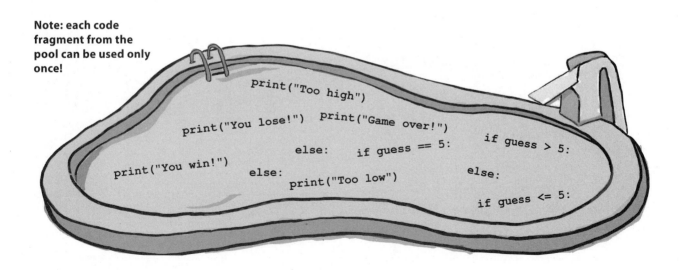

```
print("Too high")
print("You lose!")    print("Game over!")
                                              if guess > 5:
              else:      if guess == 5:
print("You win!")                                  else:
          else:
                   print("Too low")
                                           if guess <= 5:
```

Pool Puzzle Solution

Your **task** was to take the Python code fragments from the pool and place them into the blank lines in the game. You could **not** use the same code fragment more than once, and you didn't need to use all the code fragments. Your **goal** was to complete the guessing game program.

Hint: Don't forget to indent.

```python
print("Welcome!")
g = input("Guess the number: ")
guess = int(g)
if guess == 5:

    print("You win!")

else:

    if guess > 5:

        print("Too high")

    else:

        print("Too low")

print("Game over!")
```

Did you remember to indent your code deep enough?

All of this code is indented under the else part of the original if part.

This piece of code from the first version of this program is no longer needed.

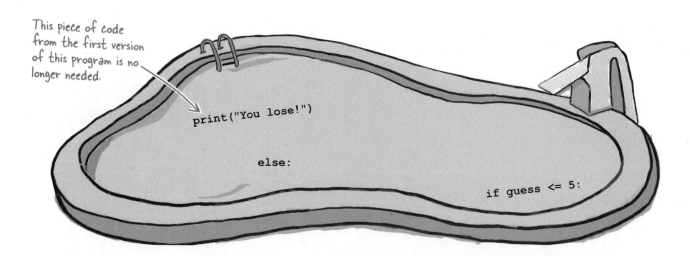

```python
print("You lose!")


        else:


                        if guess <= 5:
```

TEST DRIVE

So, what happens if you run the new version of the program?

Let's try a few tests. Remember, you will need to switch back to the program window for each run and choose **Run module** from the menu.

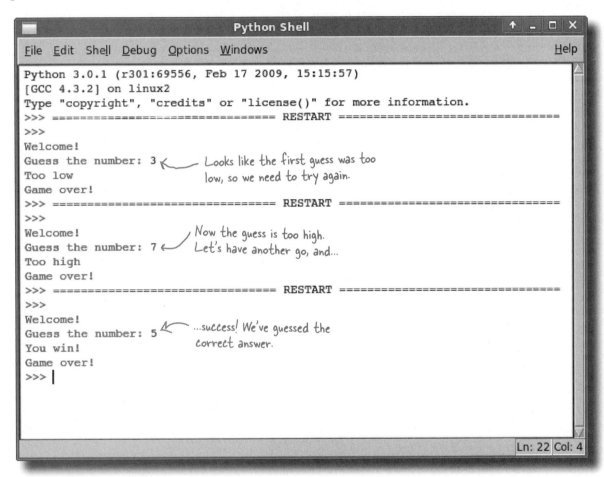

```
                                    Python Shell
 File   Edit   Shell   Debug   Options   Windows                          Help

 Python 3.0.1 (r301:69556, Feb 17 2009, 15:15:57)
 [GCC 4.3.2] on linux2
 Type "copyright", "credits" or "license()" for more information.
 >>> ============================ RESTART ============================
 >>>
 Welcome!
 Guess the number: 3          Looks like the first guess was too
 Too low                       low, so we need to try again.
 Game over!
 >>> ============================ RESTART ============================
 >>>
 Welcome!                      Now the guess is too high.
 Guess the number: 7          Let's have another go, and...
 Too high
 Game over!
 >>> ============================ RESTART ============================
 >>>
 Welcome!
 Guess the number: 5          ...success! We've guessed the
 You win!                      correct answer.
 Game over!
 >>> |

                                                              Ln: 22 Col: 4
```

The program works! But, are the users any happier?

Why do I have to keep rerunning the program? You mean I only get **one** guess?????

The users still don't like it.

The program works, and now generates extra feedback, but there's a problem. If the users want to have another guess, they have to run the program again. They *really* want the program to keep asking them for another guess until they finally get the correct answer.

Can you see what the problem is?

How do we get the computer to do something repeatedly? Should we just make a copy of the code and paste it at the end of the file? That would make sure the user is asked twice. But what if they need to make **3 guesses**? Or **4 guesses**? Or **10,000 guesses**? What about the case where the guess is correct?

The guessing game program needs to be able to run *some* code repeatedly.

Loops let you run the same piece of code over and over again

Programs often need to keep running the same piece of code many times. In addition to branches, programming languages also provide **loops**.

Loops are a little like branches. Just like branches, loops have a condition (the **loop condition**) that is either true or false. Also, like the `if` part of branches, if the loop condition is true, then a loop will run a given piece of code. For a branch, this code is called the **body**. For a loop, it's called the **loop body**.

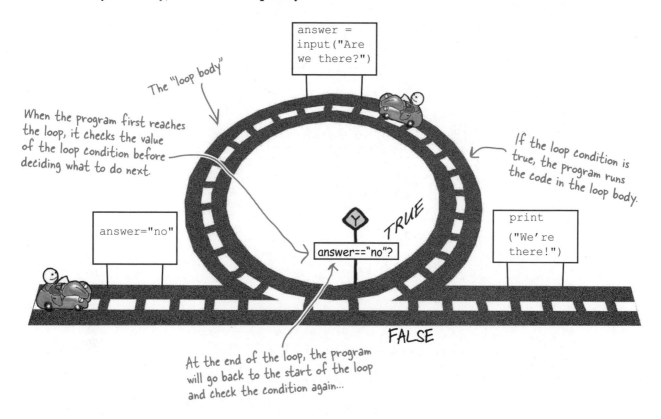

The "loop body"

```
answer =
input("Are
we there?")
```

When the program first reaches the loop, it checks the value of the loop condition before deciding what to do next.

If the loop condition is true, the program runs the code in the loop body.

```
answer="no"
```

`answer=="no"?`

TRUE

```
print
("We're
there!")
```

FALSE

At the end of the loop, the program will go back to the start of the loop and check the condition again...

The big difference between a loop and a branch is **how many times** it runs the code associated with it. A branch will run its code only once. But a loop will run the loop body, then check the loop condition again and, if it's still true, it will run the loop body again. And again. And again. In fact, it will keep running the loop body until the loop condition becomes **false**.

Python's while loop

Programming languages have lots of different ways of creating loops, but one of the simplest ways in Python is to use a **while loop**. Here's an example:

We want to make sure the loop runs the first time.

The loop condition

The loop body is the indented code following the "while" line.

```
answer = "no"
while answer == "no":
    answer = input("Are we there? ")
print("We're there!")
```

The loop body is just one line of code in this example, but the loop body can be many lines of code. It might even include branches and other loops.

This is what the loop looks like when you write it as a Python while loop. The code keeps asking the question "Are we there?" until the user types something other than no. This is what it looks like when it runs:

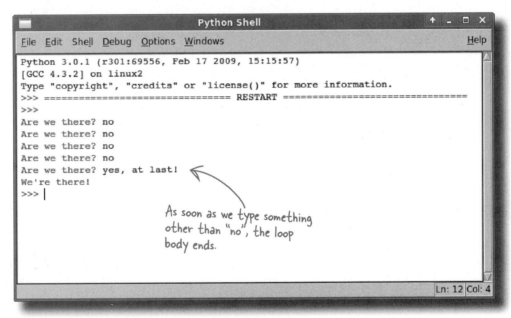

As soon as we type something other than "no", the loop body ends.

Did you notice that you had to set the value of the answer variable to something sensible before you started the loop? This is important, because if the answer variable doesn't already have the value no, the loop condition would have been false and the code in the loop body would **never** have run at all.

Bear that in mind. It might be useful in this next exercise...

 **Long Exercise**

Now, it's time to apply your programming mojo. Be warned: this exercise is kind of tricky. You need to rewrite your game program so it keeps running until the user guesses the correct answer. You will need to use all of the things you've learned in this chapter. You will need to work out the conditions for each of the branches and loops that are required.

Remember: the program needs to keep asking the user for an answer while the current guess is wrong.

Hint: If you need to test that two things have different values, use the **!=** operator.

This is the "not equal to" operator.

Write your code here.

Ready Bake Code

If you add these two lines of code to the top of your program:

```
from random import randint
secret = randint(1, 10)
```

The `secret` variable will be set to a random number between 1 and 10. Modify your program from the facing page so that instead of the answer always being 5, it will instead use a random number from 1 to 10 as the answer.

Write the next version of your program here. This version of your program uses the value of the "secret" variable as the correct answer.

....

....

....

....

....

....

....

....

....

....

....

....

....

....

Long Exercise Solution

You needed to rewrite your game program so it keeps running until the user guesses the correct answer. You needed to use all of the things you've learned in this chapter. You needed to work out the conditions for each of the branches and loops that are required.

Hint: If you need to test that two things have different values, use the **!=** operator.

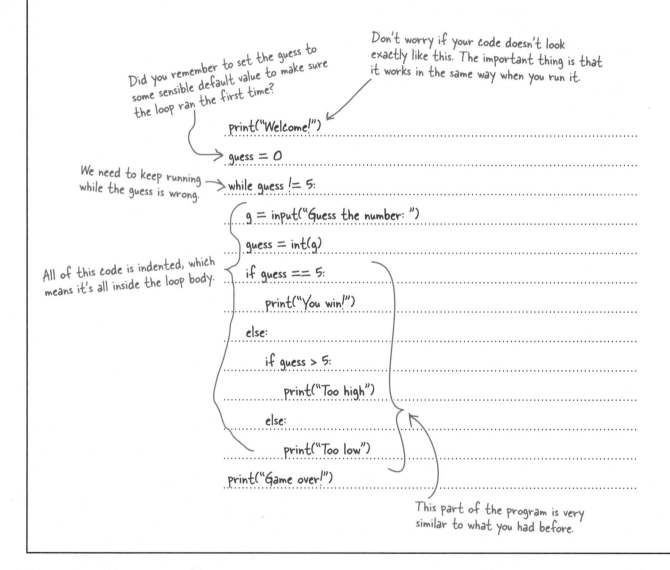

Did you remember to set the guess to some sensible default value to make sure the loop ran the first time?

Don't worry if your code doesn't look exactly like this. The important thing is that it works in the same way when you run it.

```
print("Welcome!")

guess = 0

while guess != 5:

    g = input("Guess the number: ")

    guess = int(g)

    if guess == 5:

        print("You win!")

    else:

        if guess > 5:

            print("Too high")

        else:

            print("Too low")

print("Game over!")
```

We need to keep running while the guess is wrong.

All of this code is indented, which means it's all inside the loop body.

This part of the program is very similar to what you had before.

Ready Bake Code

If you add these two lines of code to the top of your program:

```
from random import randint
secret = randint(1, 10)
```

The `secret` variable will be set to a random number between 1 and 10. You were to modify your program from the facing page so that instead of the answer always being 5, it will instead use a random number from 1 to 10 as the answer.

Here are the two lines that create the random number.

```
from random import randint
secret = randint(1, 10)
print("Welcome!")
guess = 0
while guess != secret:
    g = input("Guess the number: ")
    guess = int(g)
    if guess == secret:
        print("You win!")
    else:
        if guess > secret:
            print("Too high")
        else:
            print("Too low")
print("Game over!")
```

Now, instead of checking if the answer's 5, we check it against the random number, which is held in the "secret" variable.

TEST DRIVE

So, what happens when you run the new version of your program?

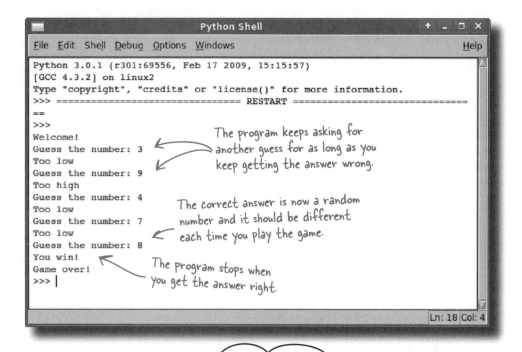

```
Python Shell                                        ↑ _ □ ✕

File  Edit  Shell  Debug  Options  Windows                    Help

Python 3.0.1 (r301:69556, Feb 17 2009, 15:15:57)
[GCC 4.3.2] on linux2
Type "copyright", "credits" or "license()" for more information.
>>> ================================ RESTART ================================
==
>>>
Welcome!
Guess the number: 3
Too low
Guess the number: 9
Too high
Guess the number: 4
Too low
Guess the number: 7
Too low
Guess the number: 8
You win!
Game over!
>>> |
                                                    Ln: 18 Col: 4
```

The program keeps asking for another guess for as long as you keep getting the answer wrong.

The correct answer is now a random number and it should be different each time you play the game.

The program stops when you get the answer right.

> This game's pretty cool. No matter how many times I play it, I still have to think to get the right answer!

Your users love the program.

And you created it all yourself. By carefully **analyzing** the problem, deciding what the feedback needed to be, and working out the intricate **looping** and **branching** logic, you've created something that really rocks.

Well done. You're on your way to becoming a real code jockey.

Your Programming Toolbox

You've got Chapter 1 under your belt. Let's look back at what you've learned so far.

Programming Tools

* Programs are created from code statements:

  commands do things.

  branches decide things.

  loops repeat things.

* Conditionals help you decide if

  something is True or False.

* Assignment sets a name to a value.

* A named value is stored in a "variable".

Python Tools

* if/else branches

* while loops

* = assignment operator

* == equality operator

* != inequality operator

* > greater than operator

* print() displays a message on screen

* input() gets and returns user input

* int() converts characters to numbers

* randint() produces a random number

2 textual data

Every string ✳ ✳ has its place

> I keep shix - hic! - honest working men. They taught me all I knew - hic! Their names are What.. and Why and... Gus... and - hic! - Jim, and Bob, and Lou.

Imagine trying to communicate without words.

All programs process data, and one of the most important types of data is **text**. In this chapter, you'll work through the basics of **textual data**. You'll automatically **search** text and get back **exactly what you're looking for**. Along the way, you'll pick up key programming concepts such as **methods** and how you can use them to **bend your data to your will**. And finally, you'll instantly **power up your programs** with the help of **library code**.

Your new gig at Starbuzz Coffee

Starbuzz Coffee has made a name for itself as the fastest growing coffee shop around. If you've seen one on your local corner, look across the street; you'll see another one.

The Starbuzz CEO is always on the lookout for ways to boost profits, and he's come up with a great idea. He wants a program that will show him the current price of coffee beans so that his buyers can make informed decisions about when to buy.

> I had a programmer do some work for me, but they're not answering their phone. They've disappeared! Think you can take over? I'll let you have the code they've already come up with.

The Starbuzz CEO →

Here's the current Starbuzz code

The previous programmer has already made a head start on
the code, and we can use this as a basis. Here's the existing
Python code, but what does it do?

*Here's the program code
in its current form.*

```
import urllib.request

page = urllib.request.urlopen("http://www.beans-r-us.biz/prices.html")
text = page.read().decode("utf8")

print(text)
```

⚛ BRAIN POWER

Take a good look at the existing Starbuzz code. What do you think it
actually does?

Test Drive

Type the code into IDLE, save the program, and run it.

```
getcoffeeprice.py - /home/barryp/HeadFirstProg/chapter2/code/g

File  Edit  Format  Run  Options  Windows                                    Help

import urllib.request

page = urllib.request.urlopen("http://beans-r-us.biz/prices.html")
text = page.read().decode("utf8")

print(text)
```

Here's the program code as entered into IDLE.

```
Python Shell

File  Edit  Shell  Debug  Options  Windows                                   Help

Python 3.0.1 (r301:69556, Feb 17 2009, 15:15:57)
[GCC 4.3.2] on linux2
Type "copyright", "credits" or "license()" for more information.
>>> ============================ RESTART ============================
>>>
<html><head><title>Welcome to the Beans'R'Us Pricing Page</title>
<link rel="stylesheet" type="text/css" href="beansrus.css" />
</head><body>
<h2>Welcome to the Beans'R'Us Pricing Page</h2>
<p>Current price of coffee beans = <strong>$5.49</strong></p>
<p>Price valid for 15 minutes from 19:42 on Wednesday 27/05/2009.</p>
</body></html>

>>>
                                                                     Ln: 14 Col: 4
```

When executed, the program produces this.

This looks like a chunk of "raw" HTML text, which is the format used to create web pages.

The code you've been left goes to the prices page on the Beans'R'Us website to get the current price of coffee beans. But instead of giving just the cost, it gives you all of the HTML text used to create the web page itself.

> Hey, that's not right! I only need to see the current price of coffee beans, not all that other stuff. Think you can give me just the cost?

The cost is embedded in the HTML

Take a closer look at the results of the program. The current price of beans is right in the middle of the output:

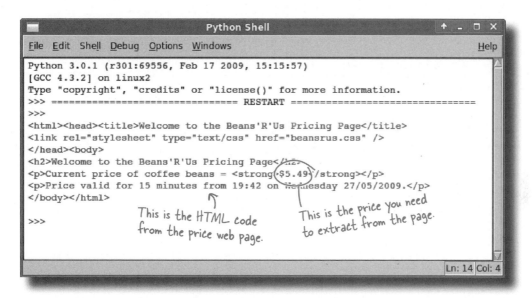

This is the HTML code from the price web page.

This is the price you need to extract from the page.

The Starbuzz CEO would find it a lot easier if you could extract the price of beans and just display that, rather than have to look for it in the HTML. But how do you do that?

A string is a series of characters

The output of the Starbuzz program is an example of a **string**. In other words, it's a series of characters like this:

Somewhere within the string is the price of coffee beans. To retrieve just the price, all you need to do is go to the right bit of the string, retrieve the characters that give the price, and display just those characters. But how?

You only need these few characters.

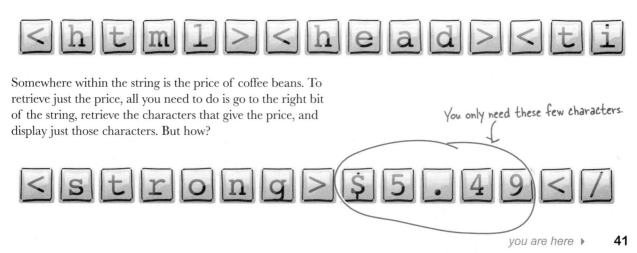

Find characters inside the text

The computer keeps track of individual characters by using **two** pieces of information: the **start** of the string and the **offset** of an individual character. The offset is *how far* the individual character is from the start of the string.

We are at the start of the string and, as we have moved zero places, the offset is 0.

The **first** character in a string has an **offset** of 0, because it is zero characters from the start. The **second** character has an **offset** of 1, and so on:

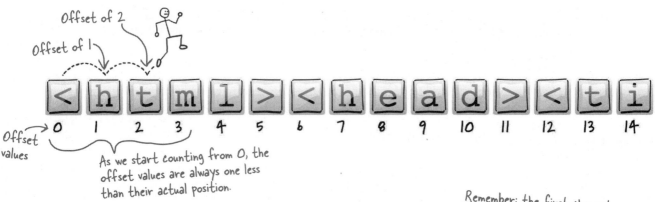

Offset of 2

Offset of 1

Offset values

0 1 2 3 4 5 6 7 8 9 10 11 12 13 14

As we start counting from 0, the offset values are always one less than their actual position.

The offset value is always 1 less than the position. Python lets you read a single character from a string by providing the offset value in square brackets after the variable name. Because the offset value is used to find a character, it is called the **index** of the character:

Remember: the first character has index 0, so we are "off by one" when referring to an individual character.

text[0] text[1] text[2] text[3] text[4] text[5] text[6] text[7] text[8] text[9] text[10] text[11] text[12] text[13] text[14]

But how do you get at more than one character?

For Starbuzz, you don't just need a single character. You need to extract the price from the string of HTML, and the price is made up of several characters.

You need to extract a smaller **substring** from a bigger string. A substring is a sequence of characters contained within another string. Specifying substrings in Python is a little like reading single characters from a string, except that you provide two index values within the square brackets:

This will read the smaller substring from the entire string contained within "s".

s[14]

s[138:147]

If you provide a single index after the variable name, you get a single character.

If you provide two index values, you extract a group of characters from the first index up to (but not including) the second index.

Sharpen your pencil

Let's work out what each of the following substring specifications mean. Imagine the variable s is set to the string below. Your job is to determine what each of the substrings provide.

`But where is Waldo?`

s[5:9]

....

s[10:12]

....

s[13:18]

....

Write down what you think "a" and "b" represent here.

In general, if you specify a substring using s[a:b], then:

a is ....   **b** is ....

Sharpen your pencil
Solution

Imagine the variable s is set to the string below. Your job was to determine what each of the substrings provide.

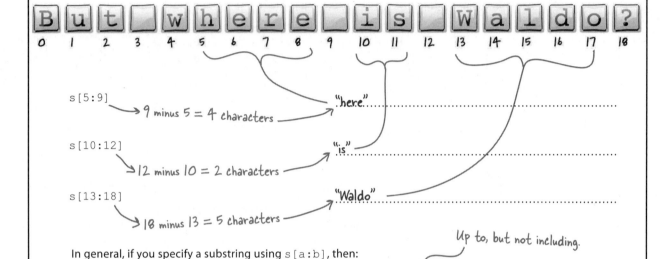

s[5:9]

→ 9 minus 5 = 4 characters → "here" ....

s[10:12]

→ 12 minus 10 = 2 characters → ".is." ....

s[13:18]

→ 18 minus 13 = 5 characters → "Waldo" ....

In general, if you specify a substring using s[a:b], then:

Up to, but not including.

a is .the index of the first character.   **b** is .the index after the last character.

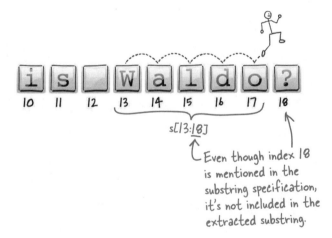

s[13:18]

↳ Even though index 18 is mentioned in the substring specification, it's not included in the extracted substring.

Watch it!

The second index value is after the last character in the substring

This is even though the first index value is the start character of the substring.

Sharpen your pencil

Remember: the 235th character in the string has index value 234.

You need to update the program to extract the price starting at the 235th character of the string. The price is four characters long. Store the price substring in a variable called `price`. Write the new version of the program here:

```
import urllib.request

page = urllib.request.urlopen("http://www.beans-r-us.biz/prices.html")
text = page.read().decode("utf8")

print(text)
```

Here's the current version of the code.

Write the new code here.

....

....

....

....

....

....

....

Sharpen your pencil
Solution

You needed to update the program to extract the price starting at the 235th character of the string. The price is four characters long and stored in a variable called `price`.

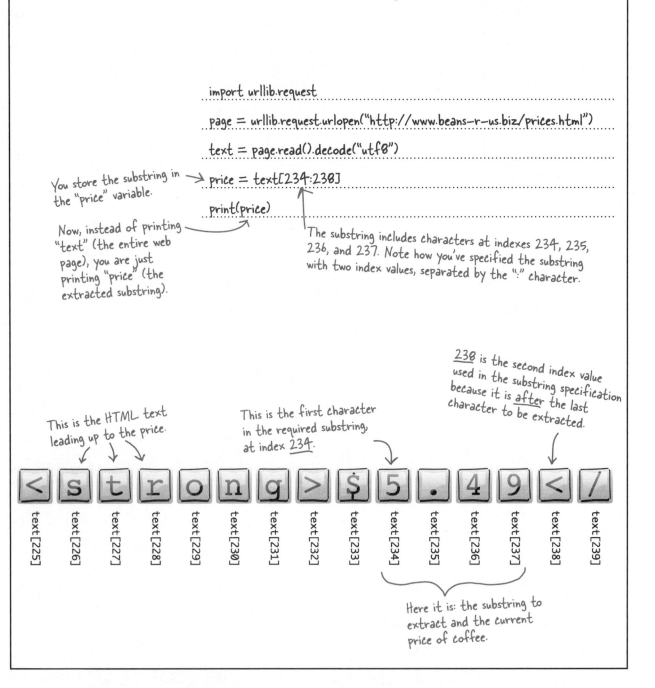

```
import urllib.request

page = urllib.request.urlopen("http://www.beans-r-us.biz/prices.html")

text = page.read().decode("utf8")

price = text[234:238]

print(price)
```

You store the substring in the "price" variable.

Now, instead of printing "text" (the entire web page), you are just printing "price" (the extracted substring).

The substring includes characters at indexes 234, 235, 236, and 237. Note how you've specified the substring with two index values, separated by the ":" character.

238 is the second index value used in the substring specification because it is <u>after</u> the last character to be extracted.

This is the HTML text leading up to the price.

This is the first character in the required substring, at index 234.

<	s	t	r	o	n	g	>	$	5	.	4	9	<	/
text[225]	text[226]	text[227]	text[228]	text[229]	text[230]	text[231]	text[232]	text[233]	text[234]	text[235]	text[236]	text[237]	text[238]	text[239]

Here it is: the substring to extract and the current price of coffee.

Test Drive

Type the code into IDLE, save the program (choose a name for
the program that is meaningful to you), and run it.

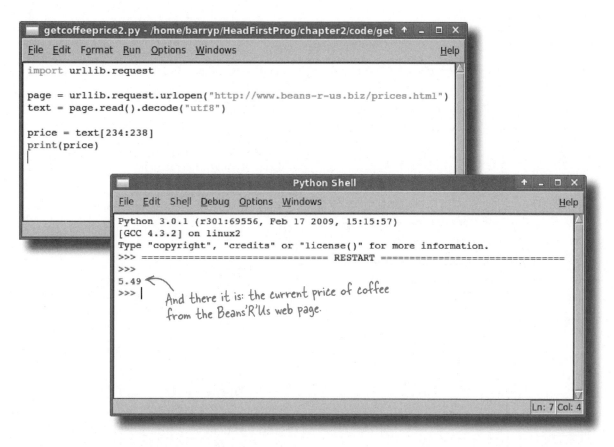

That looks a lot cleaner. Now, instead of displaying the entire
HTML text of the web page, you've cut it down to just the
piece of the string (the substring) that you need.

That's great. It's exactly
what I need! You have no
idea how much time and money
this is going to save me...

The String Exposed

This week's interview:
We ask the String what it's like being the world's most eligible datatype.

Head First: String, it's so good of you to find the time to speak to us.

String: Please, the honor is mine. Sit. Sit. Make yourself at home. Did you eat yet?

Head First: I'm fine, thank you. String, where should I begin? You are known the world over for your work. In your time you've carried the works of Shakespeare, Geothe...

String: Dan Brown.

Head First: ...all the great works of literature. And even mundane things like names and addresses. Tell me, how did you become so popular?

String: It's a question of character. Well, characters. See, before I existed, computer systems used to record text one character at a time.

Head First: That must have been rather inconvenient.

String: Inconvenient? It was a royal pain in the tuchis.

Head First: Quite.

String: Without me, handling text was like riding a pedal cycle without a saddle.

Head First: In what way?

String: It was possible to get somewhere, but the journey was kind of stressful.

Head First: You simplify things.

String: Certainly. I simplify. Instead of keeping track of a hundred, or a thousand, or a million letters, you just need keep an eye on one thing. Me!

Head First: That's a good point.

String: I like to think of myself as a front. An agent, you might say, for all the characters I work with.

Head First: People deal with you, so they don't have to deal with individual characters in memory.

String: Exactly. I'm an organizer. I keep an eye on the day to day business of the letters. If I need to be shorter or longer, I arrange for the characters to be made available.

Head First: Tell me about your substrings.

String: Ah, my substrings. Like chips off the old block. That a humble datatype should be so blessed!

Head First: A tissue?

String: Bless you. <blows nose>. Those boys are so close to me. Here's a photo. Can you see the resemblance?

Head First: Why he looks just like...

String: Ah, you guessed! Yes, my character sequence from 137 to 149. Exactly. Just like his old man. But shorter. Little more hair.

Head First: Your substrings are strings as well.

String: Certainly. Strings just like me. And they, I hope, should one day be able to produce their own substrings as well.

Head First: Yet some people are confused by your indexing.

String: What can I say? I started with nothing!

Head First: String, thank you.

String: A pleasure. Are you sure you ate?

there are no
Dumb Questions

Q: So, I can put any web address into this code and grab the associated web page from the Internet?

A: Yes, feel free to try it out for yourself.

Q: Don't I need a web browser to view web pages?

A: Yes, to view a web page in all its formatted glory—with embedded pictures, music, videos and the like—a web browser is a must-have. However, if all you want to see is the "raw" HTML, a browser is overkill.

Q: What does the import line of code do?

A: It gives the program the ability to talk to the Internet. The `urllib.request` code comes as standard with Python 3.

Q: And I guess that call to urlopen() goes and gets the web page?

A: That's right! The provided web address (or "URL" to use the proper web-speak) is fetched from the Internet and returned by the call to `urlopen()`. In this code, the fetched web page is assigned to the `page` variable.

Q: And the urllib.request bit?

A: That just tells the program to use the `urlopen()` function that comes as standard with Python 3's Internet page—reading technology. We'll have more to say about `urllib.request` in a little bit. For now, just think how lucky we all are not to have to write code to fetch web pages from the Internet.

Q: I get that the call to read() actually reads the web page from the page variable, but what's that decode("utf8") thing?

A: When the web page is fetched from the Internet, it is in a "raw" textual format. This format can be a little hard for humans to read. The call to `decode()` converts the raw web page into something that looks a little easier on the eye.

To see what we mean, try removing the call to `decode()` from the program and running the code again. Looks a little weird, doesn't it? (Don't forget to put the call to `decode()` back in before continuing.)

BULLET POINTS

- You can download the HTML of a web page as a textual **string**.

- A string is a *sequence of characters*.

- You can access individual characters in a string using an **offset**.

- The offset is known as the **index value** of the character (or just **index** for short).

- Strings within strings are called **substrings**.

- Substrings are specified using two index values—for example: `text[10:20]`.

- The first index value is the location of the first character of the substring.

- The second index value is the location **after** the last character of the substring (up to, but not including).

- Subtract the second index from the first to work out how long the substring should be.

Beans'R'Us is rewarding loyal customers

The CEO just got great news from the beans supplier.

> The supplier is so happy about all the business we're giving them that they are going to make us members of their loyalty discount program. They say it should be a simple fix. Can you look into it?

The supplier actually maintains **two prices**: one for *regular* customers and one for *loyalty program customers*. The different prices are published on different web pages:

Regular customers get their prices here. →
```
http://www.beans-r-us.biz/prices.html
```

Loyalty program customers get their prices here. →
```
http://www.beans-r-us.biz/prices-loyalty.html
```

That means you need to change the web page address in the code:

```
import urllib.request

page = urllib.request.urlopen("http://www.beans-r-us.biz/prices-loyalty.html")
text = page.read().decode("utf8")

price = text[234:238]
print(price)
```

↳ This is the new address.

Let's run it to make sure everything works OK.

Test Drive

This time when you run it, **this** happens...

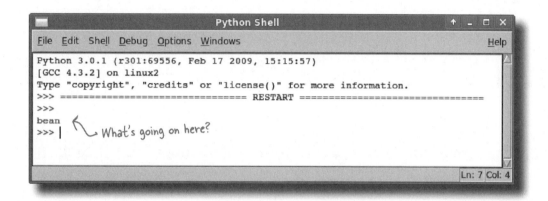

The program is no longer **displaying a price**. So what happened?

The price moved

The web page for loyalty customers is much more **dynamic** that the old web page. The page for regular customers always displays the price in a substring beginning at index 234. That's not true for the loyalty program web page. The price on that page can be almost anywhere. All you know for sure is that the price follows the substring **>$**:

The price could appear ANYWHERE in the string.

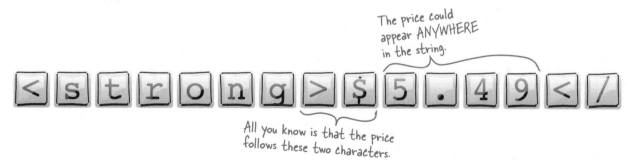

All you know is that the price follows these two characters.

You need to search for the price string.

Searching is complex

You already know how to find a substring, so you could run through the entire web page and check each two characters to see if they match >$, like this:

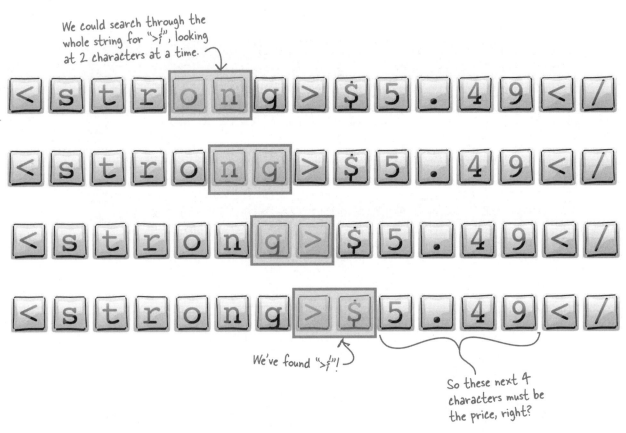

We could search through the whole string for ">$", looking at 2 characters at a time.

We've found ">$"!

So these next 4 characters must be the price, right?

You *could* do it this way... but *should* you?

There's a lot to worry about. Which two characters are you currently comparing? Where in the string are you right now? What if ">$" isn't found? Searching for substrings in strings is a little more complex than it first appears...

But if you don't want to write code to search the string, what else could you do?

Wouldn't it be dreamy if there were a simple way to search a string for a substring? But I suppose that's just a fantasy...

Python data is <u>smart</u>

The more code you write, the more you will find that you need to do the
same kind of things to the data in your variables all the time. To prevent
you from having to create the same code over and over, programming
languages provide **built-in functionality** to help you avoid writing
unnecessary code. Python data is *smart*: it can **do things**.

Let's look at an example.

Imagine you have a piece of text in a variable that you want to display in
uppercase (all CAPITAL letters):

```
msg = "Monster truck rally. 4pm. Monday."
```

You *could* write code that read through each character in the string and
printed out the matching uppercase letter. But if you're programming in a
language like Python, you can do this:

The dot means
"call the method on"
the specified variable.

"upper()" is a string method.

```
print(msg.upper())
```

```
MONSTER TRUCK RALLY. 4PM. MONDAY.
```

Here's what gets
displayed, the value of
the "msg" variable in
UPPERCASE.

But what does `msg.upper()` mean?

Well, `msg` is the string containing our piece of text. The `.upper()` that
follows it is called a string **method**. A method is just an instruction for the
string. When you call `msg.upper()`, you are telling the string to give
you an UPPERCASE version of its data.

**But is there a string method that can help you search
for a substring within a string object?**

WHAT'S MY PURPOSE?

These are some of the many built-in string methods that come with Python. Match each method to what it does. We've done one for you already.

Method

text.endswith(".jpg")

text.upper():

text.lower():

text.replace("tomorrow", "Tuesday"):

text.strip():

text.find("python"):

text.startswith("<HTML>")

What the method does

Return a copy of the string with all occurrences of one substring replaced by another.

Return a copy of the string converted to lowercase.

Return the value **True** if the string has the given substring at the beginning.

Return the value **True** if the string has the given substring at the end.

Return the first index value when the given substring is found.

Return a copy of the string with the leading and trailing whitespace removed.

Return a copy of the string converted to uppercase.

Sharpen your pencil

Which of the above methods do you need to use to locate the price substring within the Beans'R'Us web page?

....

WHAT'S MY PURPOSE? SOLUTION

These are some of the many built-in string methods that come with Python. You were to match each method to what it does.

Method

What the method does

text.endswith(".jpg")

Return a copy of the string with all occurrences of one substring replaced by another.

text.upper():

Return a copy of the string converted to lowercase.

text.lower():

Return the value **True** if the string has the given substring at the beginning.

text.replace("tomorrow", "Tuesday"):

Return the value **True** if the string has the given substring at the end.

text.strip():

Return the first index value when the given substring is found.

text.find("python"):

Return a copy of the string with the leading and trailing whitespace removed.

text.startswith("<HTML>")

Return a copy of the string converted to uppercase.

Sharpen your pencil Solution

Which of the above methods do you need to use to locate the price substring within the Beans'R'Us web page?

The "find()" method

Exercise

You need to update your price-grabbing program so that it extracts the four-character substring that follows the occurence of the ">$" characters. Write the new version of your code in the space provided.

Hints: Don't forget that the `find()` method finds the *starting position* of a substring. Once you've found ">$", use Python's **addition operator** to calculate where in the string you want to extract the substring. The addition operator is the "+" symbol.

Search for this 2-character combination.

Here's what you're really looking for.

```
coffee beans = <strong>$5.49</
strong></p><p>Price valid for
```

Exercise Solution

You needed to update your price-grabbing program so that it extracts the four-character substring that follows the occurence of the ">$" characters.

Hints: Don't forget that the `find()` method finds the *starting position* of a substring. Once you've found ">$", use Python's **addition operator** to calculate where in the string you want to extract the substring. The addition operator is the "+" symbol.

This code hasn't changed.

```
import urllib.request

page = urllib.request.urlopen("http://www.beans-r-us.biz/prices.html")
text = page.read().decode("utf8")
```

Search for the index location of the ">$" combination.

```
where = text.find('>$')
```

This is the addition operator.

The start of the actual price is another 2 index positions along the string, while the end of the price is another 4.

```
start_of_price = where + 2
end_of_price = start_of_price + 4
```

```
price = text[start_of_price:end_of_price]
```

```
print(price)
```

Did you remember to print out the price once you'd found it?

With the start and end index locations known, it's easy to specify the substring required.

Test Drive

OK, so your program should now be able to find the price, no matter where it appears in the page.

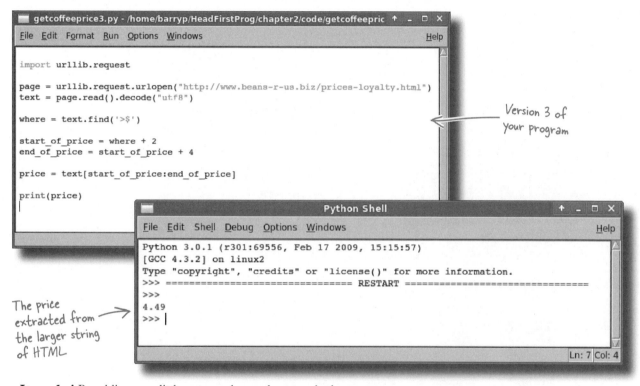

```
getcoffeeprice3.py - /home/barryp/HeadFirstProg/chapter2/code/getcoffeepric
File  Edit  Format  Run  Options  Windows                                Help

import urllib.request

page = urllib.request.urlopen("http://www.beans-r-us.biz/prices-loyalty.html")
text = page.read().decode("utf8")

where = text.find('>$')

start_of_price = where + 2
end_of_price = start_of_price + 4

price = text[start_of_price:end_of_price]

print(price)
```

Version 3 of your program

```
                              Python Shell
File  Edit  Shell  Debug  Options  Windows                              Help
Python 3.0.1 (r301:69556, Feb 17 2009, 15:15:57)
[GCC 4.3.2] on linux2
Type "copyright", "credits" or "license()" for more information.
>>> ============================== RESTART ==============================
>>>
4.49
>>> |
                                                                   Ln: 7 Col: 4
```

The price extracted from the larger string of HTML

It works! By adding very little extra code, you have made the program much smarter and more useful.

That was quick! We're back to saving money once more. Now, there's just one thing...

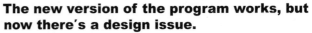

I forgot to say that I only need to know the price when it's $4.74 or lower. I don't want it to bug me when it isn't.

The new version of the program works, but now there's a design issue.

The Starbuzz CEO wants to know when the price of the beans falls below $4.74. The program needs to keep checking the Beans'R'Us website until that happens. It's time to restructure the program to add in this new feature.

Let's add a loop to the program that stops when the price of coffee is right.

Code Magnets

The program code to add the feature is sitting on the fridge door.
Your job is to arrange the magnets so that the program loops until
the price falls to $4.74 or lower.

```
text = page.read().decode("utf8")
```

```
price = 99.99
```

```
import urllib.request
```

```
price = text[start_of_price:end_of_price]
```

```
where = text.find('>$')
```

```
start_of_price = where + 2
```

```
print ("Buy!")
```

```
end_of_price = start_of_price + 4
```

```
while price > 4.74:
```

```
page = urllib.request.urlopen("http://www.beans-r-us.biz/prices.html")
```

Code Magnets Solution

The program code to add the feature was sitting on the fridge door.
You were asked to arrange the magnets so that the program loops
until the price falls to $4.74 or lower.

```python
import urllib.request

price = 99.99

while price > 4.74:

    page = urllib.request.urlopen("http://www.beans-r-us.biz/prices.html")

    text = page.read().decode("utf8")

    where = text.find('>$')
    start_of_price = where + 2

    end_of_price = start_of_price + 4

    price = text[start_of_price:end_of_price]

print ("Buy!")
```

Did you remember to indent these lines? They are inside the loop.

This line shouldn't be indented, as it's outside the loop.

TEST DRIVE

Enter the new version of the program code into an IDLE edit window and run it.

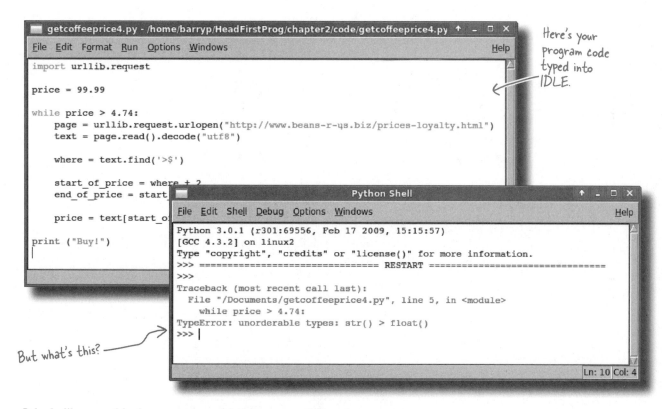

getcoffeeprice4.py - /home/barryp/HeadFirstProg/chapter2/code/getcoffeeprice4.py

File   Edit   Format   Run   Options   Windows   Help

```
import urllib.request

price = 99.99

while price > 4.74:
    page = urllib.request.urlopen("http://www.beans-r-us.biz/prices-loyalty.html")
    text = page.read().decode("utf8")

    where = text.find('>$')

    start_of_price = where + 2
    end_of_price = start

    price = text[start_o

print ("Buy!")
```

Here's your program code typed into IDLE.

Python Shell

File   Edit   Shell   Debug   Options   Windows   Help

```
Python 3.0.1 (r301:69556, Feb 17 2009, 15:15:57)
[GCC 4.3.2] on linux2
Type "copyright", "credits" or "license()" for more information.
>>> ================================ RESTART ================================
>>>
Traceback (most recent call last):
  File "/Documents/getcoffeeprice4.py", line 5, in <module>
    while price > 4.74:
TypeError: unorderable types: str() > float()
>>>
```

Ln: 10 Col: 4

But what's this?

It looks like something's gone wrong with the program. What does `TypeError` mean? What's happened?

BRAIN POWER

Look at the error message in detail. Try to identify which line in the code caused the crash and guess what a `TypeError` might be. Why do you think the code crashed?

Strings and numbers are different

The program crashed because it tried to compare a **string** with
a **number**, which is something that doesn't make a lot of sense
to a computer program. When a piece of data is classified as a
string or a number, this refers to more than just the *contents* of the
variable. We are also referring to its **datatype**. If two pieces of
data are *different types*, we can't compare them to each other.

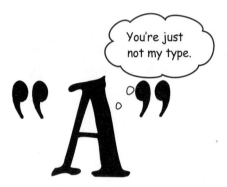

Think back to the previous chapter. You've seen this problem before,
back when you were working on the guessing game program:

This variable will be
set to a number.

"9" is a string.

```
guess = int(g)
```

The int() function converts the "9"
string into an integer, which is then
assigned to "guess".

In the guessing-game program, you needed to *convert* the user's guess
into an **integer** (a whole number) by using the `int()` function.
But coffee bean prices *aren't* whole numbers, because they contain
numbers after a decimal point. They are **floating point numbers**
or **floats**, and to convert a string to a float, you need to use a
function other than `int()`. You need to use `float()`:

```
float("4.99")
```

Like int(), but works with numbers
that contain a decimal point.

TEST DRIVE

This should be a pretty quick fix. If you use the `float()` function to convert the `price` substring, you should then be able to compare the price to 4.74:

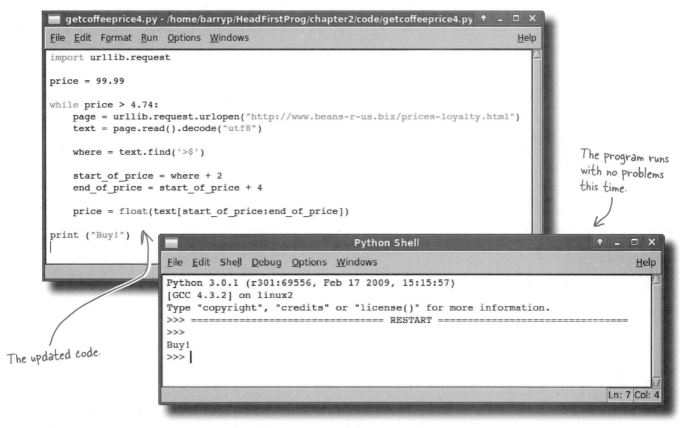

```
getcoffeeprice4.py - /home/barryp/HeadFirstProg/chapter2/code/getcoffeeprice4.py
File  Edit  Format  Run  Options  Windows                                    Help

import urllib.request

price = 99.99

while price > 4.74:
    page = urllib.request.urlopen("http://www.beans-r-us.biz/prices-loyalty.html")
    text = page.read().decode("utf8")

    where = text.find('>$')

    start_of_price = where + 2
    end_of_price = start_of_price + 4

    price = float(text[start_of_price:end_of_price])

print ("Buy!")
```

The updated code.

The program runs with no problems this time.

```
                                Python Shell
File  Edit  Shell  Debug  Options  Windows                                   Help

Python 3.0.1 (r301:69556, Feb 17 2009, 15:15:57)
[GCC 4.3.2] on linux2
Type "copyright", "credits" or "license()" for more information.
>>> =============================== RESTART ===============================
>>>
Buy!
>>> |
                                                                    Ln: 7 Col: 4
```

That's much better. Your program now waits patiently until the price falls to the right level and only then does it tell the CEO that the time is right to buy a fresh batch of coffee beans.

> This is great! Now I can get on with the rest of my day and I only hear when the price of beans drops to the right level. This'll save millions! I'll tell every outlet to use it **worldwide**.

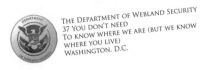

THE DEPARTMENT OF WEBLAND SECURITY
37 YOU DON'T NEED
TO KNOW WHERE WE ARE (BUT WE KNOW
WHERE YOU LIVE)
WASHINGTON, D.C.

From: The Department of Webland Security
Secret Service - Corporate Enforcement Unit

To Whom It May Concern:

A recent investigation into an apparent Distributed Denial
of Service (DDoS) attack on the www.beans-r-us.biz domain
showed that much of the traffic originated from machines
located in various Starbuzz outlets from around the world.
The number of web transactions (which reached a peak of
several hundred thousand requests worldwide) resulted in
a crash of the Beans'R'Us servers, resulting in a
significant loss of business.

In accordance with the powers invested in this office
by the United States Attorney General, we are alerting the
developer of the very dim view we take of this kind of
thing. In short:

We're watching you, Bud. Consider yourself on notice.

Yours faithfully,

Head of Internet Affairs

That sounds weird. What happened?

The program has overloaded the Beans'R'Us Server

It looks like there's a problem with the program. It's sending so many requests that it overwhelmed the Beans'R'Us website. So why did that happen? Let's look at the code and see:

Here's the code as it currently stands.

```
import urllib.request
price = 99.99
while price > 4.74:
    page = urllib.request.urlopen("http://www.beans-r-us.biz/prices.html")
    text = page.read().decode("utf8")
    where = text.find('>$')
    start_of_price = where + 2
    end_of_price = start_of_price + 4
    price = float(text[start_of_price:end_of_price])
print ("Buy!")
```

If the value of `price` isn't low enough (if it's more than 4.74), the program goes back to the top of the loop *immediately* and sends another request.

With the code written this way, the program will generate **thousands** of requests per hour. Multiply that by all the Starbuzz outlets around the world, and you can start to see the scale of the problem:

You need to delay the pricing requests. But how?

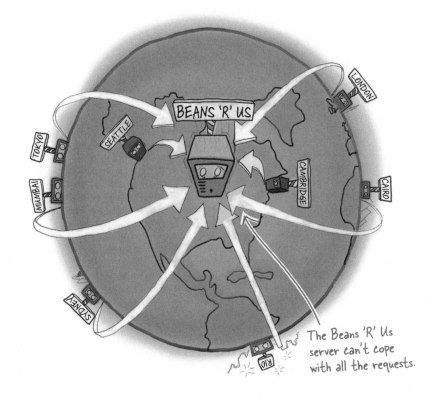

The Beans 'R' Us server can't cope with all the requests.

Time... if only you had more of it

Just when you're feeling completely lost, you get a phone call from the Starbuzz coder who wrote the original version of the program:

Zzzkzzkkvkk... Sorry, dude... vvzzz... Heavy snow... ffzzkk... Phone connection... pzzzkkkvkk.... I think you need the.... vzzzkkkk.... time library!

It seems that she can't get back because of a storm in the mountains. But she does make a suggestion. You need to regulate how often you make a request of the Beans'R'Us web server. One way to do this is to use the **time library**. This will apparently make it possible to send requests every *15 minutes* or so, which should help to lighten the load.

There's just one thing: **what's a library?**

You're already using library code

Look at the first line of the original code:

This says that we are going to use code stored in the "urllib.request" library.

```
import urllib.request
```

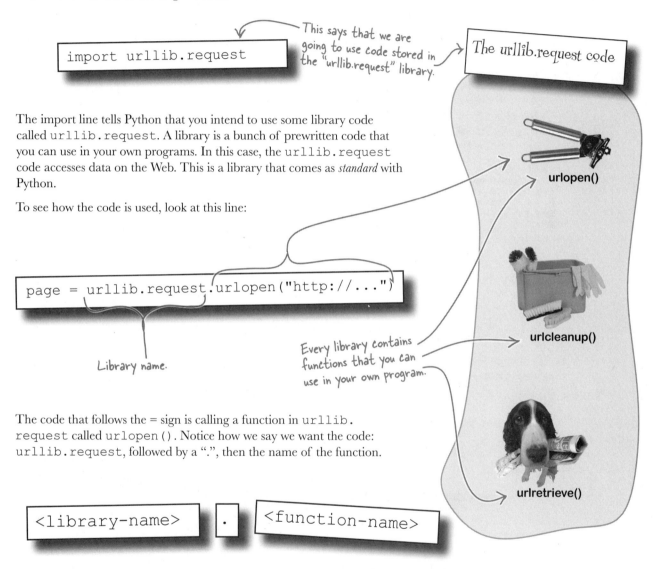

The urllib.request code

urlopen()

The import line tells Python that you intend to use some library code called urllib.request. A library is a bunch of prewritten code that you can use in your own programs. In this case, the urllib.request code accesses data on the Web. This is a library that comes as *standard* with Python.

To see how the code is used, look at this line:

```
page = urllib.request.urlopen("http://...")
```

Library name.

Every library contains functions that you can use in your own program.

urlcleanup()

The code that follows the = sign is calling a function in urllib.request called urlopen(). Notice how we say we want the code: urllib.request, followed by a ".", then the name of the function.

urlretrieve()

```
<library-name>
```
.
```
<function-name>
```

But how will the time library help us? Let's see...

Long Exercise

These are some of the functions provided by Python's built-in time library:

Python Library Documentation: time

```
time.clock()
        The current time in seconds, given as a floating
        point number.

time.daylight()
        This returns 0 if you are not currently in
        Daylight Savings Time.

time.gmtime()
        Tells you current UTC date and time (not affected
        by the timezone).

time.localtime()
        Tells you the current local time (is affected by
        your timezone).

time.sleep(secs)
        Don't do anything for the specified number of
        seconds.

time.time()
        Tells you the number of seconds since January 1st,
        1970.

time.timezone()
        Tells you the number of hours difference between
        your timezone and the UTC timezone (London).
```

You need to use **one** of these functions to help you fix your code.

But which one? Draw a circle around the function you think you might need.

With the appropriate function identified, amend the code to control how often the request for the web page is sent to the server. The Beans'R'Us webmaster has been in touch to say that their web-based pricing information is updated every 15 minutes. Fill in the blanks in the code as indicated by the dashed lines.

Hints: 15 minutes equates to 15 multiplied by 60 seconds, which is 900 seconds. Also: to use the functionality provided by a library, remember to import it first.

```python
import urllib.request

.............................................

price = 99.99
while price > 4.74:

    .............................................
    page = urllib.request.urlopen("http://www.beans-r-us.biz/prices.html")
    text = page.read().decode("utf8")
    where = text.find('>$')
    start_of_price = where + 2
    end_of_price = start_of_price + 4
    price = float(text[start_of_price:end_of_price])
print ("Buy!")
```

Long Exercise Solution

These are some of the functions provided by Python's built-in time library:

> ### Python Library Documentation: time
>
> **time.clock()**
> The current time in seconds, given as a floating point number.
>
> **time.daylight()**
> This returns 0 if you are not currently in Daylight Savings Time.
>
> **time.gmtime()**
> Tells you current UTC date and time (not affected by the timezone).
>
> **time.localtime()**
> Tells you the current local time (is affected by your timezone).
>
> **time.sleep(secs)**
> Don't do anything for the specified number of seconds.
>
> **time.time()**
> Tells you the number of seconds since January 1st, 1970.
>
> **time.timezone()**
> Tells you the number of hours difference between your timezone and the UTC timezone (London).

This looks like the best function to use.

You need to use **one** of these functions to help you fix your code.

But which one? You were to draw a circle around the function you thought you might need.

With the appropriate function identified, you were to amend the code to control how often the request for the web page is sent to the server. The Beans'R'Us webmaster has been in touch to say that their web-based pricing information is updated every 15 minutes. You were to fill in the blanks in the code as indicated by the dashed lines.

Hints: 15 minutes equates to 15 multiplied by 60 seconds, which is 900 seconds. Also: to use the functionality provided by a library, remember to import it first.

Import the library at the top of the program. This gives the program access to all the built-in functionality that the library provides.

```python
import urllib.request
import time

price = 99.99
while price > 4.74:
    time.sleep(900)
    page = urllib.request.urlopen("http://www.beans-r-us.biz/prices.html")
    text = page.read().decode("utf8")
    where = text.find('>$')
    start_of_price = where + 2
    end_of_price = start_of_price + 4
    price = float(text[start_of_price:end_of_price])
print ("Buy!")
```

Use the facilities of the time library to pause the program for 15 minutes between requests.

Order is restored

Starbuzz Coffee is off the blacklist, because their price-checking programs no longer kill the Beans'R'Us web server. The nice people at Webland Security have, rather quietly, gone away.

Coffee beans get ordered when the price is right!

I love the taste of this coffee, and I just love the cost of those beans!

Your Programming Toolbox

You've got Chapter 2 under your belt. Let's look back at what you've learned in this chapter:

Programming Tools

* Strings are sequences of individual characters.

* Individual string characters are referenced by index.

* Index values are offsets that start from zero.

* Methods provide variables with built-in functionality.

* Programming libraries provide a collection of related pre-built code and functions.

* As well as having a value, data in variables also have a "data type."

* Number is a data type.

* String is a data type.

Python Tools

* s[4] – access the 5th character of the variable "s", which is a string

* s[6:12] – access a sub-string within the string "s" (up to, but not including)

* s.find() method for searching strings

* s.upper() method for converting strings to UPPERCASE

* float() converts strings to decimal point numbers known as "floats"

* + addition operator

* > greater than operator

* urllib.request library for talking to the Web

* time library for working with dates/time

3 functions

 Let's get organized

@starbuzzceo Waiting patiently for milk...

As programs grow, the code often becomes more complex.

And complex code can be hard to read, and even harder to maintain. One way of managing this complexity is to create **functions**. Functions are **snippets of code** that you use as needed from within your program. They allow you to **separate out common actions**, and this means that they make your code **easier to read** and **easier to maintain**. In this chapter, you'll discover how a little function knowledge can **make your coding life a whole lot easier**.

Starbuzz is out of beans!

The Starbuzz buyers love the program you created in the last chapter. Thanks to your efforts, the Starbuzz CEO is only buying coffee beans when the price drops below $4.74, and his organization is saving money as a result.

But, now there's a problem: some Starbuzz outlets have *run out of beans*.

> We have a worldwide crisis! We've run out of coffee beans in some of our stores, and we've lost some customers, too. My buyers are only buying coffee when the cost is low, but if we run short on coffee supplies, I'll pay any price.

When the coffee beans start to run low in an outlet, the Starbuzz baristas need to be able to send an **emergency order** to the CEO. The outlets need some way of *immediately* requesting the purchase of coffee beans at the current price, regardless of what that price is. They also need the option of waiting for the best price, too, just like in the current program.

The program needs an extra option.

What does the new program need to do?

The new program for Starbuzz needs to give the user two options.

The first option is to watch and wait for the price of coffee beans to drop. If the user chooses this option, the program should run exactly as it did before.

The second option is for the user to place an *emergency order*. If the user chooses this option, the program should immediately display the current price from the supplier's website.

Sharpen your pencil

Here's the existing code for Starbuzz. You need to modify the program to add an emergency report feature that will immediately report the current price. Which parts of the code can you reuse to generate the emergency report? Grab your pencil and circle the part of the code you think you might reuse. Why do you think you'll need to resuse this code?

```python
import urllib.request
import time


price = 99.99
while price > 4.74:
        time.sleep(900)
        page = urllib.request.urlopen("http://www.beans-r-us.biz/prices.html")
        text = page.read().decode("utf8")
        where = text.find('>$')
        start_of_price = where + 2
        end_of_price = start_of_price + 4
        price = float(text[start_of_price:end_of_price])


print ("Buy!")
```

Sharpen your pencil
Solution

Here's the existing code for Starbuzz. You needed to modify the program to add an emergency report feature which will immediately report the current price. Which parts of the code can you reuse to generate the emergency report? You were to circle the part of the code you think you might reuse as well as state why you might need to reuse it:

```python
import urllib.request
import time


price = 99.99
while price > 4.74:
        time.sleep(900)
        page = urllib.request.urlopen("http://www.beans-r-us.biz/prices.html")
        text = page.read().decode("utf8")
        where = text.find('>$')
        start_of_price = where + 2
        end_of_price = start_of_price + 4
        price = float(text[start_of_price:end_of_price])

print ("Buy!")
```

Here's the code you can reuse.

Whether you wait for the right price or request an emergency order, you'll need this code in each case.

Does that mean we have to duplicate the code for each option? Is this a good idea?

If you just copy and paste the same code, it could make your program very long. And hard to maintain. That's why you *don't* want to duplicate the code.

Imagine if you had to maintain a program this length.

Don't <u>duplicate</u> your code...

When you need to add a new feature to a program that's similar to some other code in the program, you might be tempted to just copy and paste the code.

In practice, that's actually a pretty bad idea, because it can lead to **code bloat**. Code bloat means that you have more code in your program than you actually need. Your programs will get longer, and they'll get a lot harder to maintain.

← You'll find that code bloat is common in lots of programs, even code written by professional programmers.

> Here's the printout of the tic-tac-toe game. If you really want me to change the colors of the crosses, I'll just need to replace the code that displays each of the 9 squares. That's the same code in 9 different places. Oh, and if you want me to change the 0s...

...<u>Reuse</u> your code instead

Programming languages all come with features that allow you to **reuse code**. So what's the difference between *copying* and *reusing* code?

If you copy code, you simply duplicate it. But when you reuse code, you have a **single copy** of the code that you can **call** in all the places that you need it. Not only will your programs be shorter, but it also means that when you amend code, you will need to change it only **once** and in **one place only**.

> So you want a new gravity-bomb launcher added to each of the star-fighters? No problem. I'll change a few lines of code and every craft in the fleet will be updated.

So code reuse is a good thing. But how do you do it?

Reuse code with <u>functions</u>

Most programming languages let you create reusable, *shareable* code with **functions**. A function is a chunk of code that you separate out from the rest of your program, give a name, and then **call** from your code.

Different languages have different ways of creating functions. In Python, use the **def** keyword to *define* a new function. Here's some Python code that defines a make_smoothie() function:

A function is a boxed-up piece of reusable code.

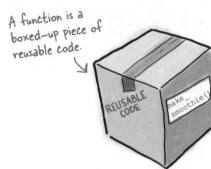

Give the function a name.

The parentheses are important, so be sure to include them.

The code you share is indented.

```python
def make_smoothie():
    juice = input("What juice would you like? ")
    fruit = input("OK - and how about the fruit? ")
    print("Thanks. Let's go!")
    print("Crushing the ice...")
    print("Blending the " + fruit)
    print("Now adding in the " + juice + " juice")
    print("Finished! There's your " + fruit + " and " + juice + " smoothie!")
```

In Python, it's important that you define the function *before* you use it, so make sure the code that *calls* (or *uses*) the function comes *after* the definition of the function:

Call the function. Note the use of parens.

```python
print("Welcome to smoothie-matic 2.0")
another = "Y"
while another == "Y":
    make_smoothie()
    another = input("How about another(Y/N)? ")
```

When the computer first encounters a call to the function, it jumps to the start of the function, runs the code it finds there... then returns to the calling piece of code. The function "answers the call" to run its code.

Every time that Python sees make_smoothie() in the code, it jumps to the code in the make_smoothie() function. It runs the code in the function until it gets to the end, and then returns to the next line in the code that called it.

Let's use functions to share code within your program.

Code Magnets

Before you amend the existing coffee bean program code, let's
see if you can create a function to display the current bean price.
Rearrange the magnets in the correct order to create the function:

We've given you a head start
by adding the first magnet.

```
page = urllib.request.urlopen("http://www.beans-r-us.biz/prices.html")
text = page.read().decode("utf8")
where = text.find('>$')
start_of_price = where + 2
end_of_price = start_of_price + 4
```

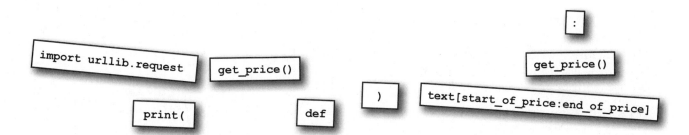

```
import urllib.request        get_price()

                    :

                                get_price()

        print(          def          )        text[start_of_price:end_of_price]
```

Code Magnets Solution

Before you amend the existing coffee bean program code, let's see if you can create a function to display the current bean price. You were to rearrange the magnets in the correct order to create the function:

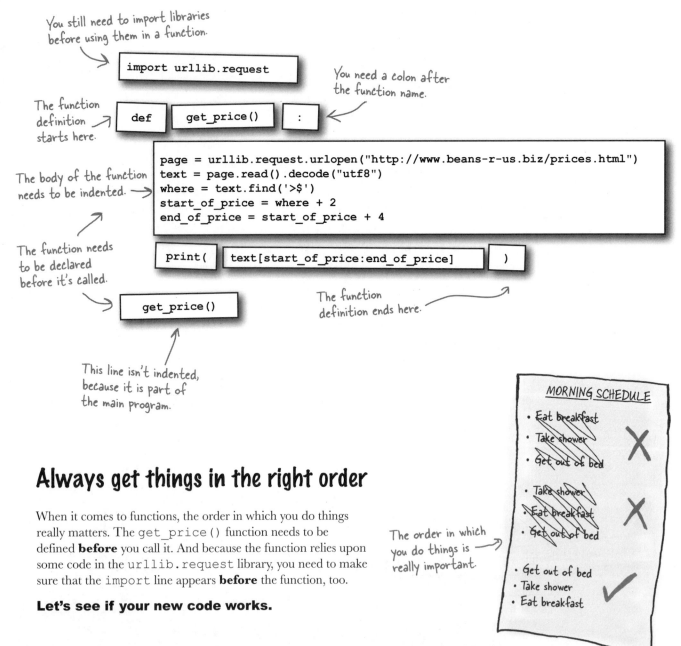

You still need to import libraries before using them in a function.

```
import urllib.request
```

You need a colon after the function name.

The function definition starts here.

```
def    get_price()    :
```

The body of the function needs to be indented.

```
page = urllib.request.urlopen("http://www.beans-r-us.biz/prices.html")
text = page.read().decode("utf8")
where = text.find('>$')
start_of_price = where + 2
end_of_price = start_of_price + 4
```

The function needs to be declared before it's called.

```
print(    text[start_of_price:end_of_price]    )
```

```
get_price()
```

The function definition ends here.

This line isn't indented, because it is part of the main program.

Always get things in the right order

When it comes to functions, the order in which you do things really matters. The `get_price()` function needs to be defined **before** you call it. And because the function relies upon some code in the `urllib.request` library, you need to make sure that the `import` line appears **before** the function, too.

Let's see if your new code works.

The order in which you do things is really important.

MORNING SCHEDULE
- Eat breakfast
- Take shower
- Get out of bed   ✗

- Take shower
- Eat breakfast
- Get out of bed   ✗

- Get out of bed
- Take shower
- Eat breakfast   ✓

Test Drive

Type the code on the opposite page into IDLE, and run it to see what happens:

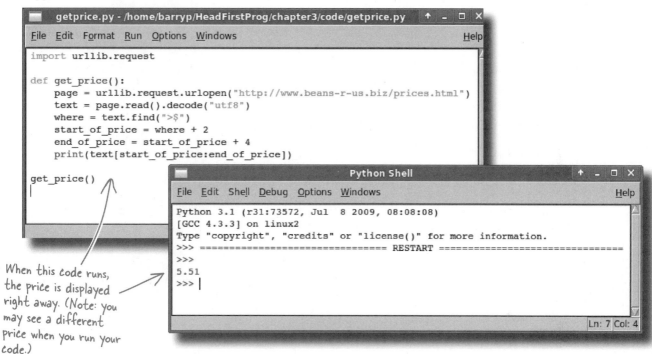

```
getprice.py - /home/barryp/HeadFirstProg/chapter3/code/getprice.py

File   Edit   Format   Run   Options   Windows                              Help

import urllib.request

def get_price():
    page = urllib.request.urlopen("http://www.beans-r-us.biz/prices.html")
    text = page.read().decode("utf8")
    where = text.find(">$")
    start_of_price = where + 2
    end_of_price = start_of_price + 4
    print(text[start_of_price:end_of_price])

get_price()
```

```
Python Shell

File   Edit   Shell   Debug   Options   Windows                            Help

Python 3.1 (r31:73572, Jul  8 2009, 08:08:08)
[GCC 4.3.3] on linux2
Type "copyright", "credits" or "license()" for more information.
>>> ================================ RESTART ================================
>>>
5.51
>>>
                                                                    Ln: 7 Col: 4
```

When this code runs, the price is displayed right away. (Note: you may see a different price when you run your code.)

The price appears immediately. You now have a function that reads the contents of the page from the supplier's website and prints out the price information.

You can reuse the function in lots of places in your program simply by calling the get_price() function. Now all you have to do is modify your existing program to use the new function.

BRAIN POWER

Look back at the original program at the start of the chapter. You know that you can use this function to produce emergency reports. But it will also need to replace the existing price-watch code. Is there a problem? Why? Why not?

> Your code prints out the price. Big deal. It's just a pity you actually need to GET the price and USE it. Your code isn't much use, just printing out the price like that, is it?

Functions are great for reusing code, but they really come into their own when they perform an action for you, then give you back some data to use in whichever way you want.

The current version of the get_price() function prints out the price of coffee beans every time it is used, or **called**. This is OK if that's what you really want it to do. The trouble is, you need the function to give you the price so that you can then decide what you want to do with it.

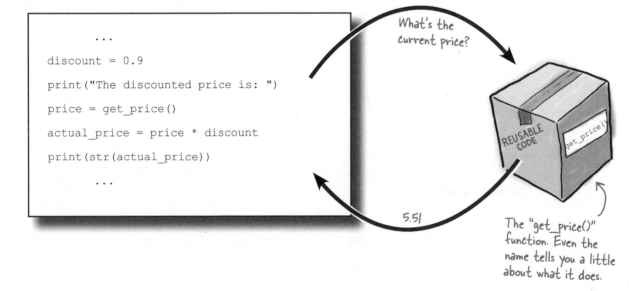

```
    ...
discount = 0.9
print("The discounted price is: ")
price = get_price()
actual_price = price * discount
print(str(actual_price))
    ...
```

What's the current price?

5.51

The "get_price()" function. Even the name tells you a little about what it does.

REUSABLE CODE   get_price()

Return data with the return command

If you use the `return()` command within a function, you can send a data value back to the calling code.

```
import urllib.request

def get_price():
        page = urllib.request.urlopen("http://www.beans-r-us.biz/prices.html")
        text = page.read().decode("utf8")
        where = text.find('>$')
        start_of_price = where + 2
        end_of_price = start_of_price + 4
        print(text[start_of_price:end_of_price])
        return(text[start_of_price:end_of_price])
```

Remove the call to "print()"...

... and replace it with a call to "return()" instead.

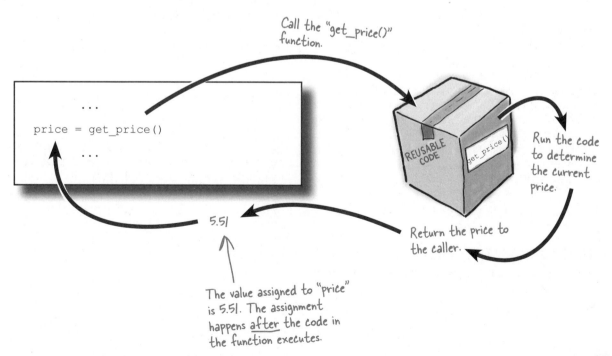

Call the "get_price()" function.

Run the code to determine the current price.

```
    . . .
price = get_price()
    . . .
```

REUSABLE CODE

get_price()

Return the price to the caller.

5.51

The value assigned to "price" is 5.51. The assignment happens *after* the code in the function executes.

there are no
Dumb Questions

Q: The return() command is just like print(), except nothing appears on screen, right?

A: Well... sort of. The `print()` command is designed to display (or *output*) a message, typically on screen. The `return()` command is designed to allow you to arrange for a function you write to provide a value to your program. Recall the use of `randint()` in Chapter 1: a random number between two values was *returned* to your code. So, obviously, when providing your code with a random number, the `randint()` function uses `return()` and not `print()`. In fact, if `randint()` used `print()` instead of `return()`, it would be pretty useless as a reusable function.

Q: So, it's a case of return() letting a function give you something back?

A: Yes, that's it, exactly.

Q: I'm not sure I'm convinced about using functions. Isn't using copy'n'paste quick and easy?

A: No, using copy'n'paste is *quick and dirty*, with the emphasis on the "dirty." When you need to repeatedly use some code, it's always better to create a function to contain and name that code. You then call (or *invoke*) the function as needed. If you later decide to change how the repeated code works, it's a no-brainer to change the code in the function **once**. If, instead, you "quickly" performed copy'n'paste five times, that's five changes you now have to make, and the chance of you missing one change or making a mistake are actually pretty high. So, don't copy'n'paste!

Q: So, using a function lets you share the repeated code in a controlled way?

A: Yes, it does. There's also a guiding principle among prgrammers known as DRY: *Don't Repeat Yourself*. Using functions lets you keep your code DRY.

Q: What happens if the function omits the return() command? Does each function have to have one?

A: No, the use of `return()` is not required. In fact, the current version of your `get_price()` function doesn't use `return()` at all. But, your function feels like it *gives* you something because it prints the current price on screen. When the `return()` command is omitted, a function returns a special *no value*. In Python, this value is called `None`.

Q: So, just to be clear, using return() is optional?

A: Yes, it is.

Q: Does return() always come at the end of the function?

A: Usually, but this is not a requirement, either. The `return()` can appear anywhere within a function and, when it is executed, control returns to the calling code from that point in the function. It is perfectly reasonable, for instance, to have multiple uses of `return()` within a function, perhaps embedded with `if` statements which then provide a way to control which `return()` is invoked when.

Q: Can return() send more than one result back to the caller?

A: Yes, it can. `return()` can provide a list of results to the calling code. But, let's not get ahead of ourselves, because lists are not covered until the next chapter. And there's a little bit more to learn about using `return()` first, so let's read on and get back to work.

Sharpen your pencil

Using the new `get_price()` function, write a new version of the price-checking program that does this:

1. Ask the user to indicate if the price is required immediately (Y/N).

2. If the user chooses "Y" for "yes," find the current price and display it on the screen.

3. Otherwise, check the price every 15 minutes until it falls below $4.74, then (and only then), display the price on screen.

....

....

....

....

....

....

....

....

....

....

....

....

....

....

....

....

....

....

Sharpen your pencil
Solution

Using the new `get_price()` function, you were asked to write a new version of the price-checking program that does this:

1. Ask the user to indicate if the price is required immediately (Y/N).

2. If the user chooses "Y" for "yes," find the current price and display it on the screen.

3. Otherwise, check the price every 15 minutes until it falls below $4.74, then (and only then), display the price on screen.

Your code may look a little different from this, but that's OK. As long as it does the same thing, you're doing fine.

```python
import urllib.request
import time

def get_price():
    page = urllib.request.urlopen("http://www.beans-r-us.biz/prices.html")
    text = page.read().decode("utf8")
    where = text.find('>$')
    start_of_price = where + 2
    end_of_price = start_of_price + 4
    return float(text[start_of_price:end_of_price])

price_now = input("Do you want to see the price now (Y/N)? ")
if price_now == "Y":
    print(get_price())
else:
    price = 99.99
    while price > 4.74:
        time.sleep(900)
        price = get_price()
    print("Buy!")
```

You need to ask the user if the price is required immediately.

If the user chooses "Y", display the value that the get_price() function gives you.

If the user decides to wait for the price to drop, get the price using the get_price() function, then use the given value to decide whether or not it's time to buy coffee.

See what happens when you run the new program. Make the required
changes in IDLE and take your new program for a spin:

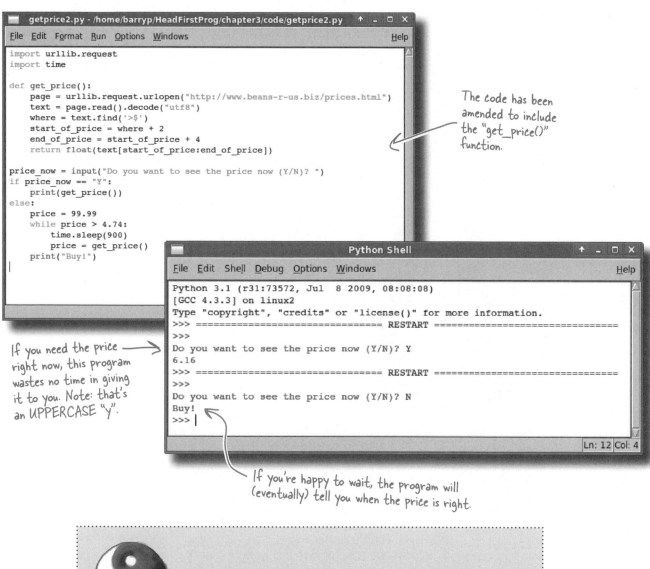

The code has been
amended to include
the "get_price()"
function.

If you need the price
right now, this program
wastes no time in giving
it to you. Note: that's
an UPPERCASE "Y".

If you're happy to wait, the program will
(eventually) tell you when the price is right.

Design principle: reuse code with functions.

This is great; it does just what I want! In fact, it's so good it's given me an idea. Since I'm on the road a lot, I'd like the price sent to my cell. Can your program tweet me?

The CEO wants the price sent to his cell phone.

Rather than have the emergency report displayed on a PC, the Starbuzz CEO would prefer to get something more immediate while he's on the road. He needs messages to be sent directly to his **Twitter** account.

BRAIN BARBELL

Sending a message to a Twitter account feels like a tall order. Where do you think you'd start looking for helpful suggestions and, quite possibly, a solution to this new problem?

Use the ~~Force,~~ Web Luke

It's pretty complicated to write a program that sends messages to a service like Twitter. Fortunately, other people have already tackled problems like this and posted their code on the Web. Here's a Python function (found on the Web) that is very similar to what you need:

This is the text of the message that will be sent.

Put your Twitter username here.

Put your Twitter password here.

```python
def send_to_twitter():
    msg = "I am a message that will be sent to Twitter"
    password_manager = urllib.request.HTTPPasswordMgr()
    password_manager.add_password("Twitter API",
                          "http://twitter.com/statuses", "...", "...")
    http_handler = urllib.request.HTTPBasicAuthHandler(password_manager)
    page_opener = urllib.request.build_opener(http_handler)
    urllib.request.install_opener(page_opener)
    params = urllib.parse.urlencode( {'status': msg} )
    resp = urllib.request.urlopen("http://twitter.com/statuses/update.json", params)
    resp.read()
```

This code looks complex but, for now, all you need to know is that it sends a message to the Twitter service. An advantage of using functions (which is illustrated here) is that they allow you to understand a program at a high level without having to initially understand all the details. This is known as working at a higher level of **abstraction**.

BRAIN POWER

This code looks like it could be useful. But is there a problem?

Why can't you just replace the `print()` calls in our existing program with calls to this function?

Do this!

To use the code you will first need to sign up for a free **Twitter** account. To register, go to:

```
https://twitter.com/signup
```

The function always sends the same message

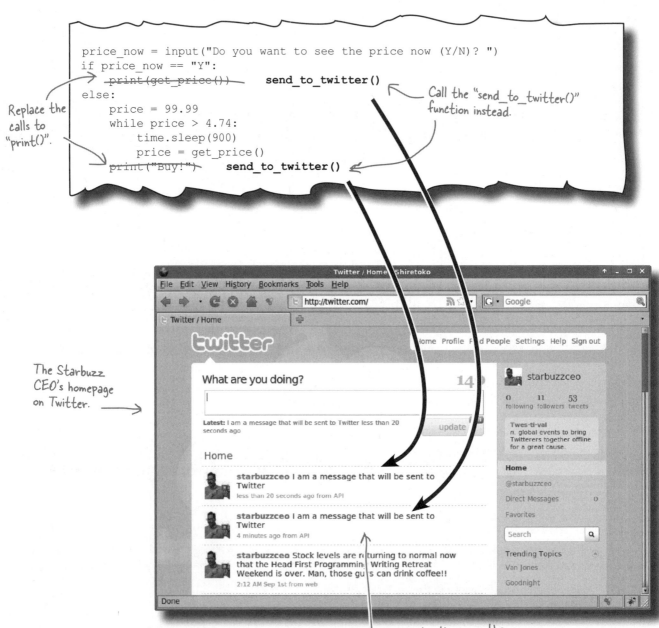

```
price_now = input("Do you want to see the price now (Y/N)? ")
if price_now == "Y":
    print(get_price())          send_to_twitter()
else:
    price = 99.99
    while price > 4.74:
        time.sleep(900)
        price = get_price()
    print("Buy!")          send_to_twitter()
```

Replace the calls to "print()".

Call the "send_to_twitter()" function instead.

The Starbuzz CEO's homepage on Twitter.

No matter which option is chosen by the user, the "send_to_twitter()" function sends the same tweet to Twitter.

Well, duh, it's pretty obvious really...
you need a version of the function
that tweets the low price and
another that tweets an emergency
order. How hard is that?

```
def send_to_twitter():
        # original code here...
```

Take the original
Twitter code and
create two new
functions.

```
def send_to_twitter_price_low():
        # original code here...
        # ...but change message to
        # buy at low price.
```

```
def send_to_twitter_emergency():
        # original code here...
        # ... but change message to
        # place an emergency order.
```

Lines that start with # are known
as comments in Python. Comments
are code annotations put there by a
coder and are meant to be read by
other coders working with the code.
Python ignores all comments, because
they aren't executable code.

BRAIN POWER

Something doesn't feel quite right about this solution.

Can you see the problem that this creates? Can you
think of a solution that fixes the problem?

Use parameters to avoid duplicating functions

Just like it's a bad idea to use copy'n'paste for repeated usages of code, it's *also* a bad idea to create multiple copies of a function with only minor differences between them. Look again at the proposed `send_to_twitter_price_low()` and `send_to_twitter_emergency()` functions on the previous page; the *only* difference between them is the message they send.

A **parameter** is a value that you send *into* your function. Think of it as the opposite of what you get when you return a value from a function:

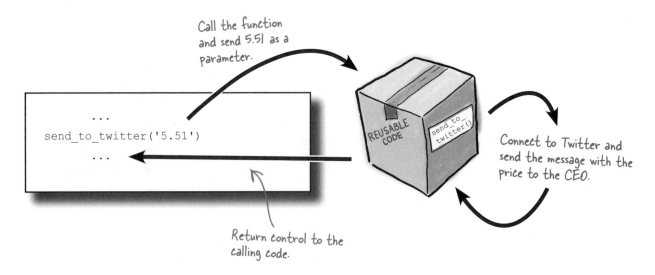

Call the function and send 5.51 as a parameter.

```
...
send_to_twitter('5.51')
...
```

Connect to Twitter and send the message with the price to the CEO.

Return control to the calling code.

The parameter's value works just like a variable *within* the function, except for the fact that its initial value is set *outside* the function code:

In this version of the function, the "msg" variable is set to the value passed in by the call to "send_to_twitter('5.51')".

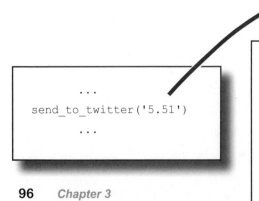

```
...
send_to_twitter('5.51')
...
```

```
def send_to_twitter(msg):
    password_manager = urllib.request.HTTPPasswordMgr()
    password_manager.add_password("Twitter API",
                        "http://twitter.com/st
    http_handler = urllib.request.HTTPBasicAuthHandler(pas
    page_opener = urllib.request.build_opener(http_handle
    urllib.request.install_opener(page_opener)
    params = urllib.parse.urlencode( {'status': msg} )
    resp = urllib.request.urlopen("http://twitter.com/sta
```

Parameters Up Close

To use a parameter in Python, simply put a variable name between the parentheses that come *after* the definition of the function name and *before* the colon. Then within the function itself, simply use the variable like you would any other:

The parameter name goes here.

```
def shout_out(the_name):
    return("Congratulations " + the_name + "!")
```

Use the parameter's value in your function's code just like any other variable.

Later, invoke the function from your code with a different parameter value each time you use the function:

```
print(shout_out('Wanda'))
msg = shout_out('Graham, John, Michael, Eric, and Terry by 2')
print(shout_out('Monty'))
```

Sharpen your pencil

Grab your pencil and update your program. Do the following:

1. Modify the `send_to_twitter()` function so that the message text is passed into the function as a parameter.

2. Update your code to make the approriate parameterized calls to `sent_to_twitter()`.

....

....

....

....

....

....

....

....

....

Sharpen your pencil
Solution

You were to grab your pencil and update your code to incorporate a version of `send_to_twitter()` that supports parameters:

```
import urllib.request
import time

def send_to_twitter(msg):
def send_to_twitter():
    msg = "I am a message that will be sent to Twitter"
    password_manager = urllib.request.HTTPPasswordMgr()
    password_manager.add_password("Twitter API",
                          "http://twitter.com/statuses", "...", "...")
    http_handler = urllib.request.HTTPBasicAuthHandler(password_manager)
    page_opener = urllib.request.build_opener(http_handler)
    urllib.request.install_opener(page_opener)
    params = urllib.parse.urlencode( {'status': msg} )
    resp = urllib.request.urlopen("http://twitter.com/statuses/update.json", params)
    resp.read()
```

The msg variable in the code needs to become a parameter of the function.

- -

```
def get_price():
    page = urllib.request.urlopen("http://www.beans-r-us.biz/prices.html")
    text = page.read().decode("utf8")
    where = text.find('>$')
    start_of_price = where + 2
    end_of_price = start_of_price + 4
    return float(text[start_of_price:end_of_price])

price_now = input("Do you want to see the price now (Y/N)? ")

if price_now == "Y":
    print(get_price()) send_to_twitter(get_price())
else:
    price = 99.99
    while price > 4.74:
        time.sleep(900)
        price = get_price()
    print("Buy!")
    send_to_twitter("Buy!")
```

You just need to replace the print() calls with send_to_twitter() calls.

Test Drive

Now you've amended the program code, it's time to see if it works. Make sure the amended code is in IDLE, and then press F5 to run your program.

To begin, let's send an emergency message:

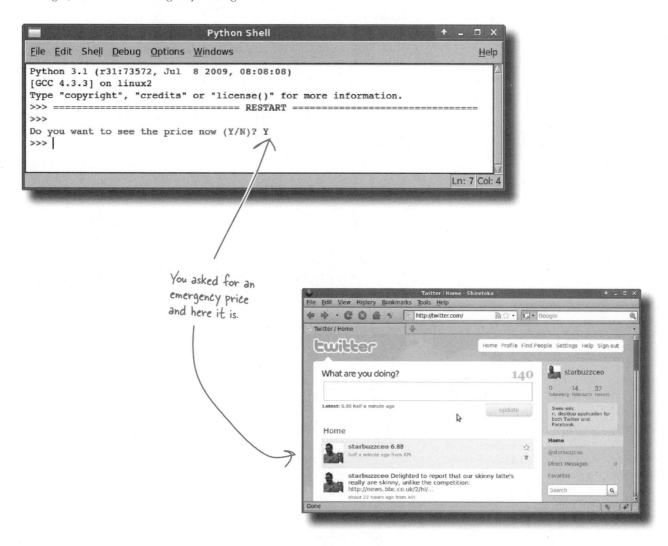

You asked for an emergency price and here it is.

```
Python 3.1 (r31:73572, Jul  8 2009, 08:08:08)
[GCC 4.3.3] on linux2
Type "copyright", "credits" or "license()" for more information.
>>> ============================ RESTART ============================
>>>
Do you want to see the price now (Y/N)? Y
>>>
```

That worked. But what about the price-watch option...?

TEST DRIVE

CONTINUED...

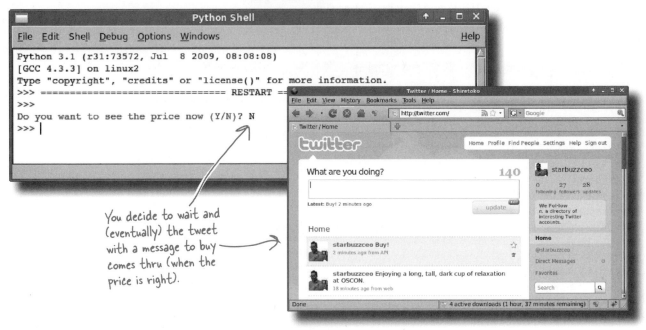

You decide to wait and (eventually) the tweet with a message to buy comes thru (when the price is right).

That works as well. You're ready to go live!

Beep, beep... was that someone's phone?

Great, an emergency order! I'll quickly place a call before we run out of beans again...

No matter where the Starbuzz CEO is, if he has his cell nearby, he gets the message.

---
there are no
Dumb Questions

Q: Can I still call the Twitter function like this: send_to_twitter()? Or do I always have to provide a value for the msg parameter?

A: As it's written, the parameter is required by the function. If you leave it out, Python will complain and refuse to run your code further.

Q: Can parameters to functions be optional?

A: Yes. In most programming languages (including Python), you can provide a default value for a parameter, which is then used if the calling code doesn't provide any value. This has the effect of making the parameter optional, in that it either takes its value from the one provided by the caller, or uses the default value if the caller does not provide anything.

Q: Can there be more than one parameter?

A: Yes, you can have as many as you like. Just bear in mind that a function with a gazillion parameters can be hard to understand, let alone use.

Q: Can all the parameters be optional?

A: Yes. As an example, Python's built-in `print()` function can have up to three optional parameters, in addition to the stuff to print (which is *also* optional). To learn more, open up a Python Shell prompt and type `help(print)` at the >>> prompt.

Q: Doesn't all that optional stuff get kinda confusing?

A: Sometimes. As you create and use functions, you'll get a feel for when to make parameters mandatory and when to make them optional. If you look at the description of `print()` again, you'll see that in most usage scenarios `print()` takes a single parameter: the thing to display. It is only when extra, less common, functionality is required that the other parameters are needed.

Q: The description of print() mentions "keyword arguments." What are they?

A: The word "argument" is another name for "parameter," and it means the same thing. In Python, an argument can have an optional "keyword" associated with it. This means that the parameter has been given a name that the calling code can use to identify which value in its code is associated with which parameter in the function.

Continuing to use `print()` as an example, the `sep`, `end`, and `file` parameters (a.k.a. keyword arguments) each have a default value, so they are all optional. However, if you need to use only one of them in the calling code, you need some way to identify which one you are using, and that's where the keyword arguments come in. There are examples of these optional features of `print()` and other such functions later in the book. Don't sweat the details right now, though.

Someone decided to mess with your code

About time I changed the Twitter password. Hmmm... Interesting code, but it would be great if it printed a message every time it sent a tweet. I think I'll just improve it a little...

One of the Starbuzz coders decided that the password should be set at the start of the program, where it can be easily amended in the future. This is what she added:

STARBUZZ
CORP
" BE INSPIRED
GET TOTALLY WIRED"

```
import urllib.request
import time


def set_password():
    password="C8H10N4O2"      ← This is the new password.

                        The coder wants to set the
set_password()    ←    password at the top of the
                        file where it's easy to find.

def send_to_twitter(msg):                              Use the value of
    password_manager = urllib.request.HTTPPasswordMgr()   "password" here.
    password_manager.add_password("Twitter API",            ↓
              "http://twitter.com/statuses", "starbuzzceo", password)
```

So, later in the program, the code uses the password variable. That means that next time the password needs to be changed, it will be easier to find it in the code because it is set right near the top of the file.

Test Drive

Add the new password code to the top of the program and then run it through IDLE:

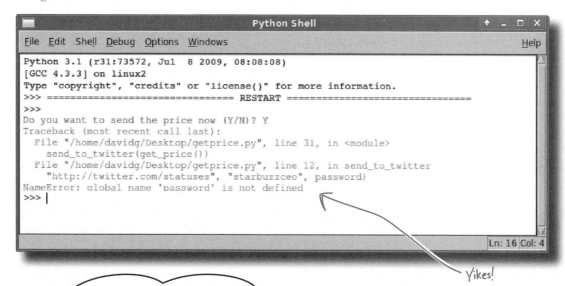

Yikes!

Oh no! It crashes! What happened?!? Our order system has stopped working worldwide! If we don't get information on where we need coffee orders soon, this could be the end of Starbuzz... Help!

The program has crashed and it can no longer send out messages to the CEO. Stores across the globe are running short on beans and it's up to you to fix the code.

BRAIN POWER

Look at the error message that was generated when the program crashed. What do you think happened?

The rest of the program can't see
the password variable

The program crashed because, for some reason, the program couldn't find a variable called `password`. But that's a little odd, because you define it in the `set_password()` function:

```
def set_password():
    password="C8H10N4O2"       ← This code sets the password.

set_password()   ← This code calls for the password to be set.

def send_to_twitter(msg):
    password_manager = urllib.request.HTTPPasswordMgr()
    password_manager.add_password("Twitter API",
              "http://twitter.com/statuses", "starbuzzceo", password)
```

This code uses the password... but for some reason, it can't see it. ↓

So what happened? Why can't the `send_to_twitter()` function see the `password` variable that was created in the `set_password()` function?

Programming languages record variables using a section of memory called the **stack**. It works like a notepad. For example, when the user is asked if she wants to send a price immediately, her answer is recorded against the `price_now` variable:

When you call a function, the computer creates a fresh list of variables

But when you call a function, Python starts to record any new variables created in the function's code on a *new* sheet of paper on the stack:

← New stack frame

LOCAL variables used by the function

STACK FRAME FOR: set_password()

VARIABLES

NAME | VALUE
password | "C8H1ON4O2"

```
def set_password():
    password="C8H10N4O2"
```

The calling code's variables are still here.

This new sheet of paper on the stack is called a new **stack frame.** Stack frames record all of the new variables that are created within a function. These are known as **local variables**.

The variables that were created before the function was called are still there if the function needs them; they are on the *previous* stack frame.

But why does the computer record variables like this?

Your program creates a new stack frame each time it calls a function, allowing the function to have its own separate set of variables. If the function creates a new variable for some internal calculation, it does so on its own stack frame without affecting the already existing variables in the rest of the program.

This mechanism helps keep things organized, but it has a side-effect that is causing problems...

When a variable's value can be seen by some code, it is said to be "in scope."

When you leave a function, its variables get thrown away

Each time you call a function, Python creates a new stack frame to record new variables. But what happens when the function ends?

The computer throws away the function's stack frame!

File this under G, for "garbage."

STACK FRAME FOR: getprice.py

VARIABLES

NAME   VALUE

price_now   "y"

STACK FRAME FOR: set_password()

VARIABLES

NAME   VALUE

password   "C8HJONJ40a"

Remember: the stack frame is there to record **local** variables that *belong* to the function. They are *not designed* to be used elsewhere in the program, because they are *local to the function*. The whole reason for using a stack of variables is to allow a function to **create** local variables that are *invisible* to the rest of the program.

And that's what's happened with the password variable. The first time Python saw it was when it was created in the set_password() function. That meant the password variable was created on the set_password() function's stack frame. When the function ended, the stack frame was thrown away and Python completely forgot about the password variable. When your code then tries later to use the password variable to access Twitter, you're outta luck, because it can't be found anymore...

When a variable's value CANNOT be seen by some code, it is said to be "out of scope."

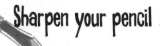

Sharpen your pencil

This is the start of the program. Write a modified version of this code that will allow the send_to_twitter() function to see the password variable.

Hint: you might **not** need to use a function.

```
import urllib.request
import time

def set_password():            You need to rewrite this section.
    password="C8H10N4O2"

set_password()

def send_to_twitter(msg):
    password_manager = urllib.request.HTTPPasswordMgr()
    password_manager.add_password("Twitter API",
                    "http://twitter.com/statuses", "starbuzzceo", password)
    http_handler = urllib.request.HTTPBasicAuthHandler(password_manager)
    page_opener = urllib.request.build_opener(http_handler)
    urllib.request.install_opener(page_opener)
    params = urllib.parse.urlencode( {'status': msg} )
    resp = urllib.request.urlopen("http://twitter.com/statuses/update.json", params)
        resp.read()
```

Write your new →
version here.

....

....

....

....

....

Sharpen your pencil
Solution

This is the start of the program. You were to write a modified version of this code that will allow the `send_to_twitter()` function to see the `password` variable.

Hint: you might **not** need to use a function.

```
import urllib.request
import time

def set_password():
    password="C8H10N4O2"

set_password()

def send_to_twitter(msg):
    password_manager = urllib.request.HTTPPasswordMgr()
    password_manager.add_password("Twitter API",
                "http://twitter.com/statuses", "starbuzzceo", password)
    http_handler = urllib.request.HTTPBasicAuthHandler(password_manager)
    page_opener = urllib.request.build_opener(http_handler)
    urllib.request.install_opener(page_opener)
    params = urllib.parse.urlencode( {'status': msg} )
    resp = urllib.request.urlopen("http://twitter.com/statuses/update.json", params)
    resp.read()
```

You needed to rewrite this section.

This is all you need to do: just create the variable.

password="C8H10N4O2"

Because the "password" variable is created outside a function, it is available anywhere in the program. The "send_to_twitter()" function should now be able to see it.

TEST DRIVE

The fixed version of the code has been loaded onto machines in every Starbuzz store worldwide. It's time to try out the code and see if you can get the ordering system working again:

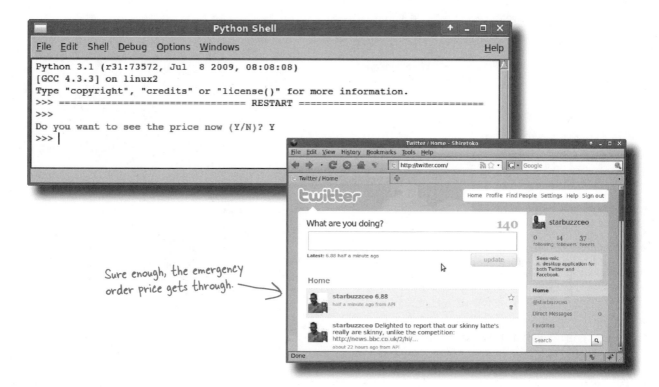

Sure enough, the emergency order price gets through.

It works! Because you are creating the `password` outside of a function, it is available **globally** throughout the Python program file. The `password` variable will be recorded against the initial stack frame, so the `send_to_twitter()` function will *now* be able to see it.

Let's see how the updated code is affecting the rest of Starbuzz.

Starbuzz is fully stocked!

With the coffee beans fully stocked, there's plenty of time for the more important things in life ...

Show of hands who wants a skinny latte?

... and there are a lot of happy Starbuzz customers, too.

From Cambridge to Cambodia, from Seattle to Sierra Leone, the orders are being placed and the beans are being delivered.

You did a great job. Your system tracks live prices from the Web and automatically sends messages to the CEO wherever he is on Earth. You are really using the power of functions to keep your code **clean**, **concise,** and **clear**. By correctly using variable scope, you even made it easy to keep the password up-to-date.

Well done!

Phew! You really saved the day! And the company! For a while there, I thought we were sunk... but you got us back up and running.

Your Programming Toolbox

You've got Chapter 3 under your belt. Let's look back at what you've learned in this chapter:

Programming Tools

* Avoid code duplication with functions.
* Parameters are variables that you can pass to functions.
* Functions can return values.
* Computers use stack frames to record and track variables.
* When you call a function, a new stack frame is created for the function to use.
* Stack frames (and local variables) are thrown away when you exit a function.
* A variable is said to be "in scope" whenever it's value can be seen by some code.

Python Tools

* Use "def" to create functions.
* Use return() to send a value back to the code that called the function.
* Pass parameters to functions by placing them between parentheses.

4 data in files and arrays

Sort it out

As your programs develop, so do your data handling needs.

And when you have lots of data to work with, using an individual variable for each piece of data gets really old, really quickly. So programmers employ some rather awesome containers (known as **data structures**) to help them work with lots of data. More times than not, all that data comes from a file stored on a hard disk. So, how can you work with data in your files? Turns out it's a breeze. Flip the page and let's learn how!

Surf's up in Codeville

The annual Codeville Surf-A-Thon is more popular than ever this year.

Because there are so many contestants, the organizers asked you to write a Python program to process the scores. Eager to please, you agreed.

The trouble is, even though the contest is over and the beach is now clear, you can't hit the waves until the program is written. Your program has to work out the highest surfing scores. Despite your urge to surf, a promise is a promise, so writing the program has to come first.

Surf-A-Thon

The scoreboard is currently empty. Wonder who won today's contest?

Find the highest score in the results file

After the judges rate the competitors, the scores are stored in a file called `results.txt`. There is one line in the file for each competitor's score. You need to write a program that reads through each of these lines, picks out the score, and then works out the highest score in the Surf-A-Thon.

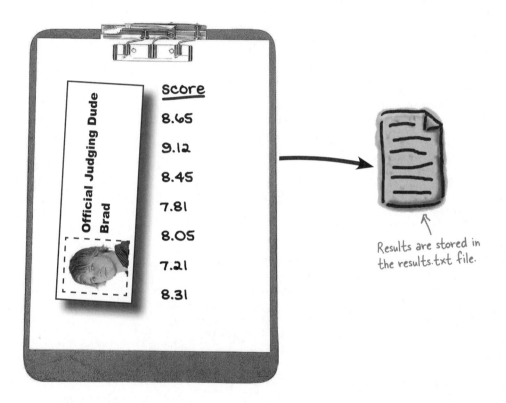

Results are stored in the results.txt file.

It sounds simple enough, except for one small detail. You've written programs to read data from the Web, and read data that's been typed in at the keyboard, but you haven't yet written any code that reads data stored in a file.

Iterate through the file with the <u>open</u>, <u>for</u>, <u>close</u> pattern

If you need to read from a file using Python, one way is to use the built-in open() command. Open a file called results.txt like this:

The opened file is assigned to a file handle, called "result_f" here.

result_f = open("results.txt")

Put the actual name of the file to open here.

The call to open() creates a **file handle**, which is a shorthand that you'll use to refer to the file you are working with within your code.

Because you'll need to read the file *one line at a time*, Python gives you the for loop for just this purpose. Like while loops, the for loop runs repeatedly, running the loop code once for each of the items *in* something. Think of a for loop as your very own custom-made data shredder:

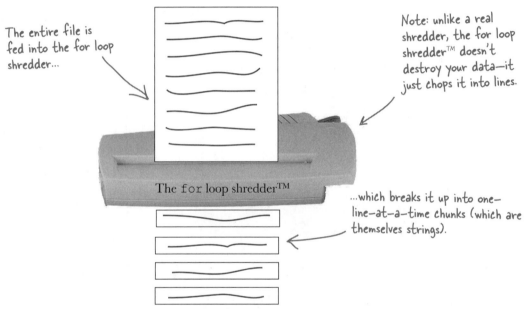

The entire file is fed into the for loop shredder...

Note: unlike a real shredder, the for loop shredder™ doesn't destroy your data—it just chops it into lines.

The for loop shredder™

...which breaks it up into one-line-at-a-time chunks (which are themselves strings).

Each time the body of the for loop runs, a variable is set to a string containing the current line of text in the file. This is referred to as **iterating** through the data in the file:

Open the file and give it a file handle.

The "each_line" variable is set to the next line from the file on each iteration. The for loop stops when you run out of lines to read.

```
result_f = open("results.txt")
for each_line in result_f:
    print(each_line)
result_f.close()
```

Do something with the thing you've just read from the file. In this case, you print out the line. Notice that the for loop's code is indented.

Close the file (through the file handle) when you're done with it.

Code Magnets

You need to complete the code to find the highest score in the `results.txt` file. Remember: the `for` loop creates a string from each line in the file.

Hint: For the program to work, you will need to convert the string into a number.

```
highest_score = 0

result_f = open("results.txt")

for line in result_f:

    if ............(..............) ........ ........................... :

                ........................ = ............. ( ............. )

result_f.close()

print("The highest score was:")

print(highest_score)
```

Code Magnets Solution

You needed to complete the code to find the highest score in the `results.txt` file. Remember: the `for` loop creates a string from each line in the file.

Hint: For the program to work, you needed to convert the string into a number.

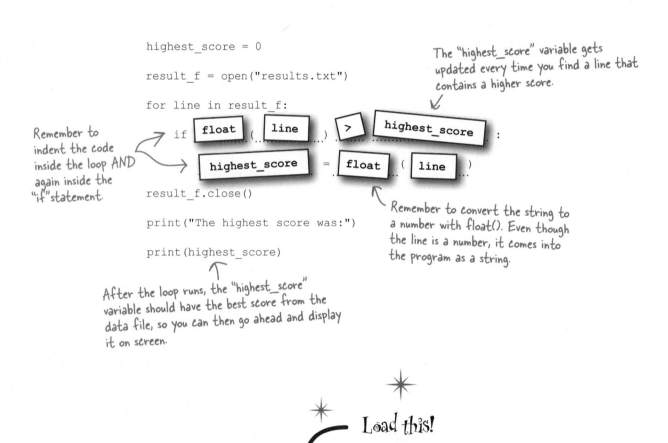

```
highest_score = 0

result_f = open("results.txt")

for line in result_f:
    if float( line ) > highest_score :
        highest_score = float( line )
result_f.close()

print("The highest score was:")

print(highest_score)
```

The "highest_score" variable gets updated every time you find a line that contains a higher score.

Remember to indent the code inside the loop AND again inside the "if" statement.

Remember to convert the string to a number with float(). Even though the line is a number, it comes into the program as a string.

After the loop runs, the "highest_score" variable should have the best score from the data file, so you can then go ahead and display it on screen.

Load this!

To successfully run this program, you need to grab a copy of the `results.txt` data file from the *Head First Programming* website. Be sure to put the data file in the same directory (or folder) that contains your code.

Test Drive

It's time to see if the program works. Use IDLE to create a new file using the code from the previous page, save your program as high_score.py, and then run it by pressing the F5 key:

Here's the program typed into IDLE.

```
highest_score = 0
result_f = open("results.txt")
for line in result_f:
    if float(line) > highest_score:
        highest_score = float(line)
result_f.close()
print("The highest score was:")
print(highest_score)
```

Oh, no, something's gone south here...

```
Python 3.1.1 (r311:74480, Aug 18 2009, 07:03:45)
[GCC 4.3.3] on linux2
Type "copyright", "credits" or "license()" for more information.
>>> ============================== RESTART ==============================
>>>
Traceback (most recent call last):
  File "/home/barryp/HeadFirstProg/chapter4/code/high_score.py", line 4, in <module>
    if float(line) > highest_score:
ValueError: could not convert string to float: Johnny 8.65
>>> |
```

Look's like you are trying to convert something that didn't look like a number.

Oh dear. It looks like something's gone wrong! The program has crashed with a ValueError, whatever that is.

BRAIN POWER

Study the error message produced by Python. Is there something wrong with the Python code? Is there a problem with the file? Is there something wrong with the data? What do you think happened?

The file contains more than numbers...

To see what happened, let's take another look at the judge's score sheet to see if you missed anything:

The judge's official ID badge was covering up the names.

There are two pieces of information on each line: a name and a number (the surfer's score).

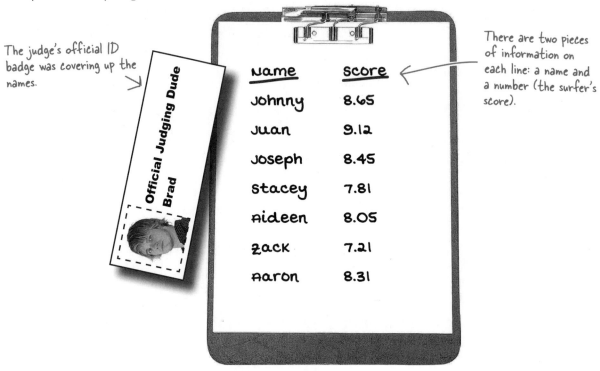

Official Judging Dude
Brad

Name	Score
Johnny	8.65
Juan	9.12
Joseph	8.45
Stacey	7.81
Aideen	8.05
Zack	7.21
Aaron	8.31

The judges also recorded the name of each surf contestant next to his or her score. This is a problem for the program only if the name was added to the `results.txt` file. Let's take a look:

The results file.

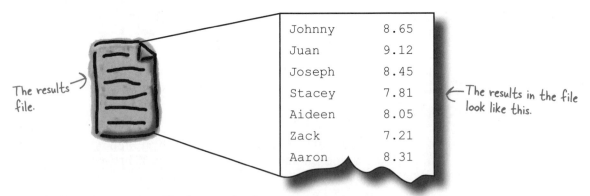

```
Johnny      8.65
Juan        9.12
Joseph      8.45
Stacey      7.81
Aideen      8.05
Zack        7.21
Aaron       8.31
```

The results in the file look like this.

Sure enough, the `results.txt` file also contains the contestant names. And that's a problem for our code because, as it iterates through the file, the string you read is no longer *just a number*.

Split each line as you read it

Each line in the `for` loop represents a single string containing two pieces of information:

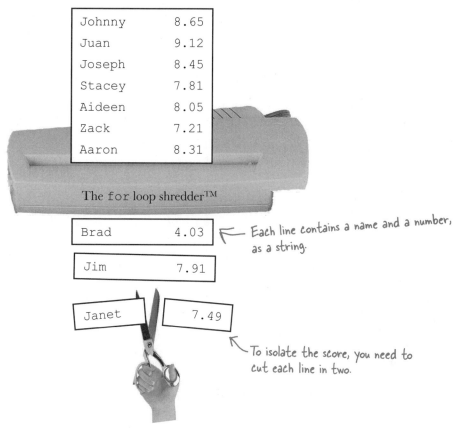

Johnny	8.65
Juan	9.12
Joseph	8.45
Stacey	7.81
Aideen	8.05
Zack	7.21
Aaron	8.31

The `for` loop shredder™

Brad	4.03

Each line contains a name and a number, as a string.

Jim	7.91

Janet	7.49

To isolate the score, you need to cut each line in two.

You need to somehow extract the score from the string. In each line, there is a name, followed by a space, followed by the score. You already know how to extract one string from another; you did it for Starbuzz back in Chapter 2. And you could do something similar here using the `find()` method and index manipulation, searching for the position of a *space* (' ') character in each line and then extracting the substring that follows it.

Programmers often have to deal with data in strings that contain several pieces of data separated by spaces. It's so common, in fact, that Python provides a special string method to perform the cutting you need: `split()`.

And you'll find that other programming languages have very similar mechanisms for breaking up strings.

Python strings have a built-in `split()` method.

The split() method cuts the string

Imagine you have a string containing several words assigned to a variable. Think of a variable as if it's a *labeled jar*:

> rock_band = "Al Carl Mike Brian"

A single variable is assigned...

...a single string, which contains four words.

A variable, a labeled jar.

A string, contained in a variable (jar).

The rock_band string, like all Python strings, has a split() method that returns a collection of substrings: one for each word in the original string.

Using a programming feature called **multiple assignment**, you can take the result from the cut performed by split() and assign it to a collection of variables:

The left side of the assignment operator lists the variables to assign values to.

> (rhythm, lead, vocals, bass) = rock_band.split()

The right side of the assignment operator contains the call to the split() method.

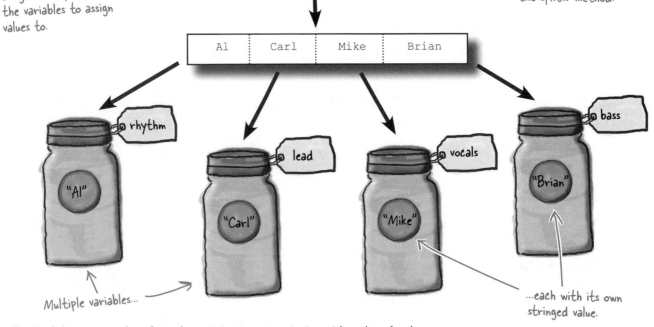

| Al | Carl | Mike | Brian |

Multiple variables...

...each with its own stringed value.

Each of the return values from the split() on rock_band is assigned to its own separately named variable, which allows you then to work with each word in whatever way you want. Note that the rock_band variable still exists and that it still contains the original string of four names.

Looks like you can use multiple assignment and split() to extract the scores from the results.txt file.

Exercise

Here is the current version of the program:

```
highest_score = 0
result_f = open("results.txt")
for line in result_f:
    if float(line) > highest_score:
        highest_score = float(line)
result_f.close()
print("The highest score was:")
print(highest_score)
```

Write the extra code required to take advantage of the `split()` method and multiple assignment in order to create variables called `name` and `score`. Then use them to complete the program to find the highest score.

....
....
....
....
....
....
....
....
....
....
....
....
....
....

Here is the current version of the program:

```
highest_score = 0
result_f = open("results.txt")
for line in result_f:
    if float(line) > highest_score:
        highest_score = float(line)
result_f.close()
print("The highest score was:")
print(highest_score)
```

You were to write the extra code required to take advantage of the `split()` method and multiple assignment in order to create variables called `name` and `score`, then use them to complete the program to find the highest score.

Add in the call to the split() method to cut the line in two, creating the "name" and "score" variables.

The only code changes required are within the for loop. The rest of the program remains unchanged.

```
for line in result_f:
    (name, score) = line.split()
    if float(score) > highest_score:
        highest_score = float(score)
```

You are no longer comparing the line to the highest score, so be sure to compare the "score" variable instead.

TEST DRIVE

So what happens when you run *this* version of the code within IDLE ? Let's amend the code and see:

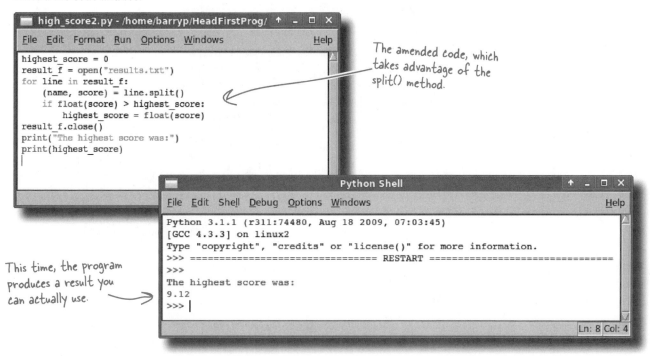

```
high_score2.py - /home/barryp/HeadFirstProg/

File  Edit  Format  Run  Options  Windows          Help

highest_score = 0
result_f = open("results.txt")
for line in result_f:
    (name, score) = line.split()
    if float(score) > highest_score:
        highest_score = float(score)
result_f.close()
print("The highest score was:")
print(highest_score)
```

The amended code, which takes advantage of the split() method.

```
Python Shell

File  Edit  Shell  Debug  Options  Windows          Help

Python 3.1.1 (r311:74480, Aug 18 2009, 07:03:45)
[GCC 4.3.3] on linux2
Type "copyright", "credits" or "license()" for more information.
>>> ================================ RESTART ================================
>>>
The highest score was:
9.12
>>> |

Ln: 8 Col: 4
```

This time, the program produces a result you can actually use.

It works! The program reads each line from the file as a string, extracts the score using the `split()` method, and then uses it to find the highest score in the file. The organizers are so excited to hear that the program is finished that they immediately display the result on the large scoreboard at the back of the beach.

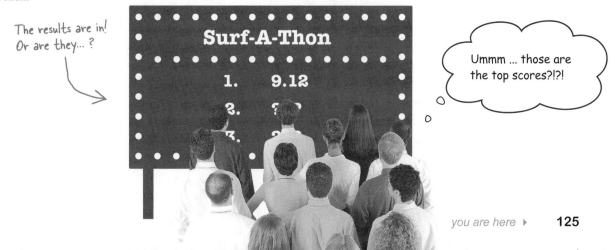

The results are in! Or are they... ?

Surf-A-Thon

1.   9.12
2.   ?
3.   ?

Ummm ... those are the top scores?!?!

But you need more than one top score

As soon as the top score appears, people start to wonder what the second and third highest scores are:

You are missing some scores here... the 2nd and 3rd scores are a mystery.

Surf-A-Thon

1. 9.12
2. ???
3. ???

What about second and third place?

It seems that the organizers didn't tell you everything you needed to know. The contest doesn't just award a prize for the winner, but also honors those surfers in second and third place.

Our program currently iterates through each of the lines in the `results.txt` file and works out the highest score. But what it actually needs to do is keep track of the *top three scores*, perhaps in three separate variables:

Looks like you need extra variables for the second and third highest scores.

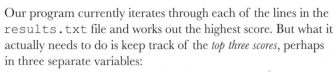

highest_score

"9.12"

second_highest

?

third_highest

?

Keeping track of 3 scores makes the code more complex

So how will you keep track of the extra scores? You could do something like this:

This is NOT real Python code. It's what programmers call "pseudo-code." They use it when they are sketching out ideas and working out a program's logic.

```
set the highest_score to 0
set the second_highest to 0
set the third_highest to 0
iterate through each of the scores:
    if the score > highest_score:
        set the third_highest to second_highest
        set the second_highest to highest_score
        set the highest_score to score
    otherwise if the score > second_highest:
        set the third_highest to second_highest
        set the second_highest to score
    otherwise if the score > third_highest:
        set the third_highest to score
```

You can see that there's a lot more logic here, because the program needs to "think" a bit more. Unfortunately, turning this logic into code will make the program longer and harder to change in the future. And, let's be honest, it's somewhat more difficult to understand what's actually going on with the logic as shown here.

How could you make this simpler?

Sharpen your pencil

Think about what would make the program easier to write. Check the box that you think would have the greatest impact:

☐ If there were no names in the file, only numbers

☐ If the data were ordered highest to lowest

☐ If the scores came before the names in the file

☐ If you knew exactly how many lines are in the file

Sharpen your pencil Solution

You were think about what would make the program easier to write and check the box that you think would have the greatest impact:

☐ If there were no names in the file, only numbers

☑ If the data were ordered highest to lowest

☐ If the scores came before the names in the file

☐ If you knew exactly how many lines are in the file

An ordered list makes code much simpler

If you had some way of reading the data from the file and then producing an ordered copy of the data, the program would be a lot simpler to write. Ordering data within a program is known as "sorting:"

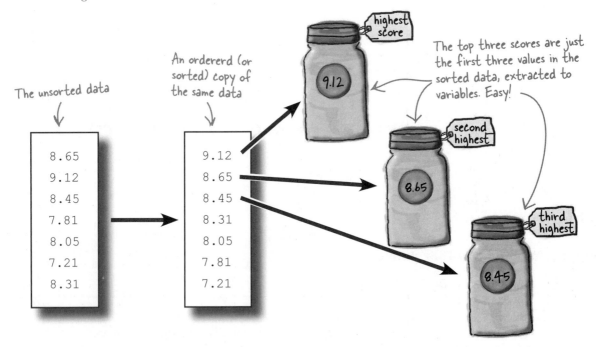

The unsorted data

An orderd (or sorted) copy of the same data

highest score — 9.12

The top three scores are just the first three values in the sorted data, extracted to variables. Easy!

second highest — 8.65

third highest — 8.45

But how do you order, or *sort*, your data? What happens to the original data in the file? Does it remain unsorted or is it sorted, too? Can the data even be sorted on disk and, if so, does this make things easier, faster, or slower?

Sorting sounds tricky... is there a "best" way?

Sorting is easier in memory

If you are writing a program that is going to deal with a lot of data, you need to decide where you need to keep that data while the program works with it. Most of the time, you will have two choices:

1 **Keep the data in files on the disk.**
If you have a very large amount of data, the obvious place to put it is on disk. Computers can store far more data on disk than they can in memory. Disk storage is **persistent**: if you yank the power cord, the computer doesn't forget the information written on the disk. But there is one real problem with manipulating data on disk: it can be very **slow**.

2 **Keep the data in memory.**
Data is much quicker to access and change if it's stored in the computer's memory. But, it's not persistent: data in memory disappears when your program exits, or when the computer is switched off (unless you remember to save it to a file, in which case it *becomes* persistent).

Keep the data in memory

If you want to sort a lot of data, you will need to shuffle data around quite a lot. This is much faster in memory than on disk.

Of course, before you sort the data, you need to read it into memory, perhaps into a large number of individual variables:

You have lots of lines of data, so you'll need lots of variables... right?!?

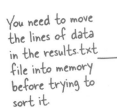

You need to move the lines of data in the results.txt file into memory before trying to sort it.

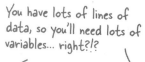

Do you have a big cupboard?!? Because that's a lot of jars...

BRAIN POWER

You are going to have a problem if you attempt to move all those lines of data into the computer's memory. What type of problem do you think you'll have?

You can't use a separate variable for each line of data

Programming languages use *variables* to give you access to data in memory. So if you are going to store the data from the results.txt file in memory, it makes sense that you'll need to use lots of variables to access all the data, right?

But how many variables do you need?

Imagine the file just had three scores in it. You could write a program that read each of the lines from the file and stored them in variables called first_score, second_score, and third_score:

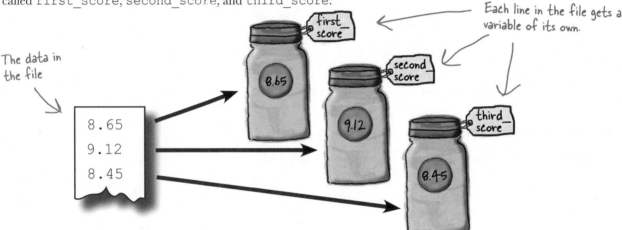

The data in the file

Each line in the file gets a variable of its own.

first_score
second_score
third_score

8.65
9.12
8.45

But what if there were four scores in the file? Or five? Even worse, what if there were *10,000* scores? You'd soon run out of variable names and (possibly) memory in your computer, not to mention the wear and tear on your fingers.

Well, the As are done and that's the first volume of all the entries from the Encyclopedia Galactica stored in memory. Time to tackle the Bs, then the Cs, Ds, Es....

Sometimes, you need to deal with a whole bundle of data, all at once. To do that, most languages give you the *array*.

An array lets you manage a whole train of data

So far, you've used variables to store only a *single piece of data*. But sometimes, you want to refer to a whole bunch of data all at once. For that, you need a new type of variable: the **array**.

An array is a "collection variable" or **data structure**. It's designed to group a whole bunch of data items together in one place and give them a name.

Think of an array as a data train. Each car in the train is called an **array element** and can store a single piece of data. If you want to store a number in one element and a string in another, you can.

Here comes the data train.

Each car holds a single piece of data.

You might think that as you are storing all of that data in an array, you still might need variables for each of the items it stores. But this is not the case. An array is itself *just another variable*, and you can give it its own variable name:

```
my_array = [7, "24", "Fish", "hat stand"]
```

All aboard the my_array express!

my_array

7

"24"

"Fish"

"hat stand"

Even though an array contains a whole bunch of data items, the array itself is a *single variable*, which just so happens to contain a collection of data. Once your data is in an array, you can treat the array just like any other variable.

So how do you use arrays?

Python gives you arrays with <u>lists</u>

Sometimes, different programming languages have different names for roughly the same thing. For example, in Python most programmers think *array* when they are actually using a Python **list**. For our purposes, think of Python lists and arrays as the *essentially* same thing.

Python coders typically use the word "array" to more correctly refer to a list that contains only data of one type, like a bunch of strings or a bunch of numbers. And Python comes with a built-in technology called "array" for just that purpose. However, as lists are very similar and much more flexible, we prefer to use them, so you don't need to worry about this distinction for now.

You create an array in Python like this:

```python
my_words = ["Dudes", "and"]
```

Give the array a name.

Assign a list of values to it.

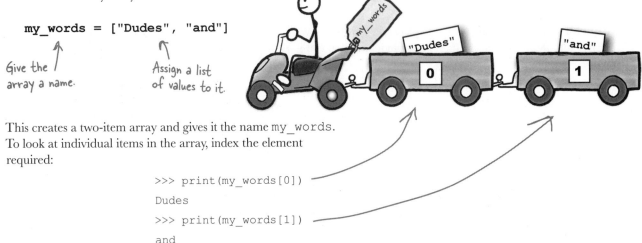

This creates a two-item array and gives it the name `my_words`. To look at individual items in the array, index the element required:

```python
>>> print(my_words[0])
Dudes
>>> print(my_words[1])
and
```

You can read individual pieces of data from inside the array using an **index**, just like you read individual characters from **inside a string**.

As with strings, the index for the *first* piece of data is 0. The second piece has index 1, and so on.

Arrays can be extended

But what if you need to add some extra information to an array? Like strings, arrays come with a bunch of built-in methods. Use the `append()` method to add an extra element onto the end of the array:

```python
>>> my_words.append("Bettys")
>>> print(my_words[2])
Bettys
```

The array has grown by one data element.

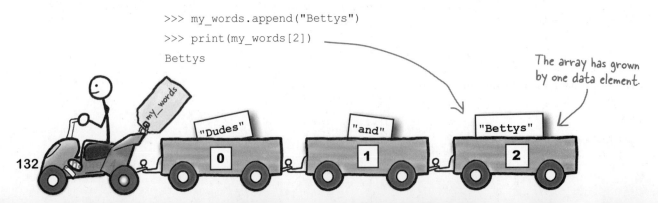

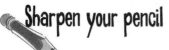

Sharpen your pencil

Rewrite your program so that each time you read a new score you append it to the end of an array called `scores`.

Then amend the code to print out the first **3** scores in the list.

Here's the code as it currently stands.

```
highest_score = 0
result_f = open("results.txt")
for line in result_f:
    (name, score) = line.split()
    if float(score) > highest_score:
        highest_score = float(score)
result_f.close()
print("The highest score was:")
print(highest_score)
```

Hint: To create an empty array of scores use `scores = []`.

....

....

....

....

....

....

....

....

....

....

....

....

Sharpen your pencil
Solution

You were to rewrite the program so that each time you read a new score you append it to the end of an array called `scores`.

You were then to amend the code to print out the first **3** scores in the list.

Here's the code as it currently stands.

```
highest_score = 0
result_f = open("results.txt")
for line in result_f:
    (name, score) = line.split()
    if float(score) > highest_score:
        highest_score = float(score)
result_f.close()
print("The highest score was:")
print(highest_score)
```

Start with an empty array.

```
scores = []
```

Process the data in the file as before...

```
result_f = open("results.txt")
for line in result_f:
    (name, score) = line.split()
```

...but, this time, append the scores to an array.

```
scores.append(float(score))
result_f.close()
print("The top scores were:")
```

With the data safely stored in the array, print out the first 3 array elements.

```
print(scores[0])
print(scores[1])
print(scores[2])
```

TEST DRIVE

The program should now store all of the information from the file into the `scores` array before displaying just the top three scores. Let's run the program within IDLE and see what happens:

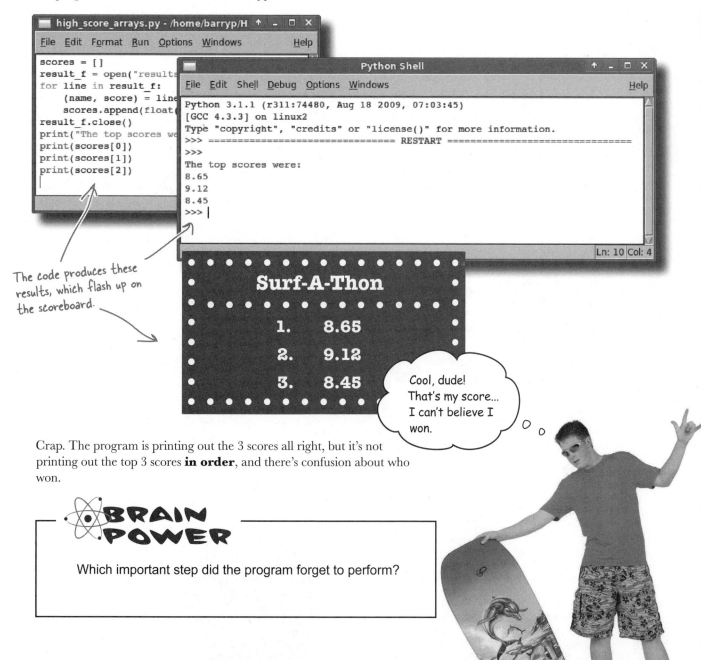

The code produces these results, which flash up on the scoreboard.

```
scores = []
result_f = open("results
for line in result_f:
    (name, score) = line
    scores.append(float(
result_f.close()
print("The top scores we
print(scores[0])
print(scores[1])
print(scores[2])
```

```
Python 3.1.1 (r311:74480, Aug 18 2009, 07:03:45)
[GCC 4.3.3] on linux2
Type "copyright", "credits" or "license()" for more information.
>>> ================================ RESTART ================================
>>>
The top scores were:
8.65
9.12
8.45
>>>
```

Surf-A-Thon

1.   8.65
2.   9.12
3.   8.45

Cool, dude! That's my score... I can't believe I won.

Crap. The program is printing out the 3 scores all right, but it's not printing out the top 3 scores **in order**, and there's confusion about who won.

BRAIN POWER

Which important step did the program forget to perform?

Sort the array before displaying the results

The array is storing the scores in the order they were read from the file. However, you still need to *sort* them so that the highest scores appear *first*.

You could sort the array by comparing each of the elements with each of the other elements, and then swap any that are in the wrong order.

The boxes in the array are stored in a random order.

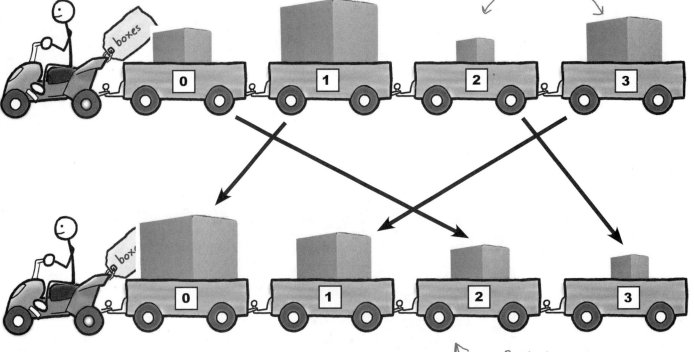

By closely examining the array of boxes, you can sort them by arranging the boxes in biggest-to-smallest order.

That looks complicated. Aren't we doing all this to make the code simpler and easier to maintain? I wonder if the array has any built-in methods that might help...?

Arrays in Python have a whole host of methods that make many tasks easier.

Let's see which ones might help.

WHAT'S MY PURPOSE?

These are some of the methods that come built into every array. See
if you can match up the descriptions with the method names. Draw in
the missing connecting lines. We've done one for you to get you started:

Method	What the method does
count()	Sorts the array into a specified order (low to high)
extend()	Removes and returns the last array item
index()	Adds an item at any index location
insert()	Looks for an item and returns its index value
pop()	Reverses the order of the array
remove()	Tells you how many times a value is in the array
reverse()	Adds a list of items to an array
sort()	Removes and returns the first array item

(index() is connected to "Looks for an item and returns its index value")

BRAIN BARBELL

Can you work out which *two* methods you need to employ to allow
you to sort the data in the order that you need?

WHAT'S MY PURPOSE? SOLUTION

These are some of the methods that come built into every array. You were to match up the descriptions with the method names:

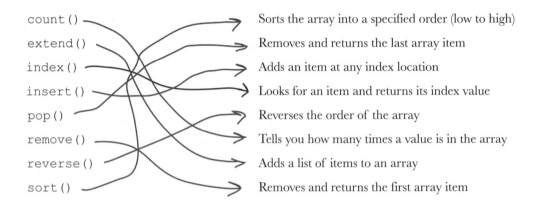

Method	What the method does
count()	Sorts the array into a specified order (low to high)
extend()	Removes and returns the last array item
index()	Adds an item at any index location
insert()	Looks for an item and returns its index value
pop()	Reverses the order of the array
remove()	Tells you how many times a value is in the array
reverse()	Adds a list of items to an array
sort()	Removes and returns the first array item

BRAIN BARBELL SOLUTION

You were to work out which *two* methods you needed to employ to allow you to sort the data in the order that you needed.

The sort() and reverse() methods look the most useful. You need to use reverse() after you sort() the data, because the default ordering used by sort() is *lowest-to-highest*, the opposite of what you need.

Sort the scores from highest to lowest

You now need to add the two method calls into your code that will sort the array. The lines need to go *between* the code that reads the data into the list and *before* the code that displays the first three elements:

The array starts off in a random order. It's "unsorted."

Sharpen your pencil

Here is the existing program. Add in the missing code that sorts the data, highest-to-lowest.

```
scores = []
result_f = open("results.txt")
for line in result_f:
    (name, score) = line.split()
    scores.append(float(score))
result_f.close()
```

Put the extra code here.

```
......................................
......................................
```

```
print("The top scores were:")
print(scores[0])
print(scores[1])
print(scores[2])
```

Sharpen your pencil
Solution

Here is the existing program. You were to add in the missing code that sorts the data, highest-to-lowest.

```
scores = []
result_f = open("results.txt")
for line in result_f:
    (name, score) = line.split()
    scores.append(float(score))
result_f.close()
```

At this point in the code, the array is in memory but it's not in the order you need. It's unsorted.

```
scores.sort()

scores.reverse()
```

These two method calls will sort the data into the required order.

```
print("The top scores were:")
print(scores[0])
print(scores[1])
print(scores[2])
```

Now that the array is sorted, the first three elements contain the high scores.

After the call to sort() and reverse(), the array is sorted in the order you need.

Geek Bits

It was very simple to sort an array of data using just two lines of code. But it turns out you can do even better than that if you use an **option** with the sort() method. Instead of using these two lines:

```
scores.sort()
scores.reverse()
```

you could have used just one, which gives the same result: `scores.sort(reverse = True)`

TEST DRIVE

Update your program in IDLE and run it. Look what happens:

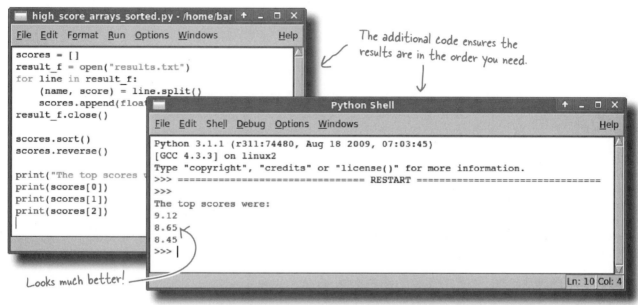

The additional code ensures the results are in the order you need.

```
high_score_arrays_sorted.py - /home/bar
File  Edit  Format  Run  Options  Windows              Help
scores = []
result_f = open("results.txt")
for line in result_f:
    (name, score) = line.split()
    scores.append(float
result_f.close()

scores.sort()
scores.reverse()

print("The top scores
print(scores[0])
print(scores[1])
print(scores[2])
```

```
Python Shell
File  Edit  Shell  Debug  Options  Windows              Help
Python 3.1.1 (r311:74480, Aug 18 2009, 07:03:45)
[GCC 4.3.3] on linux2
Type "copyright", "credits" or "license()" for more information.
>>> ================================ RESTART ================================
>>>
The top scores were:
9.12
8.65
8.45
>>>
                                                              Ln: 10 Col: 4
```

Looks much better!

The program works great!

The scores are in *descending* order, and the program is really not much longer
than when it found just one score. Using arrays allows us to solve a **much
harder** problem with very little extra code. And instead of using lots of
complex logic and lots of variables, you have straightforward logic and only
one variable: the scores array.

Surf-A-Thon

1. 9.12
2. 8.65
3. 8.45

Dude, those are some sweet scores.

And the winner is...?

It's time for the award ceremony.

The prizes are lined up and the scores are on the scoreboard.
There's just one problem.

Nobody knows which surfer got which score.

You know the winning
scores, but the winnng
surfers remain a mystery...

Winners

Surf-A-Thon

1.   9.12

2.   8.65

3.   8.45

1st

2nd

3rd

You somehow forgot the surfer names

With your rush to catch some waves before the light is gone, you forgot about the other piece of data stored in the `results.txt` file: the name of each surfer.

Without the names, you can't possibly know which score goes with which name, so the scoreboard is only half-complete.

The trouble is, your array stores one data item in each element, not two. Looks like you still have your work cut out for you. There'll be no catching waves until this issue is resolved.

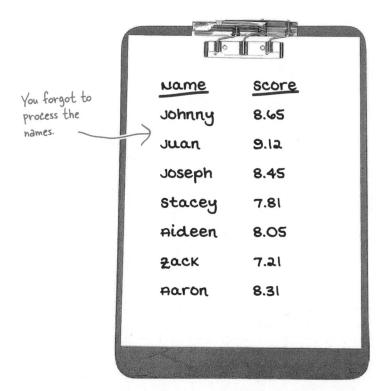

You forgot to process the names.

Name	Score
Johnny	8.65
Juan	9.12
Joseph	8.45
Stacey	7.81
Aideen	8.05
Zack	7.21
Aaron	8.31

How do you think you can remember the names and the scores for each surfer in the contest?

Once you've thought about this problem, turn over to Chapter 5 and see if you can resolve this issue.

Your Programming Toolbox

You've got Chapter 4 under your belt. Let's look back at what you've learned in this chapter:

Programming Tools

* files – reading data stored on disk
* arrays – a collection variable that holds multiple data items that can be accessed by index
* sorting – arranging a collection in a specific order

Python Tools

* open() – open a file for processing
* close() – close a file
* for – iterate over something
* string.split() – cut a string into multiple parts
* [] – the array index operator
* array.append() – add an item to the end of an array
* array.sort() – sort an array, lowest-to-highest
* array.reverse() – change the order of an array by reversing it

5 hashes and databases

Putting data in its place

> To surf one's data properly, one must constantly practice one's pose...

Arrays aren't the only show in town when it comes to data.

Programming languages come with other data-arranging goodies too, and our chosen tool, Python, is no exception. In this chapter, you'll **associate** values with names using a data structure commonly called the **hash** (better known as *dictionary* to Python-folk). And when it comes to working with **stored data**, you'll read data from an *external database system* as well as from regular text-based files. All the world's awash with data, so turn the page and start applying your ever-expanding programming skills to some cool data-processing tasks.

Who won the surfing contest?

In the previous chapter, you worked out the top three scores, but they're not much use without the names of the surfers that achieved those scores. There will no be surfing for you until you've finished the program.

Here's the code so far:

```
scores = []
result_f = open("results.txt")
for line in result_f:
    (name, score) = line.split()
    scores.append(float(score))
result_f.close()
scores.sort()
scores.reverse()
print("The top scores were:")
print(scores[0])
print(scores[1])
print(scores[2])
```

You still don't know *who* won.

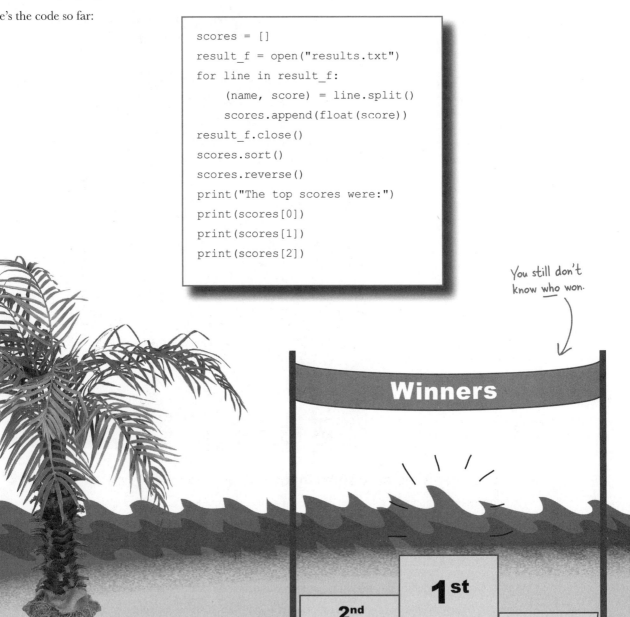

Winners

1st

2nd

3rd

The fix is easy.
Just use two arrays.
How hard is that?

Sharpen your pencil

Rewrite your current program to use two arrays: one to keep
track of the scores, the other to keep track of the surfer names.

....

....

....

....

....

....

....

....

....

....

....

....

....

....

....

....

Sharpen your pencil
Solution

You were to rewrite your current program to use two arrays: one to keep track of the scores, the other to keep track of the surfer names.

As well as the scores array, you now need a names array, too. →

```
scores = []

names = []

result_f = open("results.txt")

for line in result_f:

    (name, score) = line.split()

    scores.append(float(score))

    names.append(name)

result_f.close()

scores.sort()

scores.reverse()

names.sort()

names.reverse()

print("The highest scores were:")

print(names[0] + ' with ' + str(scores[0]))

print(names[1] + ' with ' + str(scores[1]))

print(names[2] + ' with ' + str(scores[2]))
```

Append the surfer's name to the names array.

Remember to sort the names array. →

Load this!

Don't forget to download `results. txt` from the *Head First Programming* website before continuing.

TEST DRIVE

With the `results.txt` file saved to the same directory as your program, enter this
code into IDLE and see what happens. Remember to save your program, then press
F5 to run it.

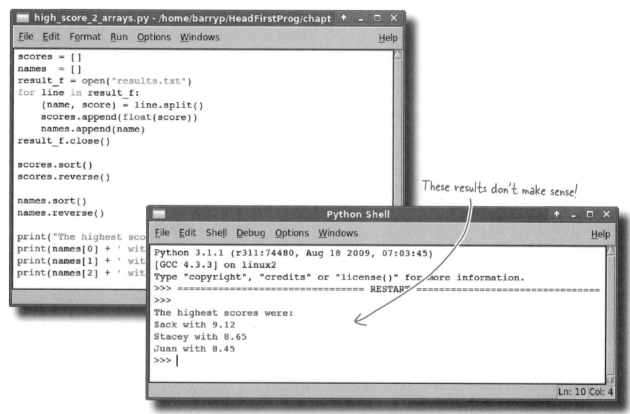

```
high_score_2_arrays.py - /home/barryp/HeadFirstProg/chapt
File  Edit  Format  Run  Options  Windows                          Help

scores = []
names  = []
result_f = open("results.txt")
for line in result_f:
    (name, score) = line.split()
    scores.append(float(score))
    names.append(name)
result_f.close()

scores.sort()
scores.reverse()

names.sort()
names.reverse()

print("The highest sco
print(names[0] + ' wit
print(names[1] + ' wit
print(names[2] + ' wit
```

These results don't make sense!

```
                              Python Shell
File  Edit  Shell  Debug  Options  Windows                         Help

Python 3.1.1 (r311:74480, Aug 18 2009, 07:03:45)
[GCC 4.3.3] on linux2
Type "copyright", "credits" or "license()" for more information.
>>> ================================= RESTART =================================
>>>
The highest scores were:
Zack with 9.12
Stacey with 8.65
Juan with 8.45
>>> |
                                                                Ln: 10 Col: 4
```

Those results look a little strange. Zack is only a novice surfer but, according
to the results from your program, Zack has the highest score. It looks like the
association between the surfer names and their scores is somehow lost... and if
you think about it, this is exactly what's happening.

The two arrays are independent of each other: one contains scores, the other
names. When the data is in the file, the surfer name and the scores are associated
with each other because they appear *on the same line*. However, once the split
occurs and the data is in the arrays, the association is **severed**. Sorting one array
has no effect on the ordering of the other. No wonder your results are a little off
the wall.

How do you fix this?

Associate the name with the score

Using two arrays just won't cut it. You need some other data structure to hold your data in such a way that the *association* between the surfers' name and their score is *maintained*.

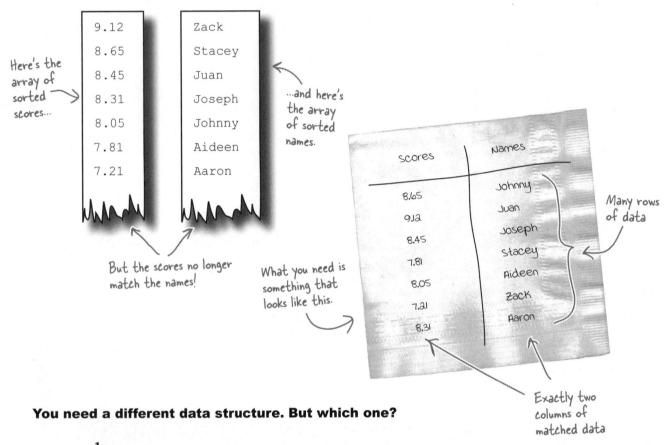

Here's the array of sorted scores...

```
9.12
8.65
8.45
8.31
8.05
7.81
7.21
```

```
Zack
Stacey
Juan
Joseph
Johnny
Aideen
Aaron
```

...and here's the array of sorted names.

But the scores no longer match the names!

What you need is something that looks like this.

Scores	Names
8.65	Johnny
9.12	Juan
8.45	Joseph
7.81	Stacey
8.05	Aideen
7.21	Zack
8.31	Aaron

Many rows of data

Exactly two columns of matched data

You need a different data structure. But which one?

the Scholar's Corner

Data Structure A standard method of organizing a collection of data items in your computer's memory. You've already met one of the classic data structures: the array.

Match the data structure names on the left with their descriptions on the right. We've already done one for you. Which one do you think you'll need to use for the surfer data?

Array   A variable that allows data to enter at one end of a collection and leave at the other end, supporting a first-in, first-out mechanism

Linked list   A variable that contains data arranged as a matrix of multiple dimensions (but typically, only two)

Queue   A variable that has exactly two columns and (potentially) many rows of data

Hash   A variable with multiple indexed slots for holding data

Set   A variable that creates a chain of data where one data item points to another data item, which itself points to another data item, and another, and so on and so forth

Multi-dimensional array   A variable that contains a collection of unique data items

WHAT'S MY PURPOSE?
SOLUTION

You were asked to match the data structure names on the left with their descriptions on the right. You were also to identify which one you thought you might need to use for the surfer data.

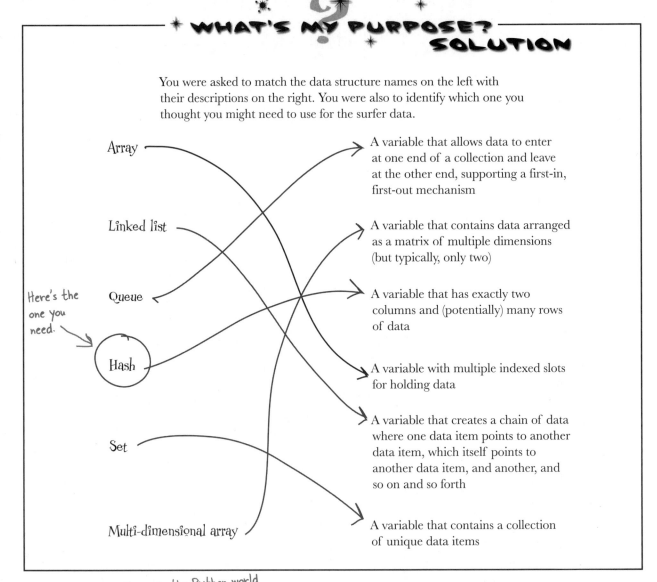

Array

Linked list

Queue

Here's the one you need.

Hash

Set

Multi-dimensional array

A variable that allows data to enter at one end of a collection and leave at the other end, supporting a first-in, first-out mechanism

A variable that contains data arranged as a matrix of multiple dimensions (but typically, only two)

A variable that has exactly two columns and (potentially) many rows of data

A variable with multiple indexed slots for holding data

A variable that creates a chain of data where one data item points to another data item, which itself points to another data item, and another, and so on and so forth

A variable that contains a collection of unique data items

Known in the Python world as a "dictionary."

Use a hash

You need to use a data structure that maintains the *association* between the surfer score and the surfer name, which is exactly what a hash gives you. There are lots of surfers with lots of scores, and you need to maintain the association between the two pieces of information.

Let's take a look at how hashes work.

Geek Bits

Hashes go by different names in different programming languages: *mapping, dictionary, associative array,* and *key-value list,* to name a few. In this book, we'll stick to using the name *hash.*

This cuts down on the amount of typing and saves our poor fingers!

Associate a key with a value using a hash

Start with an empty hash:

Note the use of curly brackets here.

```
scores = {}
```

An empty hash is assigned to a variable called "scores".

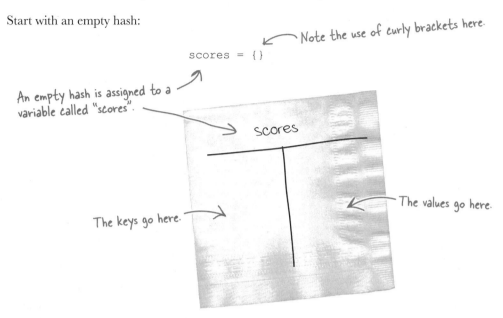

scores

The keys go here.

The values go here.

You add data to an existing hash by *describing the association* between the key and the value. Here's how to associate a surfers' name with their score:

Put the key inside the square brackets...

```
scores[8.45] = 'Joseph'
```

...and put the value to the right of the assignment operator.

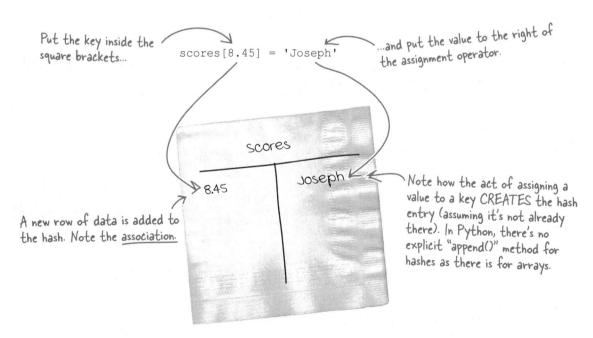

scores

8.45

Joseph

A new row of data is added to the hash. Note the <u>association</u>.

Note how the act of assigning a value to a key CREATES the hash entry (assuming it's not already there). In Python, there's no explicit "append()" method for hashes as there is for arrays.

Iterate hash data with <u>for</u>

Let's add some additional rows of data to your hash:

```
scores[9.12] = 'Juan'
scores[7.21] = 'Zack'
```

The new rows have been added.

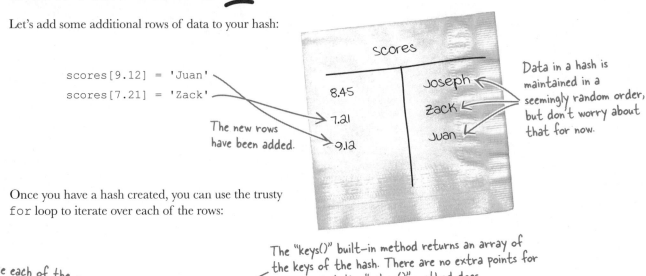

Data in a hash is maintained in a seemingly random order, but don't worry about that for now.

Once you have a hash created, you can use the trusty `for` loop to iterate over each of the rows:

Take each of the keys in the hash in turn...

The "keys()" built-in method returns an array of the keys of the hash. There are no extra points for guessing what the "values()" method does.

```
for key in scores.keys():
    print(scores[key] + ' had a score of ' + str(name_part))
```

...and display a custom message using the data in each row of the hash.

When referring to a value associated with a key, use square brackets (just like you did with array data).

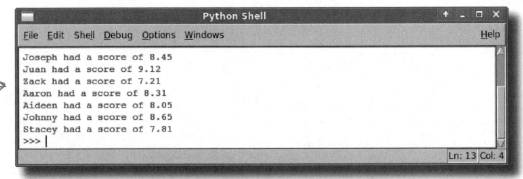

Here's what would display on screen (assuming all the data in "results.txt" was available to the hash).

```
Python Shell
File  Edit  Shell  Debug  Options  Windows                    Help

Joseph had a score of 8.45
Juan had a score of 9.12
Zack had a score of 7.21
Aaron had a score of 8.31
Aideen had a score of 8.05
Johnny had a score of 8.65
Stacey had a score of 7.81
>>>

                                              Ln: 13 Col: 4
```

Another hash method, called `items()`, returns each *key-value pair* in turn, and can be used with the `for` loop, too:

The "items()" method returns each key-value pair.

```
for score, surfer in scores.items():
    print(surfer + ' had a score of ' + str(score))
```

Whichever method you use to iterate over your hash's data is up to you, because using `items()` or `keys()` produces the same output.

Code Magnets

Rearrange the code magnets at the bottom of the page to complete the program shown below. Rather than using two arrays, this program stores the results from the surfing contest in a hash:

```python
result_f = open("results.txt")
for line in result_f:
    (name, score) = line.split()


result_f.close()

print("The top scores were:")



```

```python
scores[score] = name
```

```python
for each_score in scores.keys():
```

```python
print('Surfer ' + scores[each_score] + ' scored ' + each_score)
```

```python
scores = {}
```

Code Magnets Solution

You were to rearrange the code magnets at the bottom of the page to complete the program shown below. Rather than using two arrays, this program stores the results from the surfing contest in a hash:

You need to start with an empty hash, as opposed to an empty array.

```
scores = {}
result_f = open("results.txt")
for line in result_f:
    (name, score) = line.split()
    scores[score] = name
result_f.close()

print("The top scores were:")
for each_score in scores.keys():
    print('Surfer ' + scores[each_score] + ' scored ' + each_score)
```

After splitting out the name and the score, use the value of "score" as the key of the hash and the value of "name" as the value.

You'll find out soon why the "score" and not the "name" is used (in this case) as the key of the hash.

Use a for loop to process the contents of the hash.

Display each row from the hash, describing the association.

---

there are no Dumb Questions

Q: Can I append data to a hash just like I did with an array?

A: Yes, and no. There's no `append()` method for hashes like the one included with every array. To add a new row of data to an existing hash, use code similar to that used in the solution, above. Hashes do have their own set of methods, but `append()` is not one of them.

Q: Can I use anything as the key of a hash?

A: No, you can't. The rules Python applies here can be complex (as they can be in other programming languages, too). The best advice we can give you is to stick with numbers and strings as keys. Trust us: this isn't as restrictive as it first sounds and is, by far, the best/easiest strategy to follow.

TEST DRIVE

Take the code from the previous exercise and use it to create a new file in
IDLE. Call your program `scores_hash.py`. When you're ready, press
F5 to run your program.

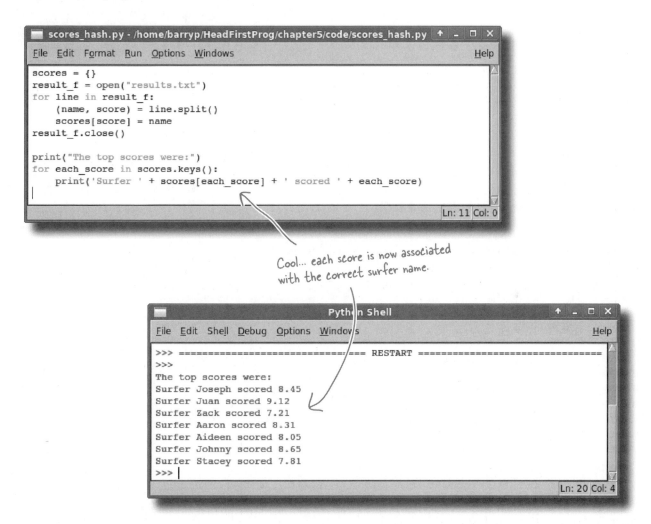

```
scores = {}
result_f = open("results.txt")
for line in result_f:
    (name, score) = line.split()
    scores[score] = name
result_f.close()

print("The top scores were:")
for each_score in scores.keys():
    print('Surfer ' + scores[each_score] + ' scored ' + each_score)
```
Ln: 11 Col: 0

Cool... each score is now associated with the correct surfer name.

Python Shell

```
>>> ===============================  RESTART  ===============================
>>>
The top scores were:
Surfer Joseph scored 8.45
Surfer Juan scored 9.12
Surfer Zack scored 7.21
Surfer Aaron scored 8.31
Surfer Aideen scored 8.05
Surfer Johnny scored 8.65
Surfer Stacey scored 7.81
>>>
```
Ln: 20 Col: 4

**Great! Your program now uses a data structure that allows
you to associate two related pieces of data together.**

The data isn't sorted

Your program now associates surfers and their scores, but it displays the data from the hash in some sort of random ordering. You need to somehow sort the data in the hash to find out who actually won the contest.

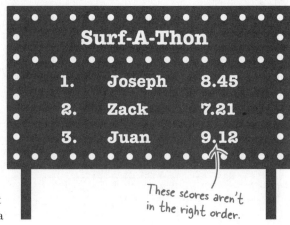

These scores aren't in the right order.

Python hashes don't have a sort() method...

In Python, hashes are optimized for speedy insertions and even speedier look-ups (searches). As a consequence, the good folks that created Python were less interested in providing a method to sort a hash, so they didn't bother.

You'll find similar design and implementation decisions in lots of different programming languages. People are different... and so are the programming languages they create.

...but there is a function called sorted()

Obviously, there's a *need* to sort a hash so, again, the good folks that created Python decided to provide a really smart built-in function that has the ability to sort *any* data structure, and they called their function `sorted()`. Here's how to use the `sorted()` function with your hash:

Use the "sorted()" function to sort the keys of the "scores" hash.

Remember: the keys in your hash are the scores, which are numbers, so we ask "sorted()" to order them highest-to-lowest using "reverse = True".

```
for each_score in sorted(scores.keys(), reverse = True):
    print('Surfer ' + scores[each_score] + ' scored ' + each_score)
```

That's one small change to one line at the bottom of your program. So, let's go ahead and **make that change**. Now that you are sorting the keys of the hash (which represent the surfer's scores), it should be clear why the scores were used as the key when adding data into the hash: you need to sort the scores, not the surfer names, so the scores need to be on the left side of the hash (because that's what the built-in `sorted()` function works with).

Do this!

Make the change to your code to use `sorted()`.

TEST DRIVE

With the one-line change applied, save your program and press F5 to run it again.

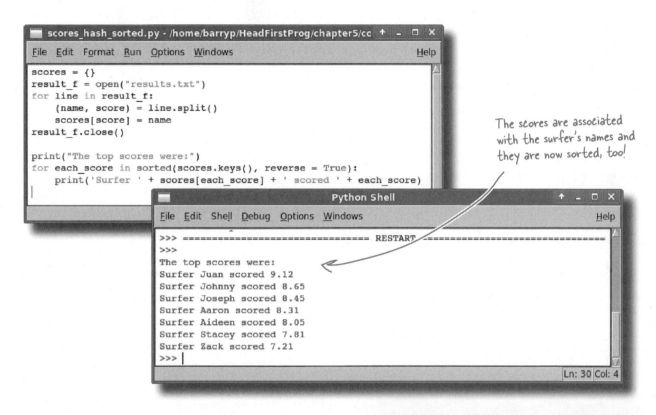

```
scores_hash_sorted.py - /home/barryp/HeadFirstProg/chapter5/cc
File  Edit  Format  Run  Options  Windows                                    Help

scores = {}
result_f = open("results.txt")
for line in result_f:
    (name, score) = line.split()
    scores[score] = name
result_f.close()

print("The top scores were:")
for each_score in sorted(scores.keys(), reverse = True):
    print('Surfer ' + scores[each_score] + ' scored ' + each_score)
```

The scores are associated with the surfer's names and they are now sorted, too!

```
                                    Python Shell
File  Edit  Shell  Debug  Options  Windows                                   Help
>>> ================================ RESTART ================================
>>>
The top scores were:
Surfer Juan scored 9.12
Surfer Johnny scored 8.65
Surfer Joseph scored 8.45
Surfer Aaron scored 8.31
Surfer Aideen scored 8.05
Surfer Stacey scored 7.81
Surfer Zack scored 7.21
>>>
                                                                   Ln: 30 Col: 4
```

Fantastic! You've identified the top 3 surfers. Time to hit those waves, dude!

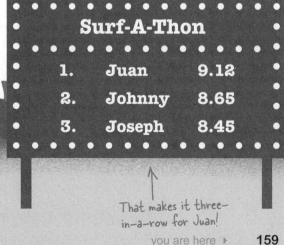

Surf-A-Thon

1.	Juan	9.12
2.	Johnny	8.65
3.	Joseph	8.45

That makes it three-in-a-row for Juan!

When data gets complex

Hot on the heels of your success with the local surfing club, you've just been contacted by the Regional Surfing Association (RSA) and they want *you* to write a new program for *them*! RSA's offering a brand-new, state-of-the-art, epoxy resin surf board as payment... once the program's working to their satisfaction, of course. ← This is too good an offer to turn down.

You've been wanting to try out an epoxy board for ages. The trouble is, they're sooooo expensive and you're a poor surfer. The waves will have to wait (yet again). But, the thoughts of surfing an epoxy board... now that's worth waiting for.

So what does RSA's data look like?

Currently, RSA's data is stored in a text file using a proprietary data format. For each surfer, there's six pieces of data recorded on each line in the file.

Here are the six pieces of data.

Here's what the data looks like:

```
101;Johnny 'wave-boy' Jones;USA;8.32;Fish;21
102;Juan Martino;Spain;9.01;Gun;36
103;Joseph 'smitty' Smyth;USA;8.85;Cruiser;18
104;Stacey O'Neill;Ireland;8.91;Malibu;22
105;Aideen 'board babe' Wu;Japan;8.65;Fish;24
106;Zack 'bonnie-lad' MacFadden;Scotland;7.82;Thruster;26
107;Aaron Valentino;Italy;8.98;Gun;19
```

```
Competition ID.
Name.
Country.
Average score.
Preferred board type.
Age.
```

← RSA's data is stored in each line, with a semicolon separating each piece of data.

RSA has tried importing this data into their favorite spreadsheet program, but that didn't really work for them. RSA wants a program that allows them to quickly **find** a surfers' data based on their Competition ID, then **display** the surfers' details like this:

```
ID:         101
Name:       Johnny 'wave-boy' Jones
Country:    USA
Average:    8.32
Board type: Fish
Age:        21
```

Each data item → is nicely labeled.

← Each data item is displayed on its own line, which makes it really easy to read (unlike the packed data file).

Sharpen your pencil

Here's one surfer's data from the file, assigned to a variable called `line`:

```
line = "101;Johnny 'wave-boy' Jones;USA;8.32;Fish;21"
```

Grab your pencil and write some code to process this line and display it on screen like this:

```
ID:          101
Name:        Johnny 'wave-boy' Jones
Country:     USA
Average:     8.32
Board type:  Fish
Age:         21
```

Hints: If you pass a string parameter to the `split()` method, the data is cut where the string parameter occurs, as opposed to the cut occurring at a space character (which is `split()`'s default behavior). Also, consider using multiple-assignment on the left side of the assignment operator when assigning more than one name-value pairing to a hash.

....
....
....
....
....
....
....
....
....
....
....
....

Sharpen your pencil
Solution

Here's one surfer's data from the file, assigned to a variable called `line`:

```
line = "101;Johnny 'wave-boy' Jones;USA;8.32;Fish;21"
```

You were to grab your pencil and write some code to process this line and display it on screen like this:

```
ID:         101
Name:       Johnny 'wave-boy' Jones
Country:    USA
Average:    8.32
Board type: Fish
Age:        21
```

Cut the line of data every time the split() method sees a semicolon.

Here's one possible solution.

```
line = "101;Johnny 'wave-boy' Jones;USA;8.32;Fish;21"
```

Create an empty hash called "s".

```
s = {}

(s['id'], s['name'], s['country'], s['average'], s['board'], s['age']) = line.split(";")
```

Use multiple-assignment to assign the split data from "line" to "s".

Display six nicely formatted messages on screen.

```
print("ID:        " + s['id'])

print("Name:       " + s['name'])

print("Country:    " + s['country'])

print("Average:    " + s['average'])

print("Board type: " + s['board'])

print("Age:        " + s['age'])
```

Test Drive

As always, you need to enter this code into IDLE before you run it. Then, save your program and take it for a spin by pressing F5.

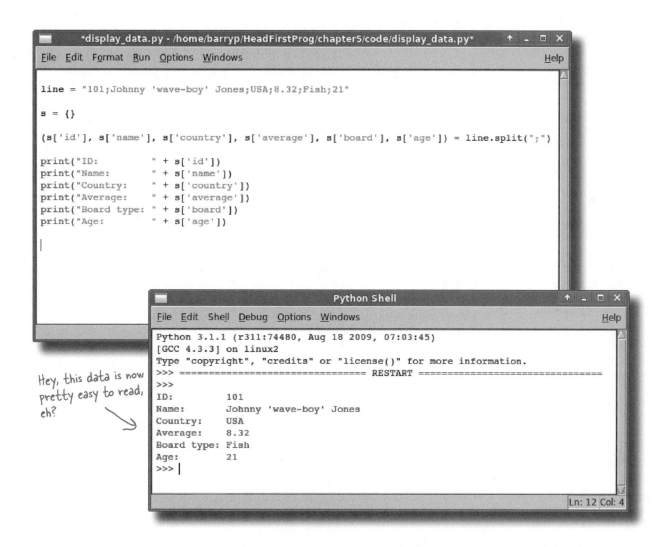

```
line = "101;Johnny 'wave-boy' Jones;USA;8.32;Fish;21"

s = {}

(s['id'], s['name'], s['country'], s['average'], s['board'], s['age']) = line.split(";")

print("ID:         " + s['id'])
print("Name:       " + s['name'])
print("Country:    " + s['country'])
print("Average:    " + s['average'])
print("Board type: " + s['board'])
print("Age:        " + s['age'])
```

Hey, this data is now pretty easy to read, eh?

```
Python 3.1.1 (r311:74480, Aug 18 2009, 07:03:45)
[GCC 4.3.3] on linux2
Type "copyright", "credits" or "license()" for more information.
>>> ================================ RESTART ================================
>>>
ID:         101
Name:       Johnny 'wave-boy' Jones
Country:    USA
Average:    8.32
Board type: Fish
Age:        21
>>>
```

Your code works for one line of data. But RSA wants to be able to display the data for any surfer, not just wave-boy's.

Return a data structure from a function

Processing one line of surfer data was pretty straightforward. But now you have to work with **all** the lines of data in the file. Your program has to make the data available *quickly* so that a request to display the details of a particular surfer can be performed as soon as possible.

You already know enough to write a function that takes the surfer ID as a parameter, searches the file one line at a time for a matching ID, and then returns the found data to the caller:

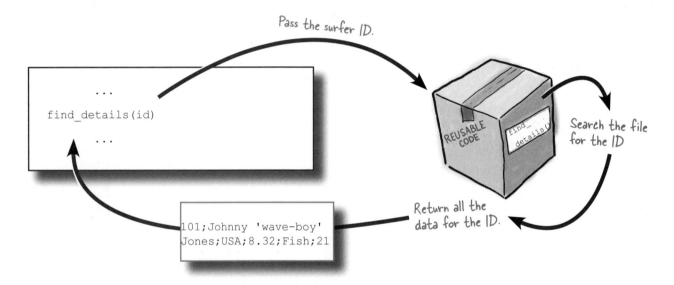

Pass the surfer ID.

find_details(id)

Search the file for the ID

Return all the data for the ID.

101;Johnny 'wave-boy' Jones;USA;8.32;Fish;21

There are really only two choices for how you return data from this function. Pass back the surfer's data either:

 As a string

or

 As a hash

But which? Returning a string requires the calling code to further process the data to extract the information it needs, which (although possible) gets messy, because the calling code is then required to cut up the string using `split()`. This is something best left to the function, because it *hides the complexity* of manipulating the data from the calling code. Returning a hash allows the calling code to simply pick out the information it needs without too much fuss and without any further processing.

Return a hash from the function to keep the calling code simple.

Code Magnets

Rearrange the code magnets to complete the function required. The following functionality is implemented:

1. Accept a single parameter (the surfer ID).

2. Process the data file one line at a time, creating a hash from the line on each iteration.

3. Compare the parameter against the ID read from the file.

4. If the IDs match, return the hash to the caller.

5. If no match is found, return an empty hash to the caller.

```
def find_details(id2find):

.............................................................................................................................................

    for each_line in surfers_f:

.............................................................................................................................................

.............................................................................................................................................

.............................................................................................................................................

            surfers_f.close()

.............................................................................................................................................

        surfers_f.close()

.............................................................................................................................................
```

```
surfers_f = open("surfing_data.csv")
```

```
return({})
```

```
s = {}
```

```
return(s)
```

```
(s['id'], s['name'], s['country'], s['average'], s['board'],
            s['age']) = each_line.split(";")
```

```
if id2find == int(s['id']):
```

Code Magnets Solution

You were to rearrange the code magnets to complete the function required. The following functionality is implemented:

1. Accept a single parameter (the surfer ID).

2. Process the data file one line at a time, creating a hash from the line on each iteration.

3. Compare the parameter against the ID read from the file.

4. If the IDs match, return the hash to the caller.

5. If no match is found, return an empty hash to the caller.

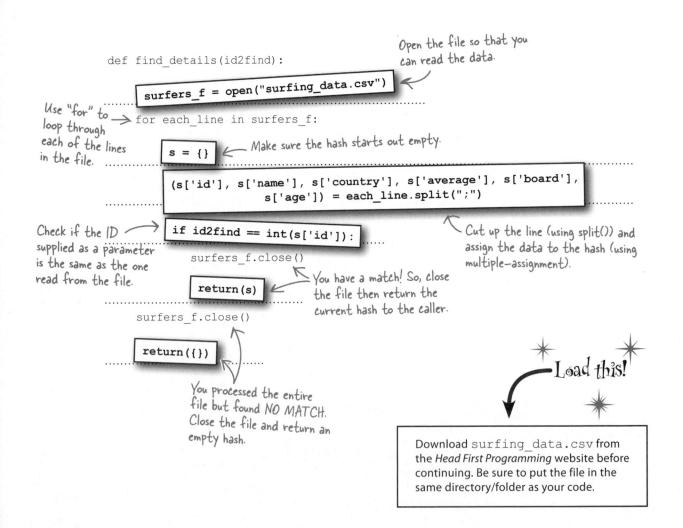

```
def find_details(id2find):
    surfers_f = open("surfing_data.csv")
    for each_line in surfers_f:
        s = {}
        (s['id'], s['name'], s['country'], s['average'], s['board'],
                s['age']) = each_line.split(";")
        if id2find == int(s['id']):
            surfers_f.close()
            return(s)
    surfers_f.close()
    return({})
```

Open the file so that you can read the data.

Use "for" to loop through each of the lines in the file.

Make sure the hash starts out empty.

Cut up the line (using split()) and assign the data to the hash (using multiple-assignment).

Check if the ID supplied as a parameter is the same as the one read from the file.

You have a match! So, close the file then return the current hash to the caller.

You processed the entire file but found NO MATCH. Close the file and return an empty hash.

Load this!

Download `surfing_data.csv` from the *Head First Programming* website before continuing. Be sure to put the file in the same directory/folder as your code.

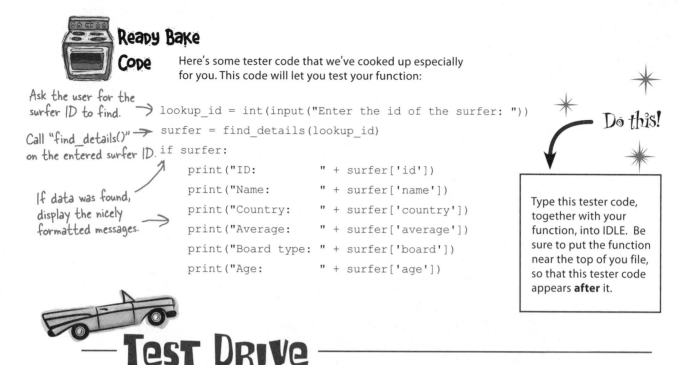

Ready Bake Code

Here's some tester code that we've cooked up especially for you. This code will let you test your function:

Ask the user for the surfer ID to find. →

Call "find_details()" on the entered surfer ID. →

```
lookup_id = int(input("Enter the id of the surfer: "))
surfer = find_details(lookup_id)
if surfer:
    print("ID:          " + surfer['id'])
    print("Name:        " + surfer['name'])
    print("Country:     " + surfer['country'])
    print("Average:     " + surfer['average'])
    print("Board type:  " + surfer['board'])
    print("Age:         " + surfer['age'])
```

If data was found, display the nicely formatted messages.

Do this!

Type this tester code, together with your function, into IDLE. Be sure to put the function near the top of you file, so that this tester code appears **after** it.

TEST DRIVE

Make sure the tester code and your function are entered into IDLE and saved to a file as a new program. Press F5 to test your function.

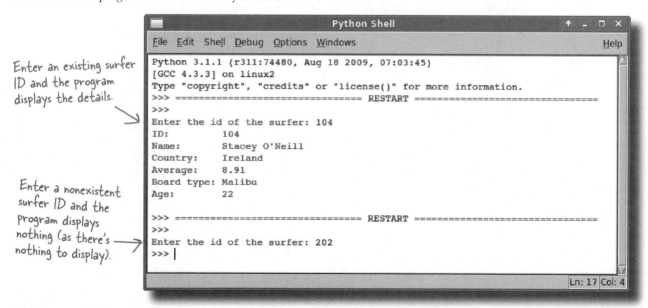

Enter an existing surfer ID and the program displays the details.

```
Python 3.1.1 (r311:74480, Aug 18 2009, 07:03:45)
[GCC 4.3.3] on linux2
Type "copyright", "credits" or "license()" for more information.
>>> ================================ RESTART ================================
>>>
Enter the id of the surfer: 104
ID:        104
Name:      Stacey O'Neill
Country:   Ireland
Average:   8.91
Board type: Malibu
Age:       22

>>> ================================ RESTART ================================
>>>
Enter the id of the surfer: 202
>>> |
```

Enter a nonexistent surfer ID and the program displays nothing (as there's nothing to display).

Great work! Your function is working well. Wonder how the RSA folks feel about it?

Here's your new board!

The RSA folks are delighted with your work.

This is exactly what we need...

Look at how quickly it pulls up each surfer's data.

I might actually get some beach time this year!

I think the guys over at TVN might want to take a look at this...

Here's your brand new board... start ripping it, dude!

Your program really hits the mark. The RSA folks can display the data from their tightly packed data file in a way that makes it easy for them to read and work with. It's fast, too.

Your use of a hash within the function was an inspired choice. The calling code only needs to be aware that a hash is being returned from the function to work with it effectively. And, as you've seen, returning a data structure (like a hash) is as easy as returning any other variable from a function.

Word of your programming skills is spreading far and wide.

Meanwhile, down at the studio...

You come highly recommended from RSA. We have a very similar requirement at TVN... would you consider selling your code to us?

Head First TVN is an up-and-coming sports network specializing in everything and anything to do with water. They are covering the National Surfing Championship and want their TV presenters to be able to use your program to access each surfer's details in much the same way that RSA did. There's just one small kink in their plans: TVN has all their data in a database system, **not** in a file.

← The TVN CEO

BRAIN POWER

Which part of your program is most likely to change if you have to get the surfer data from a database, as opposed to a file?

The code remains the same; it's the function that changes

Your program expects the find_details() function to return a hash representing the surfer's details. Rather than the function searching the file for the data, it needs to search the TVN database, convert what the database provides to a hash, and then return the hash to the calling code.

All you need to know is which database system TVN is using and how to access it from your function.

Let's base your code on TVN's code.

> I asked our technical people and they told me we use SQLite3... whatever that is. They also gave me some code for you to amend... they told me you'd know what to do with it, which is just as well because it's all gobbledygook to me!

 Ready Bake Code   Here's the TVN code:

Import the standard SQLite3 library and connect to the data in the database file (which you can download from this book's website).

Process each of the rows...

...looking for a surfer who has an ID of 104.

```
import sqlite3

db = sqlite3.connect("surfersDB.sdb")

db.row_factory = sqlite3.Row
cursor = db.cursor()
cursor.execute("select * from surfers")
rows = cursor.fetchall()
for row in rows:
    if row['id'] == 104:
        print("ID is " + str(row['id']))
        print("Name is " + row['name'])
        print("Board-type is " + row['board'])
cursor.close()
```

Grab all the surfer data from the database, assigning the data to a variable called "rows".

Print out some of the data (if we have a match).

Tidy up after yourself (always a good idea).

It is possible to improve the efficiency and power of this code if you know a little bit about SQL. We are deliberately avoiding improving TVN's SQL. However, we strongly recommend "Head First SQL" to those who want to learn more.

Sharpen your pencil

Rewrite your function to retrieve the data it needs from the TVN database. Use the ready bake code as provided by TVN's technical people as a basis for your code. Bear in mind that your program expects the data in the hash returned from the `find_details()` function to be a collection of strings.

....

....

....

....

....

....

....

....

....

....

....

....

....

....

....

....

....

....

....

Sharpen your pencil
Solution

You were to rewrite your function to retrieve the data it needs from the TVN database. You were to use the ready bake code as provided by TVN's technical people. You were to bear in mind that your program expects the data in the hash returned from the `find_details()` function to be a collection of strings.

```python
import sqlite3


def find_details(id2find):
    db = sqlite3.connect("surfersDB.sdb")
    db.row_factory = sqlite3.Row
    cursor = db.cursor()
    cursor.execute("select * from surfers")
    rows = cursor.fetchall()
    for row in rows:
        if row['id'] == id2find:
            s = {}
            s['id']      = str(row['id'])
            s['name']    = row['name']
            s['country'] = row['country']
            s['average'] = str(row['average'])
            s['board']   = row['board']
            s['age']     = str(row['age'])
            cursor.close()
            return(s)
    cursor.close()
    return({})
```

Grab all the surfer data from the database, as opposed to the file.

When a match is found...

...build the hash one key-value pair at a time.

Return the hash to the calling code (as before).

Test Drive

Change your program in IDLE to use the new version of the function (which now talks to TVN's database). Save your program under a new name and press F5 to run it.

Load this!

Download `surfersDB.sdb` from the *Head First Programming* website before running this test drive.

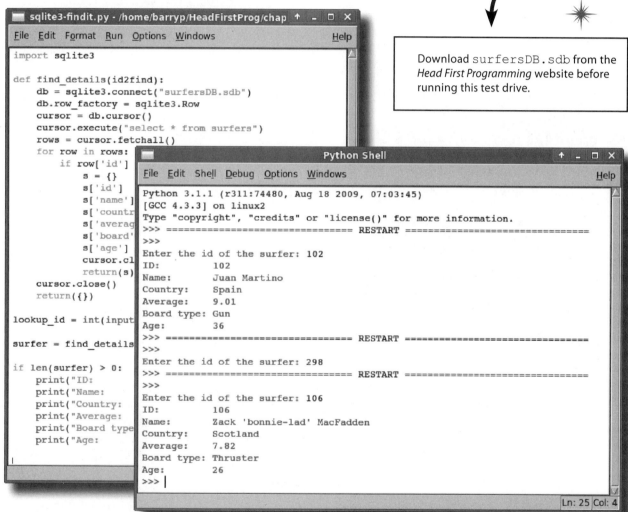

```
sqlite3-findit.py - /home/barryp/HeadFirstProg/chap

File  Edit  Format  Run  Options  Windows                    Help

import sqlite3

def find_details(id2find):
    db = sqlite3.connect("surfersDB.sdb")
    db.row_factory = sqlite3.Row
    cursor = db.cursor()
    cursor.execute("select * from surfers")
    rows = cursor.fetchall()
    for row in rows:
        if row['id']
            s = {}
            s['id']
            s['name']
            s['countr
            s['averag
            s['board'
            s['age']
            cursor.cl
            return(s)
    cursor.close()
    return({})

lookup_id = int(input

surfer = find_details

if len(surfer) > 0:
    print("ID:
    print("Name:
    print("Country:
    print("Average:
    print("Board type
    print("Age:
```

```
Python Shell

File  Edit  Shell  Debug  Options  Windows                    Help

Python 3.1.1 (r311:74480, Aug 18 2009, 07:03:45)
[GCC 4.3.3] on linux2
Type "copyright", "credits" or "license()" for more information.
>>> ================================ RESTART ================================
>>>
Enter the id of the surfer: 102
ID:        102
Name:      Juan Martino
Country:   Spain
Average:   9.01
Board type: Gun
Age:       36
>>> ================================ RESTART ================================
>>>
Enter the id of the surfer: 298
>>> ================================ RESTART ================================
>>>
Enter the id of the surfer: 106
ID:        106
Name:      Zack 'bonnie-lad' MacFadden
Country:   Scotland
Average:   7.82
Board type: Thruster
Age:       26
>>> |

                                                        Ln: 25 Col: 4
```

Now, as well as working with data in files, you can extract data from a database system. Your program fully integrates with TVN's SQLite3 technology.

The program displays similar output to before... only, this time, the data is coming from a database, NOT a file!

Send off that code to TVN, and sit back and wait for the money to roll in...

TVN's data is on the money!

With the surfing data now displayed directly from the TVN database, the sports writers no longer need to worry about all those tattered and torn competition entry forms. The data is right there on screen when they need it. They couldn't be happier. Your program has made their day.

The TVN sports writers know how to celebrate.

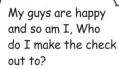

My guys are happy and so am I, Who do I make the check out to?

Your Programming Toolbox

You've got Chapter 5 under your belt. Let's look back at what you've learned in this chapter:

Programming Tools

* hash – a data structure that associates a name with a value

* s['age'] – retrieve the value associated with the 'age' name in a hash called 's'

* returning a data structure from a function

* database system – a technology, like SQLite3, that can store large quantities of data in a very efficient way

Python Tools

* {} – an empty hash

* s['wind'] = "off shore" – sets that value associated with "wind" in the "s" hash to the value "off shore"

* s.keys() – provide a list of keys for the hash called 's'

* s.items() – provide a list of keys AND values for the hash called 's'

* line.split(",") – split the string contained within the 'line' variable at every occurrence of a comma

* sorted() – a built-in function that can sort most data structures

6 modular programming

Keeping things straight

I know he said he knew a better way to do things, but this wasn't what I had in mind.

The code that you write will make its way into many programs.

And, although **sharing** is good, you need to be *careful*. One programmer might take your code and use it in an **unexpected** way, while another might change it without even letting you know. You might want to use one function in all your programs and, over time, that function's code might **change** to suit your needs. Smart programmers take advantage of *modular programming techniques* to keep their workload manageable. Let's find out how in the pages that follow...

Head First Health Club is upgrading some systems

Head First Health Club has a new CEO, and he loves new technology. He was shocked when he saw how old the sales systems were.

> Some of our technology is really ancient. I want to start by replacing the cash registers with new POS systems. Can you help?

← New CEO

The old cash registers really need to be replaced.

Old and busted

The new system will run on a PC and accept credit card payments.

The new hotness

A **point-of-sale** (POS) system is just a computer program that works like a cash register. The boss doesn't want to replace all of the cash registers immediately. He wants to begin with a trial system in the coffee bar.

← It would be nice if the systems you produce were modular in design. You'll get to that AFTER you've spent some time understanding what's required.

Let's see what the coffee bar POS needs to do.

The program needs to create a transaction file

The POS program will record credit card sales in a file called `transactions.txt`. At the end of each day, this file is sent to the bank and any money is transferred from the credit card account into the health club's bank account.

The bank has sent an example version of the file for you to see what sort of data you will need to generate:

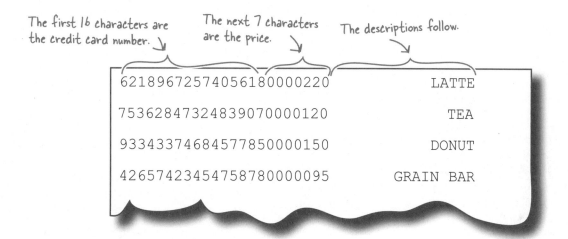

The first 16 characters are the credit card number.

The next 7 characters are the price.

The descriptions follow.

```
6218967257405618 0000220        LATTE
7536284732483907 0000120          TEA
9334337468457785 0000150        DONUT
4265742345475878 0000095    GRAIN BAR
```

The file contains **formatted data**. There's a line of text (or *record*) for each item sold. The first 16 characters of the line are the **credit card number**, followed by 7 characters that represent the sale price, excluding the decimal point (so $1.75 is written as **0000175**). The rest of the record is a description of the item being sold.

BRAIN POWER

How would you create a string of characters in the correct format for the record? Which parts of the record will be the hardest to create?

Use strings to format strings

Many programs need to create strings with particular pieces of data at particular places, so most computer languages try to make life easier for you by letting you use string **formats**.

The best way to understand string formats is with an example. Open up the Python Shell and type in this:

The first value will be inserted as a 5-character number.

The second value will be inserted as a string.

```
>>> print("There are %5d %s available" % (17, "donuts"))
```

```
There are    17 donuts available
```

The number has extra spaces added at the front, to make sure it takes up the required 5 characters.

The string-formatting operator

When Python sees a string followed by a percentage (%) symbol, it knows that it needs to consider the string as a **string format**. The values that follow the % operator are going to be inserted into the formatted string in the order specified, one value at a time. Wherever Python finds a % inside the string, it knows to insert a value.

A number format specification → **%5d**

When Python sees this, it will insert the value 17 as a 5-character whole number—that's because the "d" type specifier tells Python to print the number as a decimal. Because 17 is not 5-characters long, Python will left-pad it with 3 extra spaces at the front to make it the correct length.

A string format specification → **%s**

This symbol tells Python to insert the value "donuts" as a string. As you are not specifying a length here, the string is inserted as is.

These are just two examples of how to format values in a string. There are lots more.

> OK, this string is followed by a % symbol. So... I'll need to replace %5d with the number 17, and %s with the string "donuts".

WHAT'S MY PURPOSE?

Match each format string to what it does. We've already done one for you.

`"%s %e" % ("Value is", 16.0 ** 0.5)`   Display a string followed by 4.000000.

`"%7d" % (11232/3)`   Display a string followed by 4.000000e+00.

`"%x" % 127`   Display the value, padded with 0s.

`"%20s\n" % "Banana swirl"`   Display the result of the calculation, padded with spaces.

`"%s is $%4.2f" % ("Popsicle", 1.754)`   Pad the string out to 20 characters, then display a newline character.

`"%s %f" % ("Value is", 16.0 ** 0.5)`   Display the number as a hexidecimal (base 16).

`"%07d" % (11232/3)`   As well as a string, also display a floating point number to 2 decimal places.

Sharpen your pencil

Be careful with the decimal point in the price. →

Look back at the records you need to create for the transaction file. Each line will need to end with a newline character. If you have the credit card number, price, and description in variables called `credit_card`, `price`, and `description`, write down what you would use for the format string:

....

WHAT'S MY PURPOSE?
SOLUTION

If you have just one value to format, you don't need to surround it with parentheses.

You were to match each format string to what it does.

```
"%s %e" % ("Value is", 16.0 ** 0.5)
```
Display a string followed by 4.000000.

```
"%7d" % (11232/3)
```
Display a string followed by 4.000000e+00.

```
"%x" % 127
```
Display the value, padded with 0s.

\n means take a NEWLINE.

```
"%20s\n" % "Banana swirl"
```
Display the result of the calculation, padded with spaces.
By default, Python will pad using spaces.

This means "use 4 characters."

```
"%s is $%4.2f" % ("Popsicle", 1.754)
```
Pad the string out to 20 characters, then display a newline character.

This means "show 2 numbers after the decimal point."

```
"%s %f" % ("Value is", 16.0 ** 0.5)
```
Display the number as a hexidecimal (base 16).

Values can be the result of a calculation.

```
"%07d" % (11232/3)
```
As well as a string, also display a floating point number to 2 decimal places.

Hexadecimal numbers are used for things like colors on the Web.

Following the % with a 0 means "pad with zeroes."

Sharpen your pencil
Solution

You were to look back at the records you need to create for the transaction file and write down what you would use for the format string:

Don't worry if your answer doesn't look EXACTLY like this. Try out your answer in the Python Shell to check that it works.

Multiplying by 100 and displaying it as a whole number effectively removes the decimal point from the price.

```
"%16s%07d%16s\n" % (credit_card, price*100, description)
```

Credit card numbers should always be exactly 16 characters.

You need a newline character at the end of each line.

Code Magnets

Now that you know how to format the records in the `transactions.txt` file, it is time to write the rest of the coffee bar POS program. Complete the code below by arranging the code magnets in the correct place:

```python
def save_transaction(price, credit_card, description):
    file = open("transactions.txt", "a")
    file.write("%s%07d%s\n" % (credit_card, price * 100, description))
    file.close()

items   = ["DONUT", "LATTE", "FILTER", "MUFFIN"]
prices  = [1.50, 2.0, 1.80, 1.20]
running = True

while running:
    option = 1
    for choice in items:
.......................................................................................

        option = option + 1
    print(str(option) + ". Quit")
.......................................................................................

    if choice == option:
.......................................................................................

    else:
.......................................................................................

        save_transaction(prices[choice - 1], credit_card,.......................................)
```

The "a" means you are always going to APPEND records to the end of the file.

This is the format string you just created.

The loop will keep running while the "running" variable has the value True. To end the loop, set "running" to False.

Code magnets:

```python
credit_card = input("Credit card number: ")
```

```python
items[choice - 1]
```

```python
running = False
```

```python
choice=int(input("Choose an option: "))
```

```python
print(str(option) + ". " + choice)
```

Code Magnets Solution

Now that we know how to format the records in the `transactions.txt` file, it is time to write the rest of the coffee bar POS program. You were to complete the code below by arranging the code magnets:

```python
def save_transaction(price, credit_card, description):
    file = open("transactions.txt", "a")
    file.write("%s%07d%s\n" % (credit_card, price * 100, description))
    file.close()

items   = ["DONUT", "LATTE", "FILTER", "MUFFIN"]
prices  = [1.50, 2.0, 1.80, 1.20]
running = True


while running:
    option = 1
    for choice in items:
        print(str(option) + ". " + choice)

        option = option + 1
    print(str(option) + ". Quit")

    choice = int(input("Choose an option: "))

    if choice == option:
        running = False

    else:

        credit_card = input("Credit card number: ")

        save_transaction(prices[choice - 1], credit_card, items[choice - 1])
```

← This is the array of menu options.

← This is the matching array of menu prices.

← This code displays the program's menu.

← The user enters a menu option number to make a sale.

← This will be True if the user selects the LAST option on the menu, which is "Quit."

Test Drive

The machine has been set up in the coffee bar just in time for the boss to come in for his morning latte, so let's run the code and see what he thinks. Run the program in IDLE:

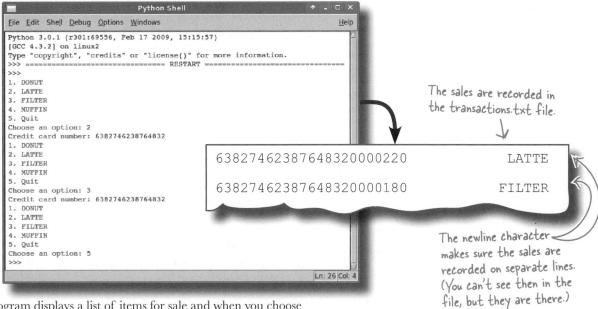

The sales are recorded in the transactions.txt file.

↓

```
6382746238764832 0000220                    LATTE

6382746238764832 0000180                    FILTER
```

The newline character makes sure the sales are recorded on separate lines. (You can't see then in the file, but they are there.)

Python Shell

```
Python 3.0.1 (r301:69556, Feb 17 2009, 15:15:57)
[GCC 4.3.2] on linux2
Type "copyright", "credits" or "license()" for more information.
>>> ============================== RESTART ==============================
>>>
1. DONUT
2. LATTE
3. FILTER
4. MUFFIN
5. Quit
Choose an option: 2
Credit card number: 6382746238764832
1. DONUT
2. LATTE
3. FILTER
4. MUFFIN
5. Quit
Choose an option: 3
Credit card number: 6382746238764832
1. DONUT
2. LATTE
3. FILTER
4. MUFFIN
5. Quit
Choose an option: 5
>>>
```

The program displays a list of items for sale and when you choose one and provide a credit card number, it adds the sale into a file called `transactions.txt`. This is the same file that the POS system in the gym uses.

> That looks pretty good. We'll try it for a couple of weeks here in the coffee bar and see how it goes.

The boss agrees to try out the system in the coffee bar, and he even agrees to **extend the trial** and let your friend create another POS for the gym, based on your code.

Things are going really well. If they continue like this, you will win the contract to replace all of the systems at the health club!

The Format String Exposed

This week's interview:
Why do appearances matter?

Head First: Format String, it's a pleasure to meet you.

Format String: The pleasure is all mine.

Head First: You're not just used in Python, are you?

Format String: Oh no. I'm really used in lots of programming languages, like C, C#, and Java. You see me crop up all over the place.

Head First: Why is that?

Format String: Well, I don't like to blow my own bugle, but I am kind of useful. Everywhere you need to generate formatted text, I can make life a lot easier for you.

Head First: Can you give us some examples?

Format String: Oh sure. If you need to send data to another system, you'll probably need me. If you want to display an error message in a specific format, I'm good at that, too.

Head First: I hate to say this, it seems so rude, but isn't it possible to do everything you do with just normal string operations?

Format String: Please, I don't take offence. Yes, you can do pretty much everything I do by writing

code and creating strings manually. But I don't think that's a great idea.

Head First: Why's that?

Format String: Two reasons: first, you might have to create a lot of code, and second, I'm a little more dynamic.

Head First: What do you mean?

Format String: Well, I'm just data. Lots of times, programmers prefer to use data instead of chunks of code, because it means they can store me away as configuration. So I get used a lot for things like internationalization.

Head First: Internationalization?

Format String: Yeah, say someone wants to display a message that someone has the top score. They could write the message in a file like "%d is the top score!". If they write a French version of the game, they just have to amend me to "%d est les points supérieurs!"

Head First: No code change necessary.

Format String: Exactly.

Head First: String Format, thanks for your time.

---

there are no Dumb Questions

Q: Those format strings look a little weird. How do I find out more about them?

A: A good reference book (we present our favorite in the appendix) will contain all you need to know and there's also lots of material on-line in the official Python docs.

Q: Are there special rules for what's acceptable as a credit card number?

A: Yes, there are. But let's not get bogged down in those type of details at this stage. Concentrate on the `save_transaction()` function and how the code interacts with it.

Q: Why does the code generate the menu in such a complex way?

A: If you study the menu generation code, you will see that when you add more items and prices, the rest of the code doesn't need to change to support the new items. The menu is generated automatically.

A late night email ruins your day

A few days after the demo, you get a late night email from the
friend who wrote the second program (based on *your* code):

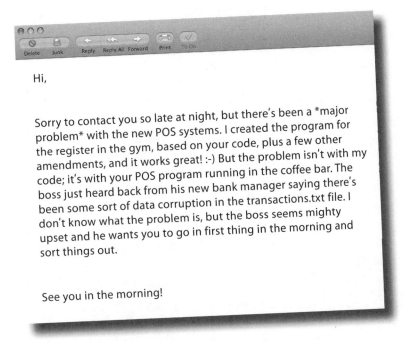

Hi,

Sorry to contact you so late at night, but there's been a *major
problem* with the new POS systems. I created the program for
the register in the gym, based on your code, plus a few other
amendments, and it works great! :-) But the problem isn't with my
code; it's with your POS program running in the coffee bar. The
boss just heard back from his new bank manager saying there's
been some sort of data corruption in the transactions.txt file. I
don't know what the problem is, but the boss seems mighty
upset and he wants you to go in first thing in the morning and
sort things out.

See you in the morning!

Something really strange has happened. Even though your code *used*
to work, it has suddenly started to go wrong. Meanwhile, your friend's
program, which is really just a **modified copy** of your program, is
working perfectly.

**Looks like you better get to the health club bright and
early tomorrow morning and see what's happened.**

$50,000... for a donut?!

When you arrive at the health club you find out exactly what's happened. The **entire day's sales** have been rejected by the bank for two reasons:

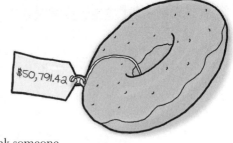

$50,791.42

1 **The credit card numbers are all fake/invalid.**
The bank was really worried about this one because they think someone must have hacked into the system to generate the messed-up credit card numbers.

2 **The prices are ridiculous.**
One of the recorded sales was for a donut that cost over **$50,000**!

And what makes it worse, this was the first time we sent the transaction file to our new bank! We only switched over the day before yesterday so that I could secure a loan for the new weight room!

This looks like a really serious problem. Let's take a look at the file that the bank rejected.

Only the sales from <u>your</u> program were rejected

The `transactions.txt` file that was sent to the bank contains all of the day's sales from both *your* POS program in the coffee bar and *your friend's* POS program in the gym. This is a section of the file:

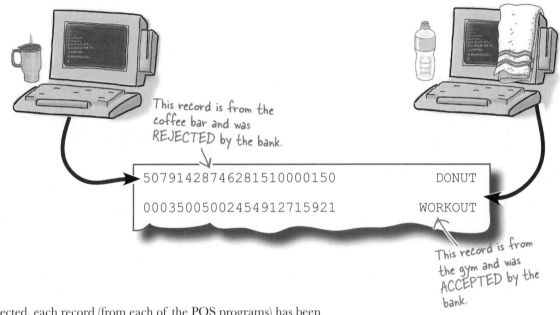

This record is from the coffee bar and was REJECTED by the bank.

`50791428746281510000150`   DONUT

`00035005002454912715921`   WORKOUT

This record is from the gym and was ACCEPTED by the bank.

As expected, each record (from each of the POS programs) has been appended to the transactions file. That bit appears to be working fine.

But, something is not quite right here...

BRAIN POWER

Study the two records carefully. Is there a difference between them that might explain why one was accepted and the other was rejected? Think about recent events. What do you think has caused this problem?

The new bank uses a new format

Your friend tells you that just after taking a copy of your code, the word came down that the health club was switching banks. Without telling *you*, your friend found out the new bank format and updated *his code* in the **gym** program.

That means that the POS program in the gym is generating records in the new bank format.

The new bank format is:

```
Price / Credit Card / Description
```

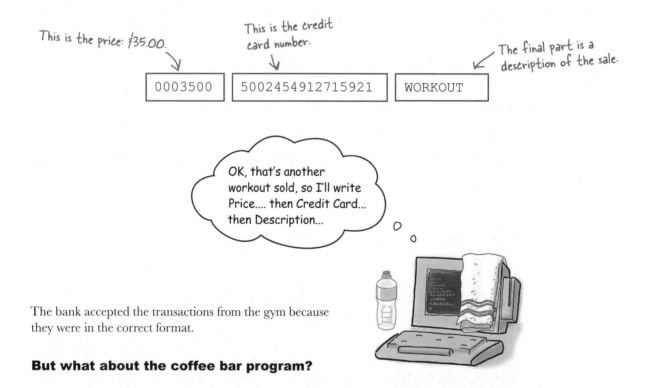

This is the price: $35.00.

This is the credit card number.

The final part is a description of the sale.

```
0003500    5002454912715921    WORKOUT
```

OK, that's another workout sold, so I'll write Price.... then Credit Card... then Description...

The bank accepted the transactions from the gym because they were in the correct format.

But what about the coffee bar program?

Your coffee bar program still uses the <u>old format</u>

Your program in the coffee bar was *never* updated after the health club switched banks. It's still doing what it always did: it's still creating files in the **old format**.

That old format wrote out the price and the credit card the *other way round*, which meant when your program wrote out a record like this:

So that's a donut. Better write Credit Card... then Price... then Description.

The credit card number

Price = $1.50

← Description

5079142874628151	0000150	DONUT

The new bank **read** the record like this:

The price... $50,791.42!

Messed up credit card number: the bank thought it was fake.

But at least the description's OK.

5079142	8746281510000150	DONUT

This is suspicious... $50,000 for a donut.... Does not compute... Fake credit card information! Security! Security!!

So it's not that somebody broke into your program and changed it. No, it's the exact opposite. Your code never picked up the change that was made to the gym program in order to support the new format.

☀BRAIN POWER

What should you do to fix it? What *shouldn't* you do?

Don't just update your copy

The code in the gym program is a *copy* of your code in the coffee bar. And copying code is a ***bad thing***. Once you have two separate copies of a piece of code, then changes need to be applied in **two places**. So how do we avoid copying code?

Smart programmers write modular code

The secret is to break your programs into smaller pieces of code called modules. What's a module? It's just a file containing code the computer can run. Every Python program you've written so far has been a single module.

But most programs you'll write will probably be split across many, many modules. And writing modular code is important because modules can be **shared between programs**.

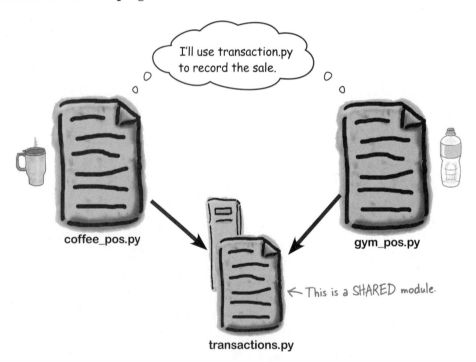

I'll use transaction.py to record the sale.

coffee_pos.py

gym_pos.py

transactions.py

← This is a SHARED module.

If you separate out the code that saves the transactions to a file and store it in a new module called `transactions.py`, that module can be shared by **both programs**. If you then ever need to change the code in `transactions.py`, **both** programs will pick up the changes automatically.

So how do you create a module...?

Remember: a module is just a file containing some Python code. So, take the code that you want to share out of the `gym_pos.py` file:

```
def save_transaction(price, credit_card, description):
    file = open("transactions.txt", "a")
```

Then save this code in a file called `transactions.py`. You have just created a new module.

...and how do you use it?

Once you've created the module, you then need to *tell the programs to use it*. When you were using *library* code you needed to *import* it. You do the same thing with your own modules. So, instead of using library code from the Standard Python Library, you're really just using library code that you've written yourself. You can add this line to the top of each of your programs:

This means "run the code in the named module."

This line needs to be added to any program that uses the "transactions.py" module.

from transactions import *

This means "treat everything inside the module as if it is code within your program."

With this line, you are telling Python that you want to run the code in the `transactions.py` file and this allows you to access whatever code the module contains *as if it is just part of your program*.

It's time to fix the programs.

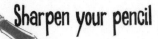

Sharpen your pencil

These are the two POS programs. Here is the code to the one used in the coffee bar (that you wrote):

This is the code to the "coffee_pos.py" program.

```python
def save_transaction(price, credit_card, description):
    file = open("transactions.txt", "a")
    file.write("%16s%07d%16s\n" % (credit_card, price * 100, description))
    file.close()


items    = ["DONUT", "LATTE", "FILTER", "MUFFIN"]
prices   = [1.50, 2.20, 1.80, 1.20]
running = True


while running:
    option = 1
    for choice in items:
        print(str(option) + ". " + choice)
        option = option + 1
    print(str(option) + ". Quit")
    choice = int(input("Choose an option: "))
    if choice == option:
        running = False
    else:
        credit_card = input("Credit card number: ")
        save_transaction(prices[choice - 1], credit_card, items[choice - 1])
```

The other program is very similar (which your friend created for use in the gym):

This is the code to the "gym_pos.py" program.

```python
def save_transaction(price, credit_card, description):
    file = open("transactions.txt", "a")
    file.write("%07d%16s%16s\n" % (price * 100, credit_card, description))
    file.close()


items   = ["WORKOUT", "WEIGHTS", "BIKES"]
prices  = [35.0, 10.0, 8.0]
running = True

while running:
    option = 1
    for choice in items:
        print(str(option) + ". " + choice)
        option = option + 1
    print(str(option) + ". Quit")
    choice = int(input("Choose an option: "))
    if choice == option:
        running = False
    else:
        credit_card = input("Credit card number: ")
        save_transaction(prices[choice - 1], credit_card, items[choice - 1])
```

Using a pencil, modify the two programs so that they use the `transactions.py` module. Then write what you think should go into the `transactions.py` module here:

....

....

....

....

Sharpen your pencil
Solution

These are the two POS programs. Here is the code to the one used in the coffee bar (that you wrote):

```
def save_transaction(price, credit_card, description):
    file = open("transactions.txt", "a")
    file.write("%16s%07d%16s\n" % (credit_card, price * 100, description))
    file.close()
from transactions import *
items    = ["DONUT", "LATTE", "FILTER", "MUFFIN"]
prices   = [1.50, 2.20, 1.80, 1.20]
running = True

while running:
    option = 1
    for choice in items:
        print(str(option) + ". " + choice)
        option = option + 1
    print(str(option) + ". Quit")
    choice = int(input("Choose an option: "))
    if choice == option:
        running = False
    else:
        credit_card = input("Credit card number: ")
        save_transaction(prices[choice - 1], credit_card, items[choice - 1])
```

The other program is very similar (which your friend created for use in the gym):

```
def save_transaction(price, credit_card, description):
    file = open("transactions.txt", "a")
    file.write("%07d%16s%16s\n" % (price * 100, credit_card, description))
    file.close()
```

```
from transactions import *
items  = ["WORKOUT", "WEIGHTS", "BIKES"]
prices = [35.0, 10.0, 8.0]
running = True


while running:
    option = 1
    for choice in items:
        print(str(option) + ". " + choice)
        option = option + 1
    print(str(option) + ". Quit")
    choice = int(input("Choose an option: "))
    if choice == option:
        running = False
    else:
        credit_card = input("Credit card number: ")
        save_transaction(prices[choice - 1], credit_card, items[choice - 1])
```

Using a pencil, you were asked modify the two programs so that they use the `transactions.py` module. You were then asked to write what you think should go into the `transactions.py` module here:

```
def save_transaction(price, credit_card, description):
    file = open("transactions.txt", "a")
    file.write("%07d%16s%16s\n" % (price * 100, credit_card, description))
    file.close()
```

↑
Make sure you use the code that
displays the PRICE first.

Test Drive

Once you have completed the exercise, you should have **three saved files**: gym_pos.py, coffee_pos.py, and transactions.py. You can now run the gym_pos.py and the coffee_pos.py programs:

gym_pos.py

coffee_pos.py

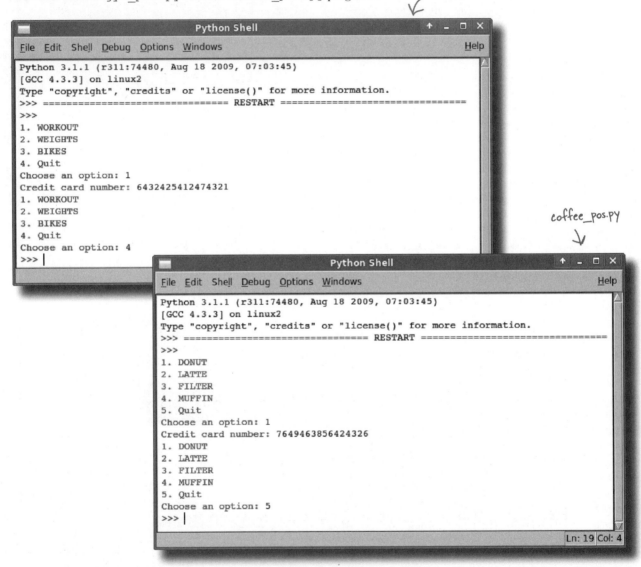

```
Python Shell
File  Edit  Shell  Debug  Options  Windows                          Help

Python 3.1.1 (r311:74480, Aug 18 2009, 07:03:45)
[GCC 4.3.3] on linux2
Type "copyright", "credits" or "license()" for more information.
>>> =============================== RESTART ================================
>>>
1. WORKOUT
2. WEIGHTS
3. BIKES
4. Quit
Choose an option: 1
Credit card number: 6432425412474321
1. WORKOUT
2. WEIGHTS
3. BIKES
4. Quit
Choose an option: 4
>>> |
```

```
Python Shell
File  Edit  Shell  Debug  Options  Windows                          Help

Python 3.1.1 (r311:74480, Aug 18 2009, 07:03:45)
[GCC 4.3.3] on linux2
Type "copyright", "credits" or "license()" for more information.
>>> =============================== RESTART ================================
>>>
1. DONUT
2. LATTE
3. FILTER
4. MUFFIN
5. Quit
Choose an option: 1
Credit card number: 7649463856424326
1. DONUT
2. LATTE
3. FILTER
4. MUFFIN
5. Quit
Choose an option: 5
>>> |
                                                          Ln: 19 Col: 4
```

The two programs look like they've worked correctly. But what about the transaction file?

The transaction file is working great, too

When you open up the `transactions.txt` file, you see this inside:

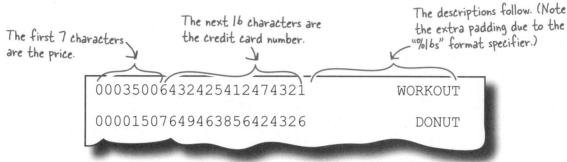

The first 7 characters are the price.

The next 16 characters are the credit card number.

The descriptions follow. (Note the extra padding due to the "%16s" format specifier.)

```
0003500643242541247432                    WORKOUT

0000150764946385642432                    DONUT
```

Both of the records, created by each of the POS programs, are now correctly formatted. That's because both programs are sharing the same piece of code to save the transactions.

> Phew! I just heard from the bank that transactions from both of the POS systems went through smoothly. That's a big relief. Good job fixing it!

Looks like you saved the day.

there are no
Dumb Questions

Q: So modules are sort of like containers for functions, right?

A: It's true that most modules are used to store a collection of related functions. However, it is perfectly acceptable to put **any** code in a module, which is then executed whenever the module is imported into your program.

Q: So when I use import, it's as if I typed the code in the module directly into my program?

A: Yes, that's a good way to think about it. Using a shared module saves you from having to type (or cut'n'paste) all that code yourself. Just import it and it's there.

Q: Do I have to use modules?

A: No, but the benefit of putting shareable code into a module starts to pay off the second you use that module in another program. Sharing code with modules is good programming practice.

The health club has a new requirement

The health club boss has a grand plan to get more customers into the health club.

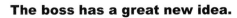

Ooh, I think we need to discount the prices in the coffee bar for the next month. There's nothing like relaxing with a latte after a tough workout, especially if the price is right. Our customers like to treat themselves, so I want to make this easy for them.

The boss has a great new idea.

The boss wants to cut 10% off all the prices in the coffee bar. If it's successful, he may want to do the same thing in other places, such as the gym.

Instead of just amending the code in the `coffee_pos.py` file, you need to create a new module called `promotion.py` that will calculate a discounted price.

Sharpen your pencil

You need to change the coffee bar POS program to apply the 10% discount to everything that's sold. You have three tasks.

1 Start by creating a new module called `promotion.py` containing one function:

```
def discount(price):
```

....

2 Complete the code in the above function so that it returns 90% of the price it is given.

3 This is the latest version of the `coffee_pos.py` module. Modify it so that it uses the new module to cut the price of everything that's sold.

```
from transactions import *

items   = ["DONUT", "LATTE", "FILTER", "MUFFIN"]
prices  = [1.50, 2.20, 1.80, 1.20]
running = True

while running:
    option = 1
    for choice in items:
        print(str(option) + ". " + choice)
        option = option + 1
    print(str(option) + ". Quit")
    choice = int(input("Choose an option: "))
    if choice == option:
        running = False
    else:
        credit_card = input("Credit card number: ")
        save_transaction(prices[choice - 1], credit_card, items[choice - 1])
```

Sharpen your pencil
Solution

You needed to change the coffee bar POS program to apply the 10% discount to everything that's sold. You had three tasks.

1 Start by creating a new module called `promotion.py` containing one function:

```
def discount(price):
    return 0.9 * price
```

Multiplying the price by 0.9 will give you a 10% discount.

2 Complete the code in the above function so that it returns 90% of the price it is given.

3 This is the latest version of the `coffee_pos.py` module. Modify it so that it uses the new module to cut the price of everything that's sold.

```
from transactions import *
from promotion import *
items   = ["DONUT", "LATTE", "FILTER", "MUFFIN"]
prices  = [1.50, 2.20, 1.80, 1.20]
running = True


while running:
    option = 1
    for choice in items:
        print(str(option) + ". " + choice)
        option = option + 1
    print(str(option) + ". Quit")
    choice = int(input("Choose an option: "))
    if choice == option:
        running = False
    else:
        credit_card = input("Credit card number: ")
        new_price=discount(prices[choice - 1])
        save_transaction(prices[choice - 1], credit_card, items[choice - 1])
                         new_price
```

You need to import the code from the "promotion.py" module.

Your code should call the "discount()" function.

"new_price" is the discounted value of the price.

TEST DRIVE

So what happens if you fire up `coffee_pos.py` in IDLE and buy a $2 latte?

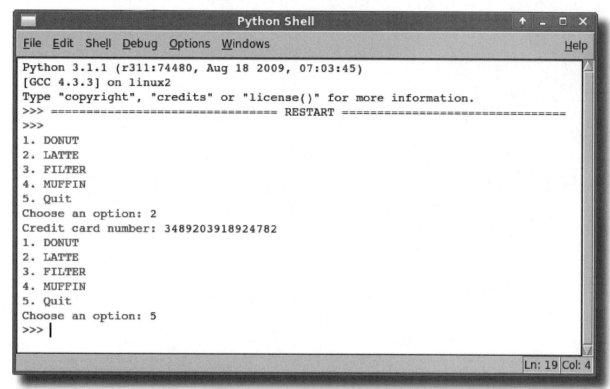

```
Python Shell                                          ↑ _ □ ✕

File  Edit  Shell  Debug  Options  Windows                        Help

Python 3.1.1 (r311:74480, Aug 18 2009, 07:03:45)
[GCC 4.3.3] on linux2
Type "copyright", "credits" or "license()" for more information.
>>> =============================== RESTART ================================
>>>
1. DONUT
2. LATTE
3. FILTER
4. MUFFIN
5. Quit
Choose an option: 2
Credit card number: 3489203918924782
1. DONUT
2. LATTE
3. FILTER
4. MUFFIN
5. Quit
Choose an option: 5
>>> |
                                                          Ln: 19 Col: 4
```

It looks like it's working on the screen. What about in the `transactions.txt` file? Will the latte still cost $2.20?

The actual price to charge is here.

00001983489203918924782   LATTE

No, the latte was discounted by 10% to $1.98, which is *exactly* what you want to record in the transactions file.

It's time to demo your code to the boss.

That's fantastic! You made the change so quickly, just in time for the doors to open. It does handle **both** kinds of discount, right?

Both kinds of discount?

It seems that there was something that the boss *forgot* to tell you. As well as deciding to cut the health club's own prices, he also got in touch with his old friend, the CEO of Starbuzz, and arranged for a special discount for everyone who shows the cashier a Starbuzz Discount Card. This is the email he received back:

Great to hear from you!

Yes, of course, you can join the Starbuzz discount scheme! A lot of people across the world are now working on systems for Starbuzz, so I think I can help your coders out. Please find attached a copy of the official Starbuzz Discount Module (tm). It's a Python module that will calculate an additional 5% discount for every customer who presents a Starbuzz Discount Card.

If we ever change the way the discount scheme works in the future, we can send you an updated module and your systems will get updated without you having to do any work at all!

Be well and keep drinking the coffee!

Your friend,

Starbuzz CEO

That's great news. Although you've heard about this extra discount late in the day, at least most of the work's already been done for you. You just need to use the Python module the Starbuzz CEO attached to his email, and your program will be set up to apply both discounts.

Let's take a look at the Starbuzz code.

The Starbuzz code

The attachment from Starbuzz was a file called `starbuzz.py`.
When you open it, you see this:

Lines that start with
are comments; Python →
will ignore them.

This is the
discount function,
as provided by
Starbuzz

```
# Official Starbuzz Discount Module
# Copyright(c) Starbuzz Corporation
# All Rights Reserved.
# This function calculates a 5% discount on a price
def discount(price):
    return 0.95 * price
```

This function returns a price
that's 5% lower than the price it
was given.

The first few lines begin with # characters; these are **comments**.
Comments are just notes added by a programmer that are intended
to be read by other programmers. Python will ignore them, because
comments are not code.

After the comments comes the Starbuzz `discount()` function. It's
just like the discount function you wrote, except instead of returning a
10% discount, it returns a 5% discount.

Your code will have to use both discounts:

●   It will apply a 10% discount to everything.

●   And if somebody presents a Starbuzz Discount Card, it will also have to
apply the 5% Starbuzz discount.

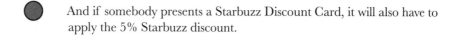

You need to change the code so that it uses both of the `discount()`
functions. Can you see a problem? What is it?

The two discount functions have the same name

Here is the promotion.py module you just created:

```
def discount(price):
    return 0.9 * price
```

And here is the starbuzz.py module:

```
# Official Starbuzz Discount Module
# Copyright(c) Starbuzz Corporation
# All Rights Reserved.
# This function calculates a 5% discount on a price
def discount(price):
    return 0.95 * price
```

Both of the modules define a function called discount(). So what happens when you try to use them? If Python sees a line of code like this:

```
new_price = discount(1.75)
```

which function will it call? The promotion discount? The Starbuzz discount? Both? Neither???

This is one of the problems of using shared code. Sometimes, there's a function in one module that has the *same name* as a function in another module. When this happens, the last function imported is the one used, which has the effect of overloading any existing function that has the same name. This can result in to hard-to-find bugs.

So what do you do?

You need to somehow qualify your function names.

Fully Qualified Names (FQNs) prevent your programs from getting confused

Imagine if you lived in a world where people had first names only:

Michael →

Michael ←

Hi, it's Michael. Say, are you free on Friday night?

Lots of people share the same first name. But people also have **surnames**. If you use a first name with a surname, things are a lot less confusing.

And it's the same thing with code. If you have two modules containing functions with the same name, the computer will get confused. But if you **fully qualify** the function name, by prefixing it with the **module name**, the computer will know exactly what you mean:

```
promotion.discount(1.75)
```

If you are going to use Fully Qualified Names (FQNs) from a module, then you will also need to change the way you import the code:

Oh, I need to apply the 10% discount from promotion.py? That's not a problem, since you're using a FQN...

coffee_pos.py

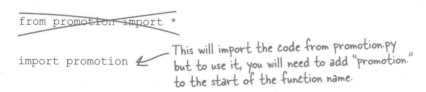

```
from promotion import *

import promotion
```
This will import the code from promotion.py but to use it, you will need to add "promotion." to the start of the function name.

Now you can fix the code to use both discounts.

Long Exercise

These are the two discount modules:

promotion.py

```
def discount(price):
    return 0.9 * price
```

starbuzz.py

```
# Official Starbuzz Discount Module
# Copyright(c) Starbuzz Corporation
# All Rights Reserved.
# This function calculates a 5% discount on a price
def discount(price):
    return 0.95 * price
```

Write a new version of `coffee_pos.py` that, after choosing a menu option, will ask if the customer has a Starbuzz Discount Card. If the answer is "Y", apply **both** the Starbuzz and the promotion discount. Otherwise, just apply the promotion discount.

Here is the latest version of `coffee_pos.py`

```
from transactions import *
from promotion import *

items  = ["DONUT", "LATTE", "FILTER", "MUFFIN"]
prices = [1.50, 2.20, 1.80, 1.20]
running = True

while running:
    option = 1
    for choice in items:
        print(str(option) + ". " + choice)
        option = option + 1
    print(str(option) + ". Quit")
    choice = int(input("Choose an option: "))
    if choice == option:
        running = False
    else:
        credit_card = input("Credit card number: ")
        new_price = discount(prices[choice - 1])
        save_transaction(new_price, credit_card, items[choice - 1])
```

Write your code
here. ↓

....
....
....
....
....
....
....
....
....
....
....
....
....
....
....
....
....
....
....
....
....
....
....

Long Exercise Solution

These are the two discount modules:

starbuzz.py

promotion.py

```
def discount(price):
    return 0.9 * price
```

```
# Official Starbuzz Discount Module
# Copyright(c) Starbuzz Corporation
# All Rights Reserved.
# This function calculates a 5% discount on a price
def discount(price):
    return 0.95 * price
```

You were asked to write a new version of `coffee_pos.py` that, after choosing an menu option, will ask if the customer has a Starbuzz Discount Card. If the answer is "Y", apply **both** the Starbuzz and the promotion discount. Otherwise, just apply the promotion discount.

Here is the latest version of `coffee_pos.py`:

```
from transactions import *
from promotion import *

items  = ["DONUT", "LATTE", "FILTER", "MUFFIN"]
prices = [1.50, 2.20, 1.80, 1.20]
running = True

while running:
    option = 1
    for choice in items:
        print(str(option) + ". " + choice)
        option = option + 1
    print(str(option) + ". Quit")
    choice = int(input("Choose an option: "))
    if choice == option:
        running = False
    else:
        credit_card = input("Credit card number: ")
        new_price = discount(prices[choice - 1])
        save_transaction(new_price, credit_card, items[choice - 1])
```

By importing the transactions module like this, you can call the functions without the module name.

You need to use this kind of import for "promotion.py" and "starbuzz.py", because you are going to qualify the function names with the module names.

```python
from transactions import *

import promotion

import starbuzz


items  = ["DONUT", "LATTE", "FILTER", "MUFFIN"]

prices = [1.50, 2.20, 1.80, 1.20]

running = True


while running:

    option = 1

    for choice in items:

        print(str(option) + ". " + choice)

        option = option + 1

    print(str(option) + ". Quit")

    choice = int(input("Choose an option: "))

    if choice == option:

        running = False

    else:

        credit_card = input("Credit card number: ")

        price = promotion.discount(prices[choice - 1])

        if input("Starbuzz card? ") == "Y":

            price = starbuzz.discount(price)

        save_transaction(price, credit_card, items[choice - 1])
```

If someone has a Starbuzz Discount Card, you need to apply the second Starbuzz discount.

Test Drive

Let's try running the new program and buy a $1.20 muffin without a discount card.

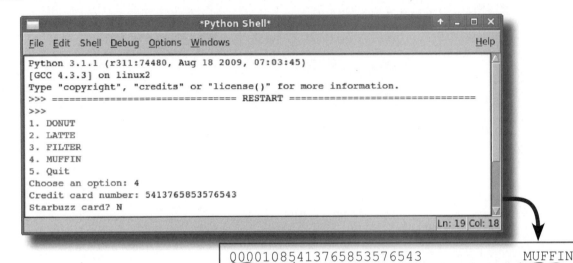

00001085413765853576543   MUFFIN

It cost $1.08 = 90% of $1.20.

It's a muffin.

But what if you try to buy a $2.20 latte using a Starbuzz card?

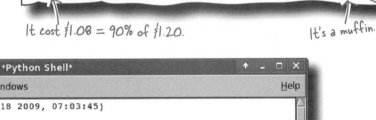

00001885413765835766543   LATTE

The code works! With the Starbuzz card, it applies two discounts. Without a Starbuzz card, your code just applies one.

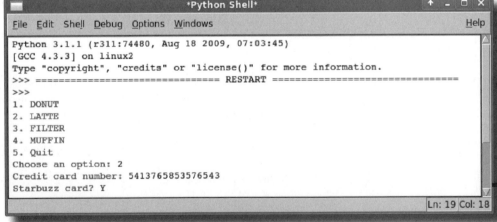

90% of $2.20 = $1.98.
5% Starbuzz discount of that gives $1.88!

It's a latte.

The discounts get the customers flooding in

Once word gets out that there are double-discounts available in
the coffee bar, the health club gets packed with customers.

> We've never been so busy! The weight
> room, the gym, the steam baths. The
> whole place is full of customers! I like
> the way you write code. I want you to
> upgrade every system in the place!

Thanks to writing **modular code**, you got the contract to
replace *all* the health club systems. Modules help you write
stable, maintainable code. The more code you write in modules,
the greater the chance that you'll be able to reuse it elsewhere.

**Breaking your code into modules turns good
programs into great programs.**

---

there are no Dumb Questions

Q: I don't get it; why do I need to use
a FQN again?

A: You use a Fully Qualified Name
(or FQN) when you need to distinguish
between two functions from different
modules that have the same name.
With the health club systems, the
`discount()` function existed within
your module *and* within the one supplied by
Starbuzz. In order to keep things straight,
you had to use a FQN.

Q: So if I hadn't used a FQN, the
wrong discount is applied to the
purchase?

A: Yes, most probably.

Q: But if I hadn't used a FQN, how
would I know which discount was used?

A: Well... that's the problem. You
wouldn't. It's hard to predict what would
happen, because it all depends on which
order the code imports its modules.

Q: So, all I need to do is keep an eye
on the order when I import modules and
everything will be OK?

A: No, that's not what we recommend.
Don't rely on what might happen. Use a
FQN so that you are always in control.

Your Programming Toolbox

You've got Chapter 6 under your belt. Let's look back at what you've learned in this chapter:

Programming Tools

✳ String formats let you use format specifiers to format strings.

✳ String specifiers let you define the type, the length, and the padding used in a format.

✳ Breaking code into separate files is called modular programming.

✳ Modular code is easier to share between programs.

✳ Writing modular code is like writing your own libraries.

✳ Fully Qualified Names (FQNs) are function names that include module names.

Python Tools

✳ Use "from ... import ✳" to run code module functions without module names.

✳ Use "import ..." if you need to qualify your function names with a module name using an FQN (which is the recommended approach in the Python community).

7 building a graphical user interface

Going all gooey

> You see, sometimes it's just not enough to build it. It has to look nice, too.

Your coding skills are great and getting better all the time.

It's just a shame your programs are not that *nice* to look at. Displaying prompts and messages on a text-based console is all well and good, but it's so 1970s, isn't it? Add some green text on a black background and your retro look will be complete. There has to be *a better way* to communicate with your users than the console, and there is: using a **graphical user interface** or **GUI** (pronounced "gooey"). Sounds cool, but complex, and it can be. But, don't fret; learning a trick or two will have your code all graphical in no time. Let's get all gooey (sorry, GUI) in this chapter.

Head First TVN now produces game shows

It's more than just sports at Head First TVN, as the station has entered the lucrative world of live game show broadcasting. Their flagship show, *Who Wants to Win a Swivel Chair*, is attracting viewing figures in the millions... not bad for a station that operates on a shoestring budget.

You've been approached by their stressed-out (but incredibly smooth) game show host to help with a program he needs. TVN was so impressed with your work last time that they are offering two free, front-row tickets to the Grand Final as payment for your work.

I can't keep track of the score and ask the questions and sound the buzzer... all by myself... can you help?

TVN's game show host.

You've had a few conversations with the host and determined a list of *program requirements*:

1. The host wants to be *prompted* after a question has been asked to press either 1 for a *correct answer* or 2 for a *wrong answer*.

2. Based on the key pressed, an appropriate *sound effect* needs to play.

3. The program needs to *remember* how many answers were correct and how many were wrong.

4. The host will end the quiz by pressing 0. Then the program will display the number of right, wrong, and asked questions.

Let's flesh out what's required in pseudo-code.

Sharpen your pencil

Use the space provided below to write the pseudo-code for the program you've been asked to write for TVN:

Write your pseudo-code here. ⟶

....
....
....
....
....
....
....
....
....
....
....
....
....
....
....
....
....
....
....
....
....

Sharpen your pencil
Solution

You were asked to use the space provided below to write the pseudo-code for the program you've been asked to write for TVN:

You need to remember how many questions were asked, how many were correct, and how many were wrong.

```
number_asked = 0
number_correct = 0
number_wrong = 0
```

Begin by asking the host to make a choice.

```
ask the host to press 1 for correct, 2 for incorrect, or 0 to end
while the host response is not 0
    if host response was 1
```

This will run if the question was answered CORRECTLY.

```
        add 1 to number_asked
        add 1 to number_correct
        play a sound effect
    if host response was 2
```

This will run if the question was answered INCORRECTLY.

```
        add 1 to number_asked
        add 1 to number_wrong
        play a sound effect
```

Ask the host at the end of each loop what he wants to do next.

```
    ask the host to press 1 for correct, 2 for incorrect, or 0 to end
```

Finally, display the scores.

```
display the values of number_asked, number_correct and
number_wrong on screen
```

Don't worry if your answer doesn't look EXACTLY like this. There are a few ways of writing the code.

Frank: I think sound is going to be a problem.

Jim: Sounds easy to me...

Joe & Frank: <groan>.

Jim: Sorry, couldn't resist that one. Seriously, though, how hard can it be to play a sound from a program?

Joe: Playing a sound is not the problem; getting it to work on multiple platforms can be. For instance, what works on Windows might not work on Mac OS X or Linux.

Jim: That's not a problem. I only use Windows, so I'll be OK.

Frank: Good for you, but the rest of us want to play, too, and we don't want to have to... um... eh... *downgrade* to Windows.

Jim: Typical: have a swipe at Windows when something doesn't work on *your* non-Windows computer.

Joe: Cool it, guys. We need to stop bickering and come up with a solution that lets us play sounds *and* works on Windows, Mac OS X, and Linux. And it has to work with Python, too.

Jim: You mean Python doesn't support sound as standard?!?

Frank: No, not really. In fact, very few programming languages support sound in a cross-platform way. This isn't just a Python problem.

Jim: So... we're outta luck then. Does that mean it's time to go home?

Joe: Not so fast, Jim! I'm pretty sure **pygame** can help here.

Jim: So... I can't go home early, but I *can* play games?

Frank: Seriously, Jim, I think Joe's right. We can use **pygame** to play our sounds in Python.

Jim: And it'll work on Windows, Mac OS X, and Linux?

Joe: Yes, I'm pretty sure it will. Granted, pygame's a set of gaming libraries for Python, but all we need to use is the bit that handles playing sounds.

Jim: Sounds great. I can't wait to see it in action.

Frank: Didn't you mean "*hear* it in action"?

Jim & Joe: <groan>.

See... sound's the problem.

You actually can't "see" sound... but, don't worry, it'll be grand.

Jim

Frank

Joe

pygame is cross platform

Before continuing with the rest of this chapter, you need to take five to download and then install the pygame technology onto your computer. The pygame technology is an example of what's known as a *third-party library*: that's extra functionality that can be added into your Python environment, but which isn't part of the standard library.

As installing pygame tends to be a very platform-specific thing, we've uploaded a set of instructions onto the *Head First Programming* website for you to follow.

STOP! Don't proceed with the rest of this chapter until you've installed pygame for Python 3 on your computer.

Ready Bake Code

Take a look at this handy pygame program, which shows how to play four sounds one after another:

Just like with other libraries, you import the library you want to use.

Create a "pygame.mixer" object and initialize the sound system.

The "wait_finish()" function loops until the channel's "get_busy()" method returns False.

The value returned from the "play()" method gets passed to "wait_finish()".

```
import pygame.mixer
sounds = pygame.mixer
sounds.init()

def wait_finish(channel):
    while channel.get_busy():
        pass


s = sounds.Sound("heartbeat.wav")
wait_finish(s.play())
s2 = sounds.Sound("buzz.wav")
wait_finish(s2.play())
s3 = sounds.Sound("ohno.wav")
wait_finish(s3.play())
s4 = sounds.Sound("carhorn.wav")
wait_finish(s4.play())
```

The "get_busy()" method checks to see if the sound is still playing.

"pass" is a Python construct that does nothing.

Load in the sound file you want to play.

Identify and play each of the sounds.

Load this!

To run this program on your computer, you obviously need pygame installed **and** you need to download the sound files for this chapter from the *Head First Programming* website. Be sure to put the sound files in the same directory/folder as your program.

─ Test Drive ───────────────────

You've successfully downloaded/installed pygame and grabbed a copy of the *Head First Programming* sound files for this chapter. Now, **test** the pygame program in IDLE to see if things are working correctly:

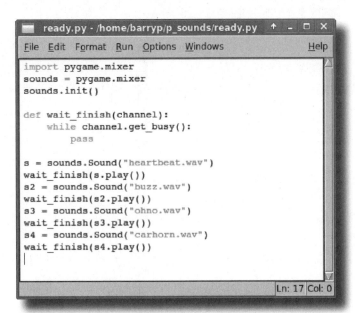

```
ready.py - /home/barryp/p_sounds/ready.py        ↑ _ □ X
File  Edit  Format  Run  Options  Windows                  Help

import pygame.mixer
sounds = pygame.mixer
sounds.init()

def wait_finish(channel):
    while channel.get_busy():
        pass

s = sounds.Sound("heartbeat.wav")
wait_finish(s.play())
s2 = sounds.Sound("buzz.wav")
wait_finish(s2.play())
s3 = sounds.Sound("ohno.wav")
wait_finish(s3.play())
s4 = sounds.Sound("carhorn.wav")
wait_finish(s4.play())
|
                                          Ln: 17  Col: 0
```

Thump!
Thump!

Buzz!

Oh no!

Beeeep!

Sounds like pygame is up and running!

I hear my cheesy sound effects... you gotta love that car horn!

Obviously, we can't show you sound in this book but trust us, this program works as billed. In fact, DON'T trust us: just be sure to run the program yourself.

there are no
Dumb Questions

Q: So pygame is a library created by some programmer other than the Python folks?

A: Yes, it's what's called a **third-party library**. It wasn't created by you or the people that bring you Python. Some other programmer(s), a third party, created pygame.

Q: And it's just given away for free?

A: Yes. Which is very nice of them, isn't it?

Q: Are there other libraries like pygame that can be added into my Python environment?

A: Yes, there are lots. To see the current list, follow the **Package Index** link from the main Python website. Python refers to third-party libraries as "packages" and, as you'll see, there are packages available for every conceivable purpose, not just playing sounds or developing games (as is the case with pygame).

Q: The sounds I downloaded are WAV files. I know that WAV is one of the standards for encoding sound, but is it the best format to use?

A: That depends on who you ask! We are using WAV files because they are used in lots of places and are well-supported on most operating systems. There are lots of file formats for sound and many of them claim to be "better" than WAV, but for what we are doing here, WAV is perfect.

Q: What's the deal with the wait_finish() function in the Ready Bake Code? I just don't get why it's there.

A: It's a function that waits for the sound to finish playing before continuing with the rest of the program.

Q: What?! Surely the sound just plays?

A: Playing with pygame in this way, although fun, masks a problem that can surface when working with sound (in any programming language). It turns out that, when asked to play a sound, the main chip inside your computer (the CPU) doesn't even bother trying. Instead, there's another, smaller chip in your computer that is specifically designed to play sounds and it is to this chip that your main chip hands the sound file to and says: "play this for me." The main chip then goes back to running your code, sees another request to play a sound, doesn't bother, hands the new sound file off to the sound chip, and repeats until your program ends. The sound chip—and this is the important part—is designed to operate in **parallel** with your main chip. While your main chip is doing something else, the sound chip is busy playing any sounds it has been asked to play. And—here's the rub—if the sound chip has been asked to play more than one sound, it attempts to play each sound *at the same time*.

Q: So the wait_finish() function is like an artificial delay after each sound?

A: No, not really a delay, more like a *pause* designed to let the sound effect play fully *before* trying to play anything else. The `wait_finish()` function **forces** your sound chip to finish with one sound before starting another. What happens is that when a sound is played, the `play()` method passes back the channel (or track) number that the sound is playing on. You can then use the channel number to ask pygame to wait for the channel to finish playing a sound before continuing, which is what the code in the Test Drive on the previous page does.

Q: And if I don't use wait_finish(), what happens then?

A: All the sounds attempt to play *at the same time* and it sounds like a jumble of sounds as opposed to one sound playing, then another, then another, and so on.

LONG EXERCISE

Now that you know how to generate a sound using pygame, it's time to write the code for TVN's program. Base your program on the pseudo-code you created earlier.

LONG EXERCISE SOLUTION

Now that you know how to generate a sound using pygame, it's time to write the code for TVN's program. You were to base your program on the pseudo-code you created earlier.

You need to import pygame's "mixer" module in order to play sounds. →

```
import pygame.mixer
```

Reuse the "wait_finish()" function from earlier. →

```
def wait_finish(channel):
    while channel.get_busy():
        pass
```

Create a mixer object and initialize the pygame sound system. →

```
sounds = pygame.mixer
sounds.init()
```

Load each of the required sounds into its own variable. →

```
correct_s = sounds.Sound("correct.wav")
wrong_s  = sounds.Sound("wrong.wav")
```

This is what you'll ask the question master each time. →

```
prompt = "Press 1 for Correct, 2 for Wrong, or 0 to Quit: "
```

Make sure the counts that you'll maintain are set to a reasonable starting value. →

```
number_asked   = 0
number_correct = 0
number_wrong   = 0
```

It would be OK to move these three lines of code to the top of the program, just so long as they have starting values before the while loop starts.

Prompt the host. → `choice = input(prompt)`

While the game → `while choice != '0':`
hasn't ended....

`    if choice == '1':`

If the answer is
correct, increment the → `        number_asked = number_asked + 1`
counters and then play
the appropriate sound. `        number_correct = number_correct + 1`

`        wait_finish(correct_s.play())`

If the answer is
incorrect, increment → `    if choice == '2':`
the counters and play
the sound effect. `        number_asked = number_asked + 1`

`        number_wrong = number_wrong + 1`

`        wait_finish(wrong_s.play())`

`    choice = input(prompt)`

`print("You asked " + str(number_asked) + " questions.")`

`print(str(number_correct) + " were correctly answered.")`

`print(str(number_wrong) + " were answered incorrectly.")`

At the end of the program,
display a summary of the
counter values.

Test Drive

Type your code into IDLE and save it under the name `gameshow.py`.
With the *Head First Programming* sounds stored in the same directory as your
program, press F5 to give it a spin.

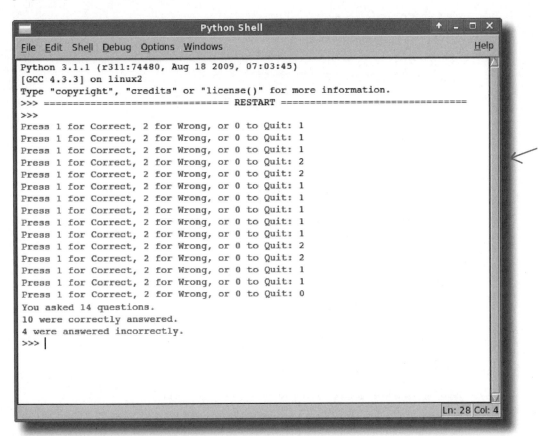

We can't show these sounds either, so go ahead and run the program to hear it working for yourself.

```
Python 3.1.1 (r311:74480, Aug 18 2009, 07:03:45)
[GCC 4.3.3] on linux2
Type "copyright", "credits" or "license()" for more information.
>>> ============================== RESTART ==============================
>>>
Press 1 for Correct, 2 for Wrong, or 0 to Quit: 1
Press 1 for Correct, 2 for Wrong, or 0 to Quit: 1
Press 1 for Correct, 2 for Wrong, or 0 to Quit: 1
Press 1 for Correct, 2 for Wrong, or 0 to Quit: 2
Press 1 for Correct, 2 for Wrong, or 0 to Quit: 2
Press 1 for Correct, 2 for Wrong, or 0 to Quit: 1
Press 1 for Correct, 2 for Wrong, or 0 to Quit: 1
Press 1 for Correct, 2 for Wrong, or 0 to Quit: 1
Press 1 for Correct, 2 for Wrong, or 0 to Quit: 1
Press 1 for Correct, 2 for Wrong, or 0 to Quit: 1
Press 1 for Correct, 2 for Wrong, or 0 to Quit: 2
Press 1 for Correct, 2 for Wrong, or 0 to Quit: 2
Press 1 for Correct, 2 for Wrong, or 0 to Quit: 1
Press 1 for Correct, 2 for Wrong, or 0 to Quit: 1
Press 1 for Correct, 2 for Wrong, or 0 to Quit: 0
You asked 14 questions.
10 were correctly answered.
4 were answered incorrectly.
>>>
```

That looks and sounds great... and I can't wait to try it out in the semifinal!

pygame Exposed
This week's interview:
Is it fun being pygame?

Head First: Hello, pygame. Nice of you to join us.

pygame: Hello. Thank you so much for giving me this opportunity to discuss my situation with you.

Head First: What situation is that?

pygame: Well, you know, just because I'm used for gaming, everyone expects me to be fun *all the time*. Life and soul of the party... never stopping to smell the roses... always on the go. <sigh> It's all too much fun, really.

Head First: Too much fun? Really?!?

pygame: Well... yes. Not a lot of people know this, but my life as pygame is hard. Not only do I have to help out regular folks with their programming problems, but there's all those gamers, too. Some of those guys *never* sleep... it's just play, play, play, play, play, play... I'm simply exhausted.

Head First: Oh, sorry to hear that. But, don't you feel good that all those programmers out there in the Python community are using you?

pygame: I guess so.

Head First: You've made a lot of programmers' lives easier. There's lots of great code written that would not have been written if it weren't for you.

pygame: Yeah, right. I do all the heavy lifting while everyone else is off doing other things.

Head First: Ah, come on, your life's not *that* bad, is it?

pygame: <sighs>

Head First: Surely you know what people are saying about you?

pygame: Now they're talking about me, too? How awful... <sobs>

Head First: Yeah, there's lots of talk, but it's all *good*. The Python programming community *loves* you, pygame.

pygame: They do? <sobs even more>

Head First: Yes. You are well-tested, well-written, and your documentation is first rate. Your support for all the major releases of Python is right on the money, too, and you work on Mac OS X, Windows, *and* Linux.

pygame: All I've ever tried to do is keep everyone happy.

Head First: And you do. We've heard so many great things about you that we are recommending you to all our friends.

pygame: Do they play games? I'm good at that, you know.

Head First: Yes, some of them do. But others just talk about the great things their applications can now do *thanks to you*, pygame.

pygame: I guess things aren't quite so bad after all?

Head First: Not at all. We're big fans!

pygame: Why, thanks. That's awesome. Do you have time for a quick game? There's this new Dungeons and Dragons that I've been dying to try...

0... 2... 1... 9... blast off!

1, 2, and 0...?!? Pressing keys? Really? That's so 1985...

Your program's looking pretty dated.

The program works, but it's not going to win a Visual Design Award any time soon. And its use of key presses makes it a little hard to use, too.

So, its *looks* could be improved and its *usability* could be better.

It sounds like you need a *graphical user interface*, or **GUI**.

Most people pronounce GUI as "gooey."

Sharpen your pencil

You need to design the look of your GUI for TVN. Draw what you think your GUI should look like in the space provided below.

Hint: Take some time to think about other GUI programs that you have used. Think about a common interface element that you could use (and draw) here.

Sharpen your pencil
Solution

You needed to design the look of the GUI for TVN. You were asked to draw what you think your GUI should look like in the space provided below.

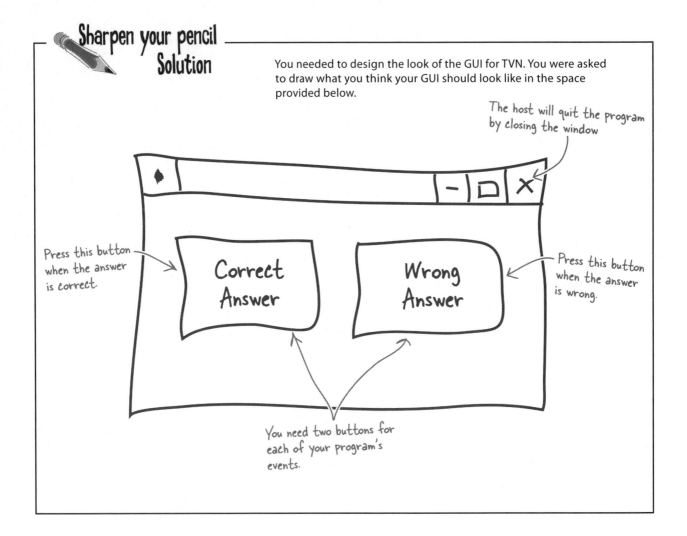

The host will quit the program by closing the window

Press this button when the answer is correct.

Correct Answer

Wrong Answer

Press this button when the answer is wrong.

You need two buttons for each of your program's events.

Frank: Since when have you been an expert on GUIs?

Jim: Isn't every Windows user?

Joe: Well, of course, everyone knows how to *use* a GUI, but we are talking about *creating* a GUI in code.

Jim: Ah... oh... um... eh... now, where shall we start?

Frank: It turns out that writing code for a GUI application is... well... just like writing any other code. If you know how to program, you know how to create a GUI. It's just a matter of **selecting** the correct GUI library, **learning** how to use it, then **writing** the code.

Joe: So we'll head off to the *Python Package Index* and grab us some GUI libraries, eh?

Frank: Not so fast. Python comes with a GUI library as standard, called tkinter.

Jim: tk-what?

Frank: tkinter. The "tk" bit refers to the fact that Python's standard GUI library is built on top of the very popular **Tk** technology. The "inter" bit is short for "interface."

Jim: So we're going to build a GUI interface in Python running on Tk using tkinter?

Frank: Yes, we are. That's not too confusing, is it?

Joe & Jim: Well... not if you say so.

Frank: The big thing with creating GUIs is understanding the *event loop*.

Joe: Ah, that's just looping code that reacts when certain things happen, isn't it? It's just like the `while` loop in the non-GUI version of TVN's program. In that code, that loop is an event loop, isn't it?

Frank: It sure is. Although the GUI event loop tends to be extra capable and can do lots more than the simple `while` loop.

Joe: That sounds complex. Is it?

Frank: No, not really. It just takes a little getting used to.

Jim: But, it's all just code, isn't it?

Frank: Yes, Python code using the tkinter library.

Joe: OK. Let's get to it, since we *already* know how to program...

Ah... GUIs. All those lovely event handlers, mouse clicks, widgets, frames, scroll bars, double clicks and—my personal favorite—the mouseover.

Jim

Frank

Joe

tkinter gives you the event loop for free

In order to process events efficiently, GUIs employ an *event loop*. Event loops watch and wait for events, calling a piece of code each time an event occurs. If you think about the current TVN Game Show program, it *already* has a very basic event loop that waits for the host to press 1, 2, or 0. The program then calls some code before waiting again for another *key-press event* from the host. To implement this in code, you used a while loop:

```
while choice != '0':
    if choice == '1':
        number_asked = number_asked + 1
        number_correct = number_correct + 1
```

In tkinter, you don't need to write a while loop like you did for your non-GUI program. In tkinter, call the mainloop() method instead:

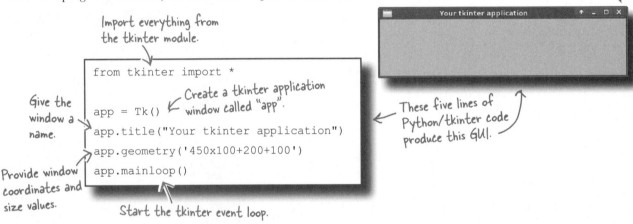

Import everything from the tkinter module.

Give the window a name.

Create a tkinter application window called "app".

Provide window coordinates and size values.

Start the tkinter event loop.

```
from tkinter import *

app = Tk()
app.title("Your tkinter application")
app.geometry('450x100+200+100')
app.mainloop()
```

These five lines of Python/tkinter code produce this GUI.

Click on the close box to terminate this application.

To add a button to your application, use code like this, being sure to put these two lines of code *before* the call to mainloop():

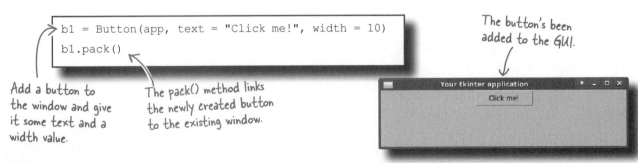

```
b1 = Button(app, text = "Click me!", width = 10)
b1.pack()
```

Add a button to the window and give it some text and a width value.

The pack() method links the newly created button to the existing window.

The button's been added to the GUI.

tkinter is packed with options

The pack() method lets you position the button in the application window. If you provide a value for the side parameter to pack(), you can control where in the window the button appears. Here are the legal values for side:

The value of "side" controls where the button is packed.

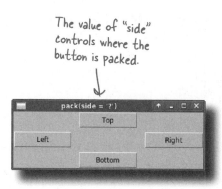

- pack(side = 'left')
  Position the button on the left side of the window.

- pack(side = 'right')
  Position the button on the right side of the window.

- pack(side = 'top')
  Position the button at the top of the window.

- pack(side = 'bottom')
  Position the button at the bottom of the window.

It is also possible to add some padding around buttons (to make them look nicer in your window):

- pack(padx = 10, pady = 10)
  Position the button with 10 pixels padding on all four sides.

Sharpen your pencil

Based on what you now know about tkinter windows and buttons, write the code to display the GUI that you need for the TVN program:

....

....

....

....

....

....

....

....

....

Sharpen your pencil
Solution

Based on what you now know about tkinter windows and buttons, you were to write the code to display the GUI that you need for the TVN program:

```
from tkinter import *
```

Create the window as in the earlier example, but change the window title and geometry values. →

```
app = Tk()

app.title("TVN Game Show")

app.geometry('300x100+200+100')
```

Create a button for the "Correct" event. →

```
b1 = Button(app, text = "Correct!", width = 10)
```

Pack one button on the left, the other on the right, and give them some padding.

```
b1.pack(side = 'left', padx = 10, pady = 10)
```

Create another button for the "Wrong" event.

```
b2 = Button(app, text = "Wrong!", width = 10)

b2.pack(side = 'right', padx = 10, pady = 10)
```

Start the event loop. →

```
app.mainloop()
```

TEST DRIVE

Let's take your first GUI program for a test drive. With your tkinter code entered into IDLE, save it as tvn.pyw and press F5 to see how it looks: ←

There's a convention in the Python world that suggests naming tkinter programs with a ".pyw" extension, as opposed to the usual ".py". This helps your operating system run your tkinter programs properly, especially on Windows.

Your code in IDLE
↓

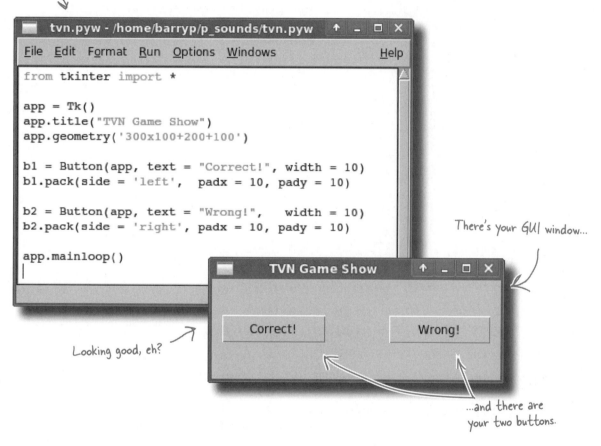

```
tvn.pyw - /home/barryp/p_sounds/tvn.pyw          ↑  _  □  X

File  Edit  Format  Run  Options  Windows                    Help

from tkinter import *

app = Tk()
app.title("TVN Game Show")
app.geometry('300x100+200+100')

b1 = Button(app, text = "Correct!", width = 10)
b1.pack(side = 'left',  padx = 10, pady = 10)

b2 = Button(app, text = "Wrong!",   width = 10)
b2.pack(side = 'right', padx = 10, pady = 10)

app.mainloop()
```

There's your GUI window...

```
                    TVN Game Show          ↑  _  □  X

        [  Correct!  ]              [  Wrong!  ]
```

Looking good, eh? ↗

...and there are your two buttons.

That's one nice, professional-looking GUI! What do the people at TVN think?

The GUI works, but doesn't do anything

Nice interface, but it doesn't work. When I click on a button, nothing happens... I don't hear anything. What happened to my cool sound effects?

The graphical user interface might be ready, but the program is not complete.

there are no Dumb Questions

Q: So all tkinter gives me is the ability to draw the GUI?

A: Well, yes, but there's quite a lot of functionality wrapped up in that small number of lines of tkinter code.

Q: That `pack()` method looks a little weird... how does it know where to put things?

A: The `pack()` method adopts a *best-guess approach* when it comes to packing your GUI widgets within your GUI application window. This usually works out, and when it doesn't, `pack()`'s parameters give you some control over the situation.

Q: That's all that `left`, `right`, `top`, **and** `bottom` stuff, isn't it?

A: Yes, as well as the `padx` and `pady` parameters. They help with widget positioning, too, by putting additonal space (or padding) around your buttons.

Q: OK, I get that, but how come nothing happens when I click on my buttons?

A: Ah, funny you should ask that...

Connect code to your button events

When you click on a button, the tkinter event loop **captures** the event and *looks for something to do with it*. The trouble is, as your program stands, you have not detailed what that something to do *is*. Your buttons have no code associated with them, so the events occur but go *unnoticed*. To *connect* code to buttons, put the code you want to run in its own function and then name the function in the button code by providing a command parameter:

Identify the function to run when the button is clicked.

```
b = Button(app, text = "Click on me!", width = 15, command = button_click)
b.pack(padx = 10, pady = 10)
```

Click!

Create a function to contain the code that runs when the event occurs.

```
def button_click():
    print("I've just been clicked!")
```

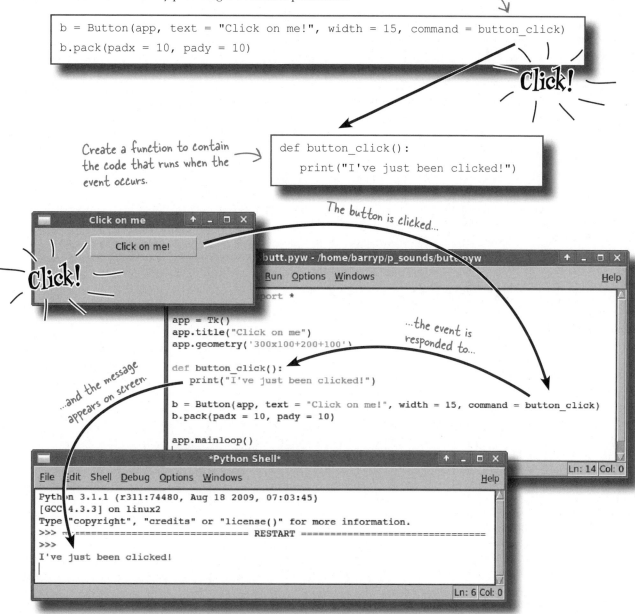

The button is clicked...

...the event is responded to...

...and the message appears on screen.

```
import *

app = Tk()
app.title("Click on me")
app.geometry('300x100+200+100')

def button_click():
    print("I've just been clicked!")

b = Button(app, text = "Click on me!", width = 15, command = button_click)
b.pack(padx = 10, pady = 10)

app.mainloop()
```

```
Python 3.1.1 (r311:74480, Aug 18 2009, 07:03:45)
[GCC 4.3.3] on linux2
Type "copyright", "credits" or "license()" for more information.
>>> ================================ RESTART ================================
>>>
I've just been clicked!
```

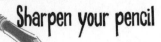

Sharpen your pencil

The code from the nongraphical version of the TVN program is on this and the facing page. Take your pencil and mark the parts of the code that you would extract and turn into functions so that you can then connect the functions to the buttons in your GUI. Mark the other parts of this program that also need to be added to the GUI version.

The nature of the interface provided by the GUI means that some of the program's requirements have changed.

Note: Don't worry about prompting the host to ask a question in the GUI. But **do worry** about maintaining a count of the number of questions answered correctly and incorrectly. (The total count is not important, either.)

How many functions do you think you need? Write their names here:

....

....

```python
import pygame.mixer

def wait_finish(channel):
    while channel.get_busy():
        pass

sounds = pygame.mixer
sounds.init()

correct_s = sounds.Sound("correct.wav")
wrong_s   = sounds.Sound("wrong.wav")
prompt = "Press 1 for Correct, 2 for Wrong, or 0 to Quit: "

number_asked    = 0
number_correct = 0
number_wrong    = 0
```

```
choice = input(prompt)
while choice != '0':
    if choice == '1':
        number_asked = number_asked + 1
        number_correct = number_correct + 1
        wait_finish(correct_s.play())
    if choice == '2':
        number_asked = number_asked + 1
        number_wrong = number_wrong + 1
        wait_finish(wrong_s.play())
    choice = input(prompt)


print("You asked " + str(number_asked) + " questions.")
print(str(number_correct) + " were correctly answered.")
print(str(number_wrong) + " were answered incorrectly.")
```

With the code you need identified, take the time to update your GUI application with the new functions and whatever other code you've extracted from the non-GUI program.

Produce a new program that is a combination of your existing GUI code and the extracted code from this program.

Sharpen your pencil
Solution

You were to take your pencil and mark the parts of the code on the previous (and facing) page to identify the code you would extract and turn into functions so that you can then connect the functions to the buttons in your GUI. You were also to mark the other parts of this program that also need to be added to the GUI version:

You were to think about how many functions you might need. You were to write their names here:

→ play_correct_sound()

play_wrong_sound() ←

You need a function to play a sound when the answer is correct...

...and another function to play a sound when the answer is wrong.

```
import pygame.mixer

def wait_finish(channel):
    while channel.get_busy():
        pass

sounds = pygame.mixer
sounds.init()

correct_s = sounds.Sound("correct.wav")
wrong_s   = sounds.Sound("wrong.wav")
prompt = "Press 1 for Correct, 2 for Wrong, or 0 to Quit: "

number_asked   = 0
number_correct = 0
number_wrong   = 0
```

The GUI program still needs to use pygame.

You still need to maintain these counters.

```
choice = input(prompt)
while choice != '0':
    if choice == '1':
        number_asked = number_asked + 1
        number_correct = number_correct + 1
        wait_finish(correct_s.play())
    if choice == '2':
        number_asked = number_asked + 1
        number_wrong = number_wrong + 1
        wait_finish(wrong_s.play())
    choice = input(prompt)

print("You asked " + str(number_asked) + " questions.")
print(str(number_correct) + " were correctly answered.")
print(str(number_wrong) + " were answered incorrectly.")
```

← Turn this code into the "play_correct_sound()" function.

← Turn this code into the "play_wrong_sound()" function.

← Displaying the summary remains a requirement, too.

With the code you need identified, you were to take the time to update your GUI application with the new functions and whatever other code you've extracted from the non-GUI program.

You were asked to produce a new program that is a combination of your existing GUI code and the extracted code from this program.

Turn the page for the updated code solution...

The GUI program's now ready for a screentest

Here's what your GUI program should look like now:

```python
from tkinter import *

import pygame.mixer

sounds = pygame.mixer
sounds.init()

correct_s = sounds.Sound("correct.wav")
wrong_s   = sounds.Sound("wrong.wav")

number_correct = 0
number_wrong   = 0

def play_correct_sound():
    global number_correct
    number_correct = number_correct + 1
    correct_s.play()

def play_wrong_sound():
    global number_wrong
    number_wrong = number_wrong + 1
    wrong_s.play()

app = Tk()
app.title("TVN Game Show")
app.geometry('300x100+200+100')

b1 = Button(app, text = "Correct!", width = 10, command = play_correct_sound)
b1.pack(side = 'left',  padx = 10, pady = 10)

b2 = Button(app, text = "Wrong!",  width = 10, command = play_wrong_sound)
b2.pack(side = 'right', padx = 10, pady = 10)

app.mainloop()

print(str(number_correct) + " were correctly answered.")
print(str(number_wrong) + " were answered incorrectly.")
```

Python's "global" keyword lets you adjust the value associated with a variable created outside the function.

The buttons are now connected to event-handling functions.

Test Drive

With the code you need extracted from the nongraphical application and added to your GUI program, press F5 in IDLE to see (and hear) if things are working any better now:

It not only looks good, but now it sounds good, too!

Ting!   Splat!

Every time you click on a button, the appropriate sound effect is heard. Great work!

there are no Dumb Questions

Q: So "event handlers" in tkinter are just functions?

A: Yes, as we said earlier in this chapter: *it's all just code*. And by putting the code you want to run in a function, it's easy to reference it using the `command` parameter associated with each button. Your user clicks the button to run the code in your function.

Q: This actually isn't too hard. I always thought building a GUI was only for advanced programmers?

A: Well... that certainly used to be the case, but things have changed (for the better). Technologies like tkinter allow every programmer to build great-looking GUIs without too much fuss. It's a case of tkinter concentrating on the GUI, while you concentrate on your code.

Q: And is it the case that, if I want to add other things to my GUI program, it's done in a similar way?

A: Yes, all you have to do is write the code.

Q: And I connect my code up to my other things using something like the command parameter that works with buttons?

A: Yes, that's all there is to it. The mechanism for the other interface elements (or *widgets*, for short) might be a little different, but the concept is the same. Once you can work with one, the rest are a lot easier to get your head around.

But TVN is still not happy

The sounds work great, the GUI looks fantastic... but where are my results? I can't find them!

The results appeared in the Python Shell, *not* in the GUI, so the host missed seeing them. When you point this out to him, he's less than impressed and makes it clear that he expects the results to appear in the GUI.

You need some way to display messages in the GUI.

The results are right there in the Python Shell. But this is NOT what the host wants.

```
                              Python Shell                          ↑ _ □ ✗
File  Edit  Shell  Debug  Options  Windows                              Help
Python 3.1.1 (r311:74480, Aug 18 2009, 07:03:45)
[GCC 4.3.3] on linux2
Type "copyright", "credits" or "license()" for more information.
>>> ============================== RESTART ==============================
>>>
12 were correctly answered.
3 were answered incorrectly.
>>> |
                                                              Ln: 8 Col: 4
```

WHAT'S MY PURPOSE?

The *interface elements* that you add to a GUI are known as **widgets**. You've met one already: the button. There are lots of others. Look at the names of some other widgets below and see if you can match them with the correct description. We've already done the first one for you.

Drop-down list ——————————————→ A widget that provides a way for large and small amounts of text to be entered

Label —————————————————————→ A separate window that pops up to request additional information from the user

Text box ————————————————→ A widget that displays a string message in a window

Menu ————————————————————→ The combination of a drop-down list and a text box

Combo box ————————————————→ A widget that allows you to select one item from a large list

Dialog box ————————————————→ A list of command options that is attached to the top of a window

Write your answer here. → Which widget do you think you need to use in your program?

....

WHAT'S MY PURPOSE?
SOLUTION

The *interface elements* that you add to a GUI are known as **widgets**.
You've met one already: the button. There are lots of others. You were
to look at the names of some other widgets below and see if you could
match them with the correct description.

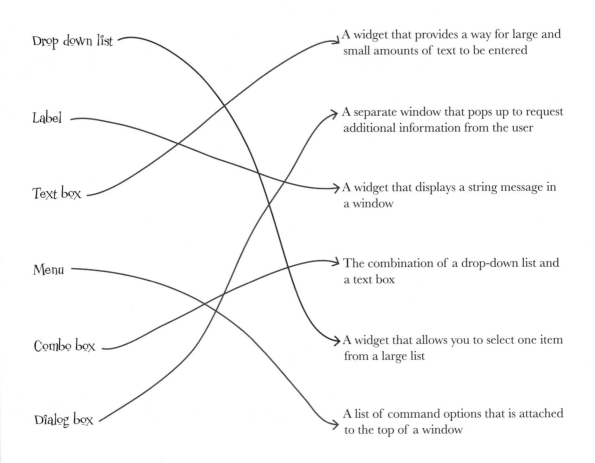

Drop down list → A widget that provides a way for large and small amounts of text to be entered

Label → A separate window that pops up to request additional information from the user

Text box → A widget that displays a string message in a window

Menu → The combination of a drop-down list and a text box

Combo box → A widget that allows you to select one item from a large list

Dialog box → A list of command options that is attached to the top of a window

You were asked to identify which widget you would use in your program.

Use the "Label" widget.

You need to add a label to your GUI in
order to display the results.

Label it

When it comes to adding a label to your GUI, use the tkinter `Label` widget. You create it in code not unlike the way you create a button. Here's the code to add a label to an existing GUI application. The label simply displays a string:

Create a new label, attach it to the main window, give it some text, and adjust the label's height.

```
l = Label(app, text='When you are ready, click on the buttons!', height = 3)
l.pack()
```

Don't forget to pack() the widget.

Put the label code before the code for the buttons and the GUI will then look like this.

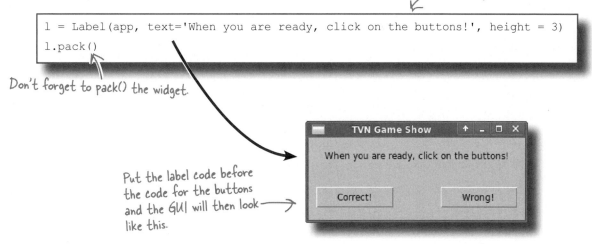

Another variation replaces the `text` parameter with `textvariable`. If you assign a *special* tkinter variable to this parameter, the label will change whenever the value of the variable changes, *automatically*:

Create an "IntVar".

Associate the "IntVar" with the label.

```
num_good = IntVar()
num_good.set(0)

l1 = Label(app, textvariable = num_good)
l1.pack(side = 'left')

    ...

num_good.set(100)
```

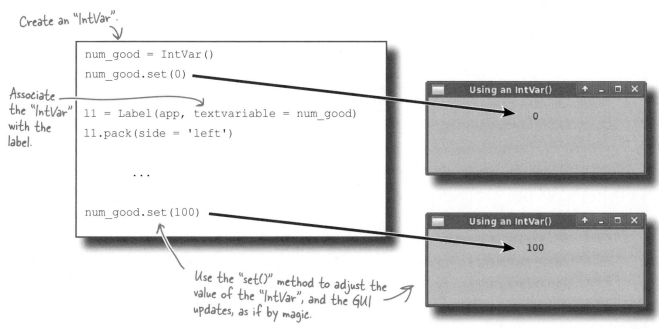

Use the "set()" method to adjust the value of the "IntVar", and the GUI updates, as if by magic.

LONG EXERCISE

Based on what you now know about adding a label to a GUI, rework your GUI code so that it uses two labels. One should display the number of correct answers and the other should display the number of wrong answers. We've left plenty of room for you to write in all the code that your program now needs.

....

....

....

....

....

....

....

....

....

....

....

....

....

....

....

....

....

....

....

....

....

....

....

....

....

....

....

....

....

....

....

....

....

....

....

....

....

....

....

Long Exercise Solution

Based on what you now know about adding a label to a GUI, you were asked to rework your GUI code so that it uses two labels. One should display the number of correct answers and the other should display the number of wrong answers. We left plenty of room for you to write in all the code that your program now needs.

Start by importing the library code you need. →
```
from tkinter import *

import pygame.mixer
```

Create the two event handlers that set the IntVar and play the appropriate sound. →
```
def play_correct_sound():

    num_good.set(num_good.get() + 1)

    correct_s.play()


def play_wrong_sound():

    num_bad.set(num_bad.get() + 1)

    wrong_s.play()
```

Create the GUI application window. →
```
app = Tk()

app.title("TVN Game Show")

app.geometry('300x110+200+100')
```

Initialize the sound system. →
```
sounds = pygame.mixer

sounds.init()
```

Load in the required sound effects. →

```
correct_s = sounds.Sound("correct.wav")

wrong_s  = sounds.Sound("wrong.wav")
```

Create two IntVars: one to count the number of correct answers and another to count the number of wrong answers. →

```
num_good = IntVar()

num_good.set(0)

num_bad = IntVar()

num_bad.set(0)
```

Display a friendly message that tells the host what to do. →

Be sure to PACK your widgets. →

```
lab = Label(app, text='When you are ready, click on the buttons!', height = 3)

lab.pack()
```

Create two labels to hold each counter and connect the labels to the relevant IntVars.

```
lab1 = Label(app, textvariable = num_good)

lab1.pack(side = 'left')


lab2 = Label(app, textvariable = num_bad)

lab2.pack(side = 'right')
```

Create each of the buttons and connect them to their relevant event handler.

```
b1 = Button(app, text = "Correct!", width = 10, command = play_correct_sound)

b1.pack(side = 'left', padx = 10, pady = 10)


b2 = Button(app, text = "Wrong!",  width = 10, command = play_wrong_sound)

b2.pack(side = 'right', padx = 10, pady = 10)
```

Start tkinter's main event loop. →

```
app.mainloop()
```

Test Drive

With your newly amended code entered into IDLE, press F5 to see and hear the GUI in all its glory:

Sweet... the fully working GUI.

TVN Game Show

When you are ready, click on the buttons!

16   Correct!   Wrong!   2

The labels are displaying running totals with each mouse click (event).

That's just perfect! The new version of the program works with my touchscreen and is so easy to use! I love it! Oh, and before I forget, here are your two front-row tickets for the Grand Final. See you then!

There it is: the host's winning TV smile!

One final decision: who are you going to take with you?

Your Programming Toolbox

You've got Chapter 7 under your belt. Let's look back at what you've learned in this chapter:

Programming Tools

* Using a third-party programming library

* Playing with a sound library

* Event loops – respond to events when they occur

* Event handler – code that executes when a certain event occurs

* GUI – a graphical user interface (looks nice, doesn't it?)

* Widget – a GUI interface element

Python Tools

* pygame – a professional-level set of gaming libraries that support sound

* pass – a piece of code that does nothing

* break – exit from a loop

* tkinter – a standard library for creating GUIs

* Tk() – a blank GUI app

* Button() – a tkinter button widget

* Label() – a tkinter label widget

* IntVar() – a tkinter integer variable that can update the GUI "as if by magic"

8 guis and data

Data entry widgets

So, you see, if we replace all our command-line data entry systems with GUIs, we can increase efficiency enough for me to afford these totally blinged-out alloys for my Hummer.

GUIs don't just process events. They also handle data.

Almost all GUI applications need to read user data, and choosing the right widgets can change your interface from *data entry hell* to *user heaven*. Widgets can accept plain text, or just present a menu of options. There are lots of different widgets out there, which means there are lots of choices, too. And, of course, making the right choice can make all the difference. It's time to take your GUI program to the **next level**.

Head-Ex needs a new delivery system

Head-Ex Deliveries is a small delivery company that's looking to expand. They know that delivery companies rely on their computer systems, so they want to have a whole new system to book deliveries around the country.

The system needs to be simple to use, so they want to use a graphical user interface (GUI). They want to give **you** the job of creating the system and even have a sweetener to make it worth your while.

I'll put you on a bonus. The more we deliver, the more you get paid!

Head-Ex employee →

They've already designed the interface

Head-Ex has been thinking about expanding their business for a while and they already have a design for the interface to the new delivery system. This is what it needs to look like:

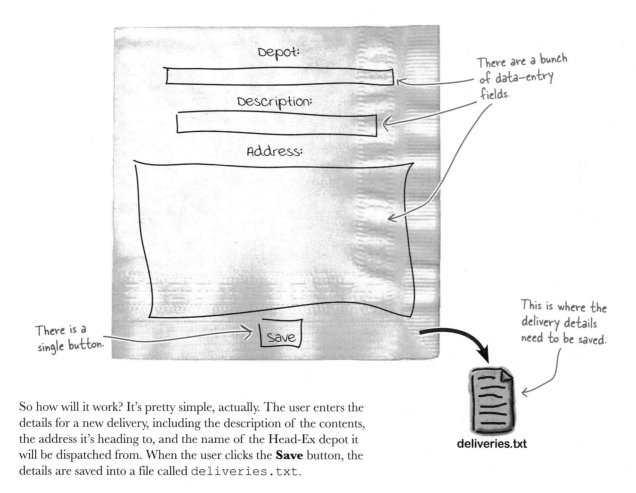

Depot:

Description:

Address:

Save

There are a bunch of data-entry fields.

There is a single button.

This is where the delivery details need to be saved.

deliveries.txt

So how will it work? It's pretty simple, actually. The user enters the details for a new delivery, including the description of the contents, the address it's heading to, and the name of the Head-Ex depot it will be dispatched from. When the user clicks the **Save** button, the details are saved into a file called `deliveries.txt`.

⚛ BRAIN POWER

What's the difference between this GUI and the ones you created before?

Read data from the GUI

Think about the GUIs you've created so far. Those apps ran code in response to *events* generated by users clicking buttons. So what's different here? Well, in addition to generating events, your users will also be **creating data**.

You need to do two things:

 You need to create an interface with places to enter text.
The Head-Ex design shows exactly what the interface will need to look like:

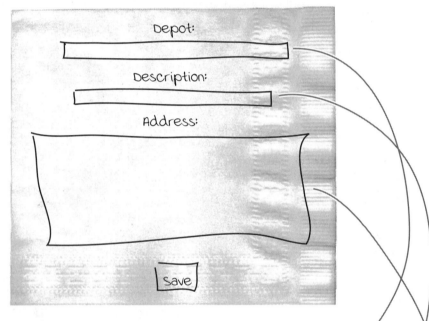

2 **You need some way of accessing that information.**
The data will need to be stored away in a file, so you need some way of **asking the interface** what text has been entered. That way, when someone clicks on the **Save** button, you'll be able to write the data to the deliveries.txt file, like this:

You will need to APPEND this information to the file whenever someone presses "Save."

The format of the file doesn't matter, as long as the depot staff can read it.

```
Depot:
Seattle, WA
Description:
Books
Address:
1 Main Street
Anytown
WA
```

The <u>Entry</u> and <u>Text</u> widgets let you enter text data into your GUI

If you look at the interface design, you'll see that there are **two** different types of text field you will need to handle: short text and longer, **multi-line** text fields. To deal with these two needs, Python's tkinter library has two different **widgets** for each data-entry type:

A TEXT FIELD is just a box on the screen that you can use to enter text.

Entry widget: for entering single lines of text

The Entry widget is what you'll use for most of the text fields. You can create an Entry widget like this:

```
my_small_field = Entry(app)
```

Remember that you always need to import the tkinter library first.

One single line of text

```
starbuzzceo@gmail.com
```

Text widget: for longer, multi-line text

Because not all text data fits on a single line, tkinter has the Text widget. Think of email messages, Wikipedia pages, and word processing documents. For large **multi-line** data, you need something other than Entry. You need Text:

```
my_large_field = Text(app)
```

You can enter large pieces of textual data in here.

Multiple lines of text

```
Costello: I mean the fellow's name. Abbott: Who.
Costello: The guy on first. Abbott: Who. Costel-
lo: The first baseman. Abbott: Who. Costello: The
guy playing... Abbott: Who is on first! Costello:
I'm asking YOU who's on first. Abbott: That's the
man's name. Costello: That's who's name? Abbott:
Yes. Costello: Well go ahead and tell me. Abbott:
That's it. Costello: That's who? Abbott: Yes.
```

We just checked... we're pretty sure Python is on first.

The Entry and Text fields should be enough to create the Head-Ex interface. But it's not enough to simply *create* the interface. You also need to *control the data* inside it.

Read and write data to text fields

When someone enters text into an `Entry` widget, Python stores that text somewhere in memory as a *string*. If you want to read the string, simply call the widget's `get()` method:

my_entry_field.get()

This will return the string "ice cream".

But what if you want to *change* the contents of the widget, can you do that too? Yes, you can: **add** text to the widget using the `insert()` method. It's a little more involved than just reading the text, because you need to say *where* you want the text inserted:

my_entry_field.insert(0, "banana ")

This is the INDEX of the insertion point.

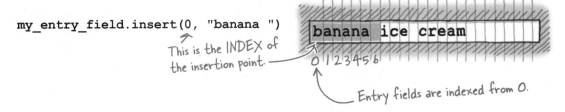

Entry fields are indexed from 0.

You need to specify the **index** of the insertion point. Indexes in `Entry` fields work just like indexes in strings: *they begin at zero*. So if you insert text at index **0**, the new text will appear *at the front of* all the text already in the field. In the same way, the `delete()` method lets you remove text from the field. You might want to delete the entire contents of the field, so tkinter gives you a handy **END** symbol that lets you delete *all* the text like this:

This will delete the entire contents.

0 is the index of the first character in the field.

The final character in the field is indexed by END.

my_entry_field.delete(0, END)

END is a special value that represents the last character in the field.

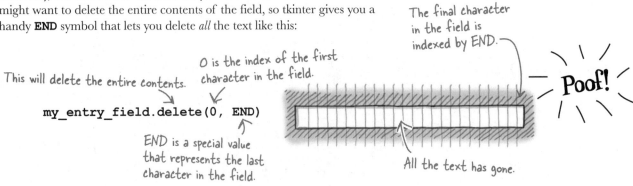

All the text has gone.

Poof!

The `get()`, `insert()`, and `delete()` methods give you complete control over the contents of *your* `Entry` field.

But what about Text fields?

Large Text fields are harder to handle

So Text fields *should* work the same way, right? Well, actually, they don't. The designers of tkinter figured people might want to access particular *lines* and *columns* in Text fields. This means that while Entry fields use a *single number* to index the contents of the field, Text fields use a string, in the form **row.column**:

Unlike Entry() fields, you can't just use get() to get the entire contents.

This means from the ROW=1 and COLUMN=0, which is the first character in the field.

This first character has index "1.0"

Row 1.

my_large_field.get("1.0", END)

This will return the entire contents of the field.

This will return ALL of the text in the Text field.

Costello: I mean the fellow's name. Abbott: Who. Costello: The guy on first. Abbott: Who. Costello: The first baseman. Abbott: Who. Costello: The guy playing... Abbott: Who is on first! Costello: I'm asking YOU who's on first. Abbott: That's the man's name. Costello: That's who's name? Abbott: Yes. Costello: Well go ahead and tell me. Abbott: That's it. Costello: That's who? Abbott: Yes.

Column 0.

Once you understand how Text indexes work, you'll see that you can *insert* and *delete* text from them in a very similar way to Entry fields:

my_large_field.delete("1.0", END)

This will clear the field.

my_large_field.insert("1.0", "Some text")

This will insert the text at the start of the field.

Now that you know how to create text fields and control the text they contain, you're ready to build the Head-Ex application.

Watch it!

Be careful how you number rows and columns in Text() fields.

Rows begin at 1, but columns begin at 0.

Code Magnets

Complete the code to create the interface. Think carefully about the widgets you will need for each of the fields.

```
from tkinter import *

app = Tk()           ← Create the GUI.
app.title('Head-Ex Deliveries')
Label(app, text = "Depot:").pack()
depot = Entry(app)
depot.pack()
```

You don't need to keep track of the labels, so no need to assign them to variables.

Recall that "pack()" adds the widgets to the window.

You'll want to keep track of the data entry fields, so assign them to variables.

Calling "pack()" without options means you leave it to tkinter to decide how best to lay things out on the GUI.

....

....

....

....

....

....

```
Button(app, text = "Save", command = save_data).pack()
```

This means the button will call the save_data() function when it's clicked.

....

Entry(app)			
	Label(app, text = "Description:")	Text(app)	description =
description			
			address
	.pack()	.pack()	
.pack()	.pack()		
	app.mainloop()	address =	
		Label(app, text = "Address:")	

 Sharpen your pencil

In addition to the GUI code, you need to write the function that will save the data from the GUI to the `deliveries.txt` file.

The **Save** button on the interface is going to call a function called `save_data()`. The function will append the data from the GUI to the end of the `deliveries.txt` file formatted like this:

```
Depot:
Seattle, WA
Description:
Books
Address:
1 Main Street
Anytown
WA
```

Then it will need to clear the fields on the form to make them ready for the next record to be entered. The function will have to appear in the program *before* the GUI code. Write the code for the function here:

Don't forget: it FIRST needs to save the data. THEN it needs to clear the fields.

....

....

....

....

....

....

....

....

....

....

....

....

....

Code Magnets Solution

You were to complete the code to create the interface. You were to
think carefully about the widgets you will need for each of the fields.

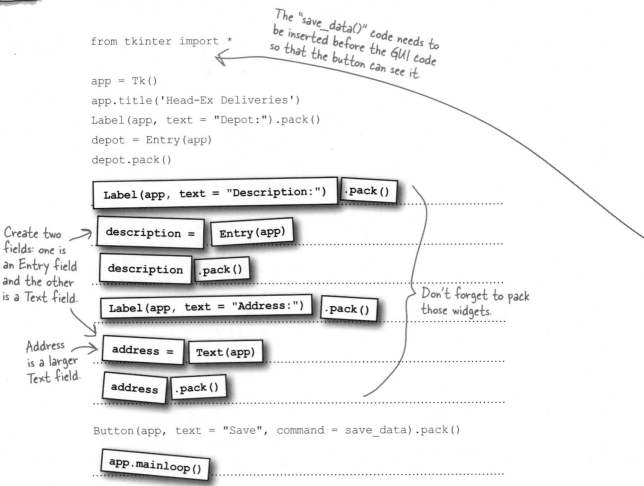

```
from tkinter import *

app = Tk()
app.title('Head-Ex Deliveries')
Label(app, text = "Depot:").pack()
depot = Entry(app)
depot.pack()
```

The "save_data()" code needs to be inserted before the GUI code so that the button can see it.

```
Label(app, text = "Description:")    .pack()
```

Create two fields: one is an Entry field and the other is a Text field.

```
description =    Entry(app)
description    .pack()
```

```
Label(app, text = "Address:")    .pack()
```

Address is a larger Text field.

```
address =    Text(app)
address    .pack()
```

Don't forget to pack those widgets.

```
Button(app, text = "Save", command = save_data).pack()
```

```
app.mainloop()
```

Sharpen your pencil
Solution

The **Save** button on the interface is going to call a function called `save_data()`. The function will append the data from the GUI to the end of the `deliveries.txt` file formatted like this:

```
Depot:
Seattle, WA
Description:
Books
Address:
1 Main Street
Anytown
WA
```

Then it will need to clear the fields on the form ready for the next record to be entered. The function will have to appear in the program *before* the GUI code. You were to write the code for the function here:

Your code may look a little different.

Append the text to the end of the file, just as you did when we wrote the POS programs for the Health Club.

```
def save_data():

    fileD = open("deliveries.txt", "a")

    fileD.write("Depot:\n")
    fileD.write("%s\n" % depot.get())

    fileD.write("Description:\n")

    fileD.write("%s\n" % description.get())

    fileD.write("Address:\n")

    fileD.write("%s\n" % address.get("1.0", END))

    depot.delete(0, END)

    description.delete(0, END)

    address.delete("1.0", END)
```

get() returns the contents of an Entry field.

get("1.0", END) returns the contents of a Text field.

Don't forget to clear the fields after saving the data.

This means "1st row, 0th column." Remember that rows start at 1 and columns from 0.

TEST DRIVE

The deliveries program is ready, so it is time for the demo. With the code entered into IDLE, press F5 to fire it up and you should see this:

Your GUI is looking good.

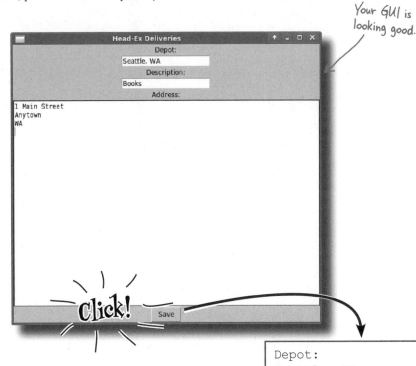

Click!

The data you enter into the text fields gets written to the file.

```
Depot:
Seattle, WA
Description:
Books
Address:
1 Main Street
Anytown
```

You can enter data into each of the fields, even the multi-line address. When you click **Save**, the fields all get cleared. When you open up the `deliveries.txt` file, you see that the data you entered into the GUI has been saved.

Cool! That's exactly what we need. I'll tell every office to start using it.

Congratulations! You've written your first GUI data-entry application.

BULLET POINTS

- `Entry` fields are used for single lines of text.

- `Text` fields are used to handle multi-line text.

- Read the contents of fields with the `get()` method.

- Add text using the `insert()` method.

- Remove text with the `delete()` method.

- `Entry` fields are indexed with a number starting at 0.

- Text fields are indexed with a string, starting at "1.0".

---

there are no
Dumb Questions

Q: Is it possible to put more than one line of text into an Entry box widget?

A: Yes, you probably could, but if you need to do this, you are much better off using a `Text` box, because they are designed to handle more than one line of text.

Q: I notice that we are calling the pack() method as part of the label creation code, whereas before we assigned the label to a variable then called pack() on the new variable. Which packing technique should I use and does it really matter?

A: No, it does not really matter which technique you use to call `pack()`. If it makes sense to pack your widgets as they are created, include the call to `pack()` as part of the creation code. If it doesn't make sense, assign the widget to a variable and do your packing whenever you need to. If you look at other examples of tkinter code on the Web, you'll see that other programmers use both techniques.

Q: Why can't we just assign a value to an Entry box using the assignment operator (=)? Why do we have to use the insert() method?

A: The `Entry` box is a widget *object*, **not** a Python variable, so using the assignment operator does not make sense here. When working with objects, you need to use the application programming interface (API) provided by and included with the object, which in this case is the `insert()` method.

Q: Why do the rows in a Text box start counting from one as opposed to zero (like everything else in Python)?

A: Beats the hell out of us. No idea.

Q: So, just to be clear, Who is on first?

A: No. *Who* is on second. *Python* is on first.

One of the Head-Ex deliveries went astray

For the first few days, the system worked great. Deliveries were correctly booked and goods were shipped. But then, something odd happened at the British delivery depot.

I'm terribly sorry, old chap, but I think these boxes were meant for the **other** Cambridge. Cup of tea?

One of the deliveries went **seriously** astray. A consignment of college football jerseys was sent to Cambridge in *England*, instead of the Cambridge in *Massachusetts*. But the system is still working fine, isn't it? So what could possibly have gone wrong?

There's no time for tea. Let's get to the bottom of this.

↑
But it was lovely
to be asked...

Users can enter <u>anything</u> in the fields

The system **is** doing exactly what it was designed to do: it lets people enter the details for depots, descriptions, and addresses. The trouble is, even though there are only a few depots, the `Entry` text fields lets the user type pretty much **anything**. There are no controls on what gets entered into the GUI.

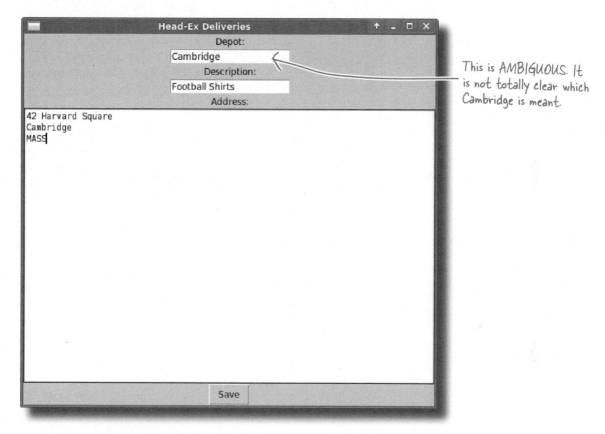

This is AMBIGUOUS. It is not totally clear which Cambridge is meant.

It wasn't obvious whether the delivery was intended for the Head-Ex depot in Cambridge, MA, or the Head-Ex depot in Cambridge, England. You need some way to prevent users from entering **ambiguous** data in the depot field.

BRAIN POWER

Think about the GUIs you've used in the past. How could you **restrict** the values that someone could enter into a GUI?

Radio buttons force users to choose a valid depot

Text fields aren't the only data-entry game in town. If you look at any GUI program, you will find a whole host of different widgets being used: sliders, buttons, check boxes. Why are there so many different types of widget? Are they just there to make the interface more interesting to use?

The reason there are so many widgets is to allow the programmer to efficiently **manage** and **control** the kind of data that people can enter.

If you want to allow a **small number** of values for a field, you can use the **radio button** widget. A *radio button* works just like the AM/FM selection buttons on your radio: press AM and the FM button pops up. Press FM and the reverse happens.

Radio buttons in a GUI program work in the same way: if you select one of the buttons, the other buttons are *automatically deselected*. That way, you can choose only **one** from a small **group** of options.

Click AM and the FM button pops up.

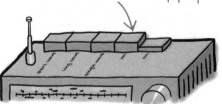

Click FM and the AM button pops up.

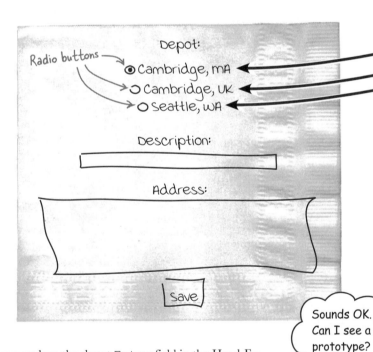

Radio buttons →

Depot:
- ⦿ Cambridge, MA
- ○ Cambridge, UK
- ○ Seattle, WA

Description:

Address:

Save

Sounds OK. Can I see a prototype?

So if you replace the depot `Entry` field in the Head-Ex program with a set of radio buttons, you prevent users from entering ambiguous depot names. That way, they will be able to choose one, *and only one*, depot.

Creating radio buttons in tkinter

You need to create three radio buttons in the interface, one for each of the depots. This is how you might do that in tkinter:

You don't need the Entry field anymore.

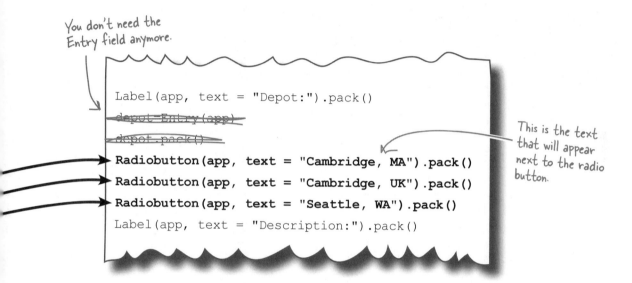

```
Label(app, text = "Depot:").pack()
depot = Entry(app)
depot.pack()
Radiobutton(app, text = "Cambridge, MA").pack()
Radiobutton(app, text = "Cambridge, UK").pack()
Radiobutton(app, text = "Seattle, WA").pack()
Label(app, text = "Description:").pack()
```

This is the text that will appear next to the radio button.

You need to remove the depot `Entry` widget and replace it with **three** `Radiobutton` widgets, one for each of the valid depots. The text given to each widget will be the text that appears alongside the radio button in the interface.

What about reading which radio button has been selected? For now, you just need to create a prototype of the interface, so there's no need to change any of the code that saves records. That's something we can deal with later.

Let's demo the new interface to the guys at Head-Ex.

Test Drive

It's time for the demo of the new version of the interface. When the guys from Head-Ex arrive, you fire up the new program in IDLE:

There's clearly something wrong with the prototype. There is only supposed to be one radio button selected at any one time, and yet the program shows *all* of the radio buttons selected together.

What happened? You need to look in a little more detail at how radio buttons actually work.

The radio buttons should work together

When you modified the code, you added the three radio buttons like this:

```
Radiobutton(app, text = "Cambridge, MA").pack()
Radiobutton(app, text = "Cambridge, UK").pack()
Radiobutton(app, text = "Seattle, WA").pack()
```

That code added three new radio buttons to the interface, but it created them as three *independent widgets*. This means that each of the radio buttons is working separately, with no knowledge of the other two.

But **the whole point** of radio buttons is that they work together. When you select one radio button, you expect all of the other radio buttons to be deselected, just like the buttons on the radio.

GUI programs often need to **synchronize** different widgets together. You do something to one widget, which results in something else happening to another widget.

So how might you get your radio buttons to cooperate?

When the AM button is selected, the FM button should be deselected.

Think about the way you want radio buttons to work. Is there something that they all need to share? What is it?

The radio buttons can share a <u>model</u>

The text fields you originally created each stored a single data item. For every widget on the screen, there was a single piece of data. But that's *not true* for your radio buttons. The **three** radio buttons will be used by the user to record just **one** thing: the depot that a delivery is sent to. The three radio buttons needs to *share a single piece of data*. And that piece of data is called the **model**.

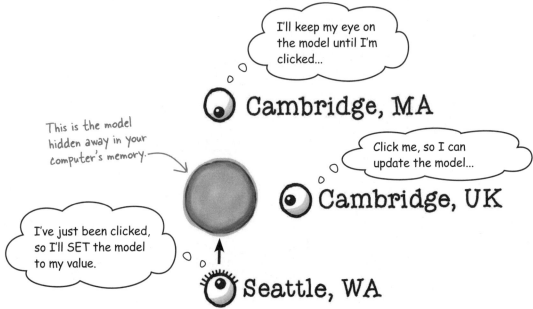

So if the Seattle radio button is **selected**, it will **update** the model with a new *value*.

You haven't set values on the radio buttons yet; you've only set text descriptions. You could set the values to be whatever you want, but it is simplest to set them to the same thing used as the description of the field:

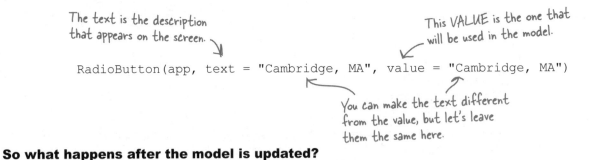

The text is the description that appears on the screen.

This VALUE is the one that will be used in the model.

```
RadioButton(app, text = "Cambridge, MA", value = "Cambridge, MA")
```

You can make the text different from the value, but let's leave them the same here.

So what happens after the model is updated?

The system tells the other widgets when the model changes

The tkinter library code will keep a track of which widgets are using which models and, whenever a model changes, tkinter will let the widgets know about it. So if we select the `Seattle, WA` radio button, it will update the model, and the other radio buttons that share the model will deselect themselves.

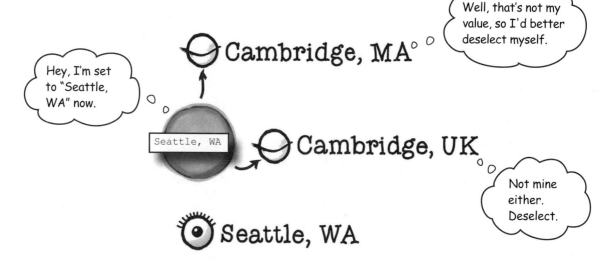

There's a special name for the way this code works:

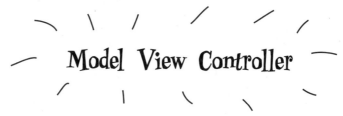

- The **model** is the data stored.

- The **view** is just a fancy name for the widget.

- And the **controller** is the code in tkinter that lets all of the views know when the model has changed.

So much for the MVC theory. Time to fix the code.

So how do you use <u>models</u> in tkinter?

Imagine you wanted to add delivery options to the program. You could use
radio buttons and do something like this:

It's important to EXPLICITLY give each button a VALUE.

```
Radiobutton(app, text = "First Class", value = "First Class").pack()
Radiobutton(app, text = "Next Business Day", value = "Next Business Day").pack()
```

You then need to create a *model* for the radio buttons to *share*. In tkinter,
models are called **control variables**, and control variables that store text
are called `StringVars`:

A StringVar is just like the IntVar from Chapter 7, except that it holds a string value.

```
service = StringVar()
service.set(None)
Radiobutton(app, text = "First Class", value = "First Class",
                    variable = service).pack()
Radiobutton(app, text = "Next Business Day", value = "Next Business Day",
                    variable = service).pack()
```

This sets the StringVar to the special value "None" which means "No value."

This code will now give us a pair of buttons that work together. If you
select one, the other will automatically become deselected:

Click the SECOND option and the FIRST will be deselected.

First Class

Next Business Day

And if you ever need to read or change the model value in the code, you just
need to call the `StringVar`'s `get()` or `set()` methods:

```
>>> print(service.get())
"Next Business Day"
```

This returns the current value of the model.

```
>>> service.set("First Class")
```

This sets the model object back to "First Class", which will automatically select the correct radio button on the screen.

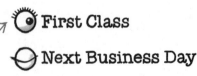

First Class

Next Business Day

Pool Puzzle

This is the section of the program that creates the depot radio buttons. See if you can complete it using the fragments of code from the pool. Be warned: you might not need **all** of the pieces...

```
Label(app, text = "Depot:").pack()

.............................................
depot.set(None)
Radiobutton(app, ...................... , ...................................... , ...................................... ).pack()
Radiobutton(app, ...................... , ...................................... , ...................................... ).pack()
Radiobutton(app, ...................... , ...................................... , ...................................... ).pack()
```

Note: each thing from the pool can be used only once!

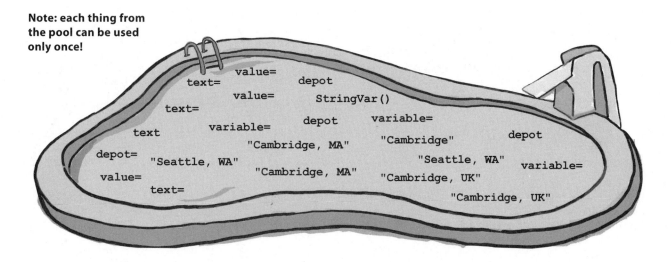

```
value=
text=                  depot
          value=              StringVar()
    text=
              variable=       depot        variable=
    text                                "Cambridge"          depot
depot=                "Cambridge, MA"
          "Seattle, WA"                        "Seattle, WA"    variable=
    value=        "Cambridge, MA"      "Cambridge, UK"
          text=                              "Cambridge, UK"
```

Sharpen your pencil

What piece of code would you use to make sure **all** of the radio buttons are cleared *after* the record is saved?

....

Pool Puzzle Solution

This is the section of the program that creates the depot radio buttons. You were asked to see if you could complete it using the fragments of code from the pool. Not **all** of the pieces were needed.

```
Label(app, text = "Depot:").pack()
depot = StringVar()
depot.set(None)
Radiobutton(app, variable = depot, text = "Cambridge, MA", value = "Cambridge, MA").pack()
Radiobutton(app, variable = depot, text = "Cambridge, UK", value = "Cambridge, UK").pack()
Radiobutton(app, variable = depot, text = "Seattle, WA", value = "Seattle, WA").pack()
```

Note: each thing from the pool can be used only once!

```
text                                    "Cambridge"
```

Sharpen your pencil
Solution

What piece of code would you use to make sure **all** of the radio buttons are cleared after the record is saved?

Because none of the radio buttons have this value, none of them will be selected. → depot.set(None)

Test Drive

Now it's time for another demo of your program. When you first fire up the program, you see that there are initially no depots selected.

That's good. Now what happens if you select the first option, then change to the third?

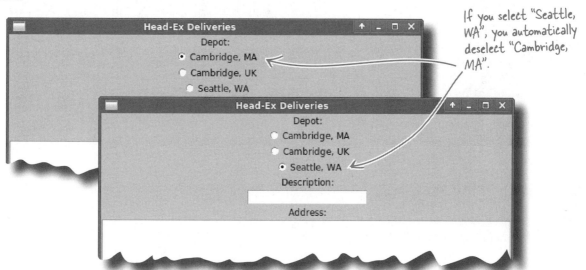

If you select "Seattle, WA", you automatically deselect "Cambridge, MA".

If you make a selection, the other radio buttons automatically deselect themselves, which is exactly what you need.

The radio buttons are working correctly.

> Phew. Now the users will always send the packages to real depots. You did a great job. Thanks!

Head-Ex's business is expanding

With the new systems in place, business is better than ever at Head-Ex. They have new trucks, more employees, and an increasing number of offices.

Head-Ex is opening depots all over the world.

But with this success comes a new problem...

There are too many depots on the GUI

The coders at Head-Ex have been amending your program to add new depots as they were opened. But there's a problem. Now there are so many depots that they can't all fit on the screen.

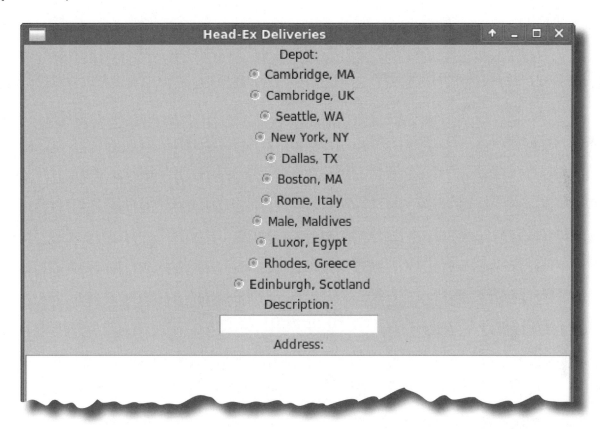

Something needs to be done to the GUI. But what?

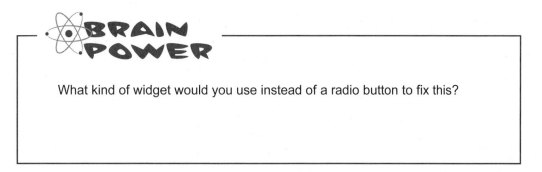

What kind of widget would you use instead of a radio button to fix this?

An <u>OptionMenu</u> lets you have as many options as needed

An **OptionMenu** or *drop-down listbox* is a widget that lets you restrict the number of options a user can choose, just like a group of radio buttons. But it has a couple of important differences.

First, it takes up a lot less space than a functionally equivalent group of radio buttons, about the same amount of space as an `Entry` text field. Second—and this is the really important characteristic—when you click it, an option menu can display a *large list of options*.

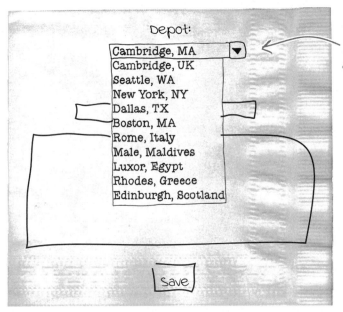

The user could select a depot from an option menu.

If the Head-Ex coders use an option menu, they will be able to increase the number of depots available, but they won't have to increase the size or complexity of their GUI.

So what needs to be changed in the code if you want to swap the radio buttons for an option menu?

It's not what *changes*, but what *stays the same*.

The <u>model</u> stays the same

Think for a moment about the model you are using with the radio buttons. It represents the name of the chosen depot, which you want to keep for the option menu. If the model stays the same, then your code, which currently looks like this:

```
depot = StringVar()
depot.set(None)
Radiobutton(app, variable = depot, text = "Cambridge, MA", value = "Cambridge, MA").pack()
Radiobutton(app, variable = depot, text = "Cambridge, UK", value = "Cambridge, UK").pack()
Radiobutton(app, variable = depot, text = "Seattle, WA",   value = "Seattle, WA").pack()
```

can be replaced with code like this:

```
depot = StringVar()
depot.set(None)
OptionMenu(app, depot, "Cambridge, MA", "Cambridge, UK", "Seattle, WA").pack()
```

The second parameter must be the model and it doesn't need the "variable =" bit.

A list of all the options that appear in the widget

This is the same model as before.

Cambridge, MA

Cambridge, MA ▼
Cambridge, UK
Seattle, WA
New York, NY
Dallas, TX
Boston, MA
Rome, Italy
Male, Maldives
Luxor, Egypt
Rhodes, Greece
Edinburgh, Scotland

But wait... you don't have to list <u>all</u> the values like that

It looks like a lot of work to put all of the options in the actual function call to `OptionMenu()`, doesn't it? After all, there's a large list of depots.

Thankfully, Python comes to the rescue. If you have the options already stored in a list:

```
depots = ["Cambridge, MA", "Cambridge, UK", "Seattle, WA"]
```

you can pass the entire list instead of separate values like this:

```
OptionMenu(app, depot, *depots).pack()
```

This ✳ means "Take the rest of the parameters from this list and insert them here."

Now let's put the pieces together.

Long Exercise

This is a version of the program that uses radio buttons.

You are going to update this program so that it uses an option menu. But the *options* need to be read from a text file.

```python
from tkinter import *

def save_data():
    fileD = open("deliveries.txt", "a")
    fileD.write("Depot:\n")
    fileD.write("%s\n" % depot.get())
    fileD.write("Description:\n")
    fileD.write("%s\n" % description.get())
    fileD.write("Address:\n")
    fileD.write("%s\n" % address.get("1.0", END))
    depot.set(None)
    description.delete(0, END)
    description.delete(0, END)
    address.delete("1.0", END)

app = Tk()
app.title('Head-Ex Deliveries')
Label(app, text = "Depot:").pack()
depot = StringVar()
depot.set(None)
Radiobutton(app, variable = depot, text = "Cambridge, MA", value = "Cambridge, MA").
pack()
Radiobutton(app, variable = depot, text = "Cambridge, UK", value = "Cambridge, UK").
pack()
Radiobutton(app, variable = depot, text = "Seattle, WA",   value = "Seattle, WA").
pack()
Label(app, text = "Description:").pack()
description = Entry(app)
description.pack()
Label(app, text = "Address:").pack()
address = Text(app)
address.pack()
Button(app, text = "Save", command = save_data).pack()
app.mainloop()
```

1 First, you need to create a function called `read_depots()` that will read the lines in a text file and return them to your code as a list.

Hint: When you read a line from the file, it might have a newline character at the end. The `rstrip()` string method will remove it for you.

This function will be inserted here.

```
def read_depots(file):
    ..............................................................................................
    ..............................................................................................
    ..............................................................................................
    ..............................................................................................
    ..............................................................................................
    ..............................................................................................
    ..............................................................................................
    ..............................................................................................
```

2 Then, you need to replace **this section of the code** with code that generates an option menu using the data from the `read_depots()` function you just created. It should use a file called `depots.txt`. Write the code here:

```
    ..............................................................................................
    ..............................................................................................
    ..............................................................................................
    ..............................................................................................
    ..............................................................................................
    ..............................................................................................
    ..............................................................................................
    ..............................................................................................
```

options added

Long Exercise Solution

This is a version of the program that uses radio buttons.

You needed to update this program so that it used an option menu. But the *options* were to be read from a text file.

```python
from tkinter import *

def save_data():
    fileD = open("deliveries.txt", "a")
    fileD.write("Depot:\n")
    fileD.write("%s\n" % depot.get())
    fileD.write("Description:\n")
    fileD.write("%s\n" % description.get())
    fileD.write("Address:\n")
    fileD.write("%s\n" % address.get("1.0", END))
    depot.set(None)
    description.delete(0, END)
    description.delete(0, END)
    address.delete("1.0", END)

app = Tk()
app.title('Head-Ex Deliveries')
Label(app, text = "Depot:").pack()
depot = StringVar()
depot.set(None)
Radiobutton(app, variable = depot, text = "Cambridge, MA", value = "Cambridge, MA").
pack()
Radiobutton(app, variable = depot, text = "Cambridge, UK", value = "Cambridge, UK").
pack()
Radiobutton(app, variable = depot, text = "Seattle, WA",   value = "Seattle, WA").
pack()
Label(app, text = "Description:").pack()
description = Entry(app)
description.pack()
Label(app, text = "Address:").pack()
address = Text(app)
address.pack()
Button(app, text = "Save", command = save_data).pack()
app.mainloop()
```

1 First, you needed to create a function called `read_depots()` to read the lines in a text file and return them as a list.

```
def read_depots(file):        Start with an
    depots = []               empty array.
    depots_f = open(file)
    for line in depots_f:
        depots.append(line.rstrip())
    return depots
```

Open the file.

Read from the file one line at a time.

Append a stripped copy of the line to the array.

Return the list to the calling code.

2 Then, you needed to replace **this section of the code** with code that generated an option menu using the data returned by the `read_depots()` function. It needed to use a file called `depots.txt`. You were to write the code here:

Call the function, passing in the name of the file to read the data from.

```
options = read_depots("depots.txt")
OptionMenu(app, depot, *options).pack()
```

Use the data to build the option menu.

Test Drive

Before you run your program, be sure to create the depots.txt file. When you start up the program in IDLE, the interface is a lot more compact and even easier to use:

A nice and neat list of depot options

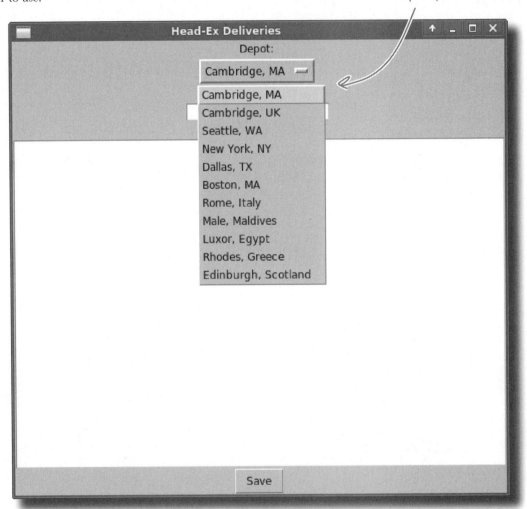

The system is working really well now. And, due to the depots being stored in a file, Head-Ex can change the list of depots in the file *without having to amend the code in any way*.

Your GUI program builds the list of depots *dynamically* and *on-demand*, which makes it very flexible indeed.

Things are going great at Head-Ex

The GUI system is easy to use, and by restricting the depots with an option menu, the quality of the entered data is spot on. This means the Head-Ex delivery service is more reliable, the number of customers is increasing, and the business is growing bigger—worldwide.

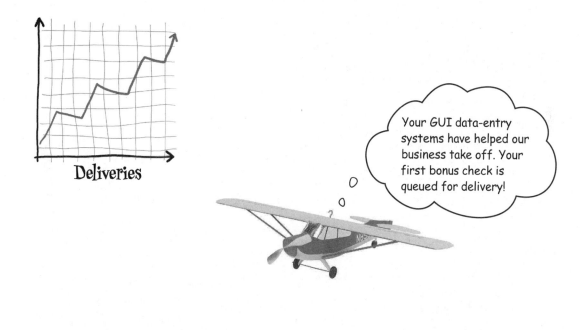

Deliveries

Your GUI data-entry systems have helped our business take off. Your first bonus check is queued for delivery!

Check out Head-Ex's ever-expanding fleet.

Using tkinter's data models, you used the power of model-view-controller to build a GUI data-entry system that really rocks.

CHAPTER 8

Your Programming Toolbox

You've got Chapter 8 under your belt.
Let's look back at what you've learned
in this chapter:

Programming Tools

* MVC — Model, View, Controller.

* Think of widgets as views.

* Use data models to keep your data separate from your views.

* Radio buttons work together if they share a model.

* Object API — the application programmer interface provided by an object.

* Populate a GUI widget dynamically and on-demand.

Python Tools

* Entry() — used by tkinter to enter small amounts of text — one line.

* Text() — handle multi-line text in tkinter.

* Entry fields are indexed from 0.

* Text fields are indexed with a "row. column" string, starting with "1.0".

* The tkinter controller — keeps the views informed about data changes.

* StringVar() — a tkinter stringed variable that can update the GUI "as if by magic."

* RadioButton() — useful for when you want to select one item from a group in tkinter.

* OptionMenu() — useful for when you want to select one item from a LARGE group of items in tkinter.

8 ½ exceptions and message boxes

Get the message?

> So when you say, "Not even if you were the last man on Earth," what do you mean?

Sometimes things just go wrong. You just need to handle it.

There will always be things beyond your control. Networks will fail. Files will disappear. Smart coders learn how to deal with those kinds of **errors** and make their programs **recover** gracefully. The best software keeps the user informed about the bad things that happen and what should be done to recover. By learning how to use **exceptions** and **message boxes**, you can take your software to the next level of reliability and quality.

What's that smell?

Just when it looked like things were going so well, there was a problem in the Head-Ex storeroom.

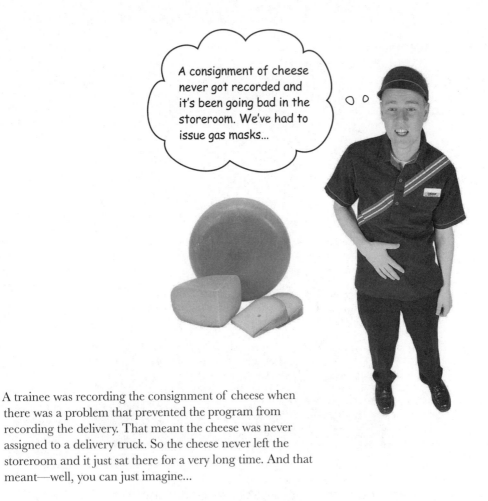

A consignment of cheese never got recorded and it's been going bad in the storeroom. We've had to issue gas masks...

A trainee was recording the consignment of cheese when there was a problem that prevented the program from recording the delivery. That meant the cheese was never assigned to a delivery truck. So the cheese never left the storeroom and it just sat there for a very long time. And that meant—well, you can just imagine...

To prevent the same thing happening again, you need to find what caused the problem.

Someone changed the file permissions

It turns out the whole thing was caused when someone from Technical Support decided to change the permissions on the `deliveries.txt` file, making it **read-only**. When the system tried to write deliveries into the file, it failed. But what's worse, it **failed silently**:

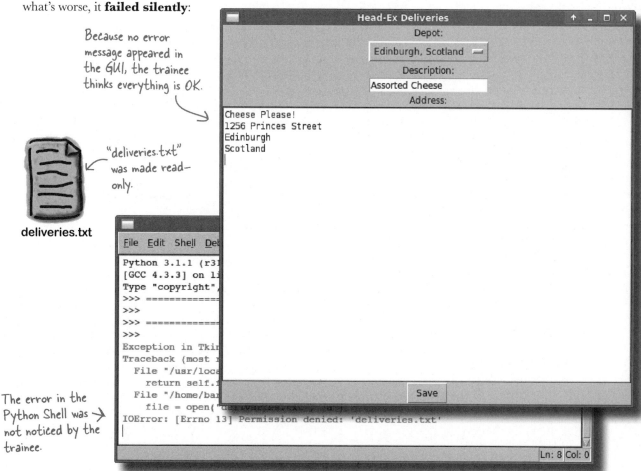

Because no error message appeared in the GUI, the trainee thinks everything is OK.

"deliveries.txt" was made read-only.

deliveries.txt

The error in the Python Shell was not noticed by the trainee.

When you were writing programs that ran in the **Python Shell**, you could always tell when it failed: a huge, ugly error message appeared. Why not with GUIs? Don't they do the same?

They do, but the trouble is that the message appears in the Shell and your user is busy looking at the nice GUI, so the ugly error can often be missed.

When using a GUI, how do you spot errors? Once spotted, what happens then?

> **Note:** To reproduce this error on your PC, you need to make your `deliveries.txt` file *read-only*. How you do this depends upon your operating system. If you are unsure how to make a file read-only, check the Web for more advice (or ask a friendly local guru). On most systems, it involves editing the *properties* of the file.

When it couldn't write to the file, the program threw an <u>exception</u>

What happens when an error occurs? Some errors are *really bad*: they cause the program to **crash**. Other, less serious errors are known as *recoverable*: the program can keep running, even though something went wrong. You can spot these situations in your code, because most programming technologies **throw** an **exception** when they occur.

Imagine a line of code that has a problem, such as the line that was trying to write to the `deliveries.txt` file. Python will spot that the append operation *failed* and, instead of running the rest of the code that follows, Python abandons ship and skips out of the code completely. That's what *throwing an exception* means: the program doesn't *crash*, but it abandons what you were trying to do and tries to recover the situation:

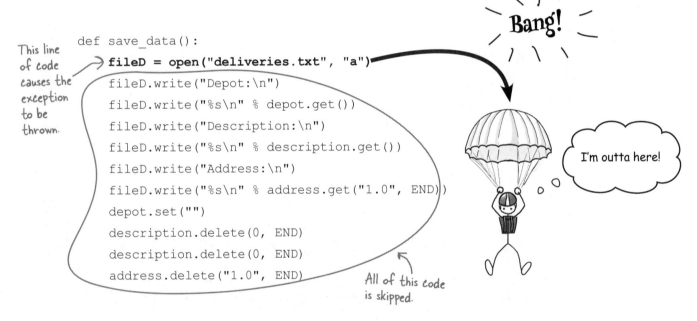

This line of code causes the exception to be thrown.

```
def save_data():
    fileD = open("deliveries.txt", "a")
    fileD.write("Depot:\n")
    fileD.write("%s\n" % depot.get())
    fileD.write("Description:\n")
    fileD.write("%s\n" % description.get())
    fileD.write("Address:\n")
    fileD.write("%s\n" % address.get("1.0", END))
    depot.set("")
    description.delete(0, END)
    description.delete(0, END)
    address.delete("1.0", END)
```

All of this code is skipped.

Bang!

I'm outta here!

But *why* skip past the rest of the code? Why not keep on running? Generally, that would be a *bad idea*. Once a line of code has gone *bad*, there's no way of knowing if it makes sense to keep running the code that follows. For example, if the Head-Ex code can't open the deliveries file to append to it, it makes no sense to continue trying to write data to the unopened file!

In order to recover, you need to start running your code from somewhere else.

Catch the exception

Python spots when an exception is *thrown*, and you can write some code to run when the exception occurs. This is called *catching the exception*. The code that you run when there's an error resulting in the thrown exception is called an **exception handler**.

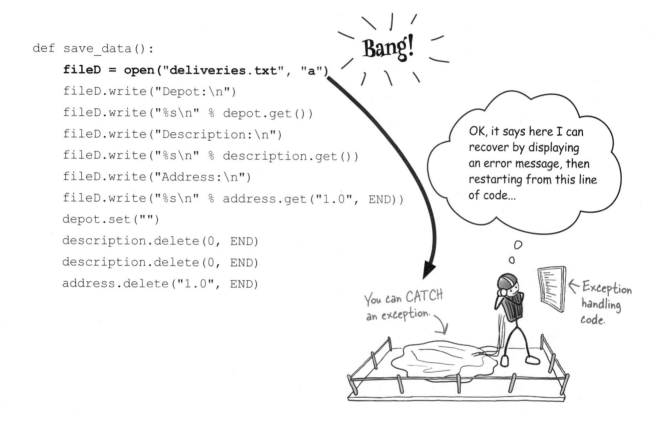

```
def save_data():
    fileD = open("deliveries.txt", "a")
    fileD.write("Depot:\n")
    fileD.write("%s\n" % depot.get())
    fileD.write("Description:\n")
    fileD.write("%s\n" % description.get())
    fileD.write("Address:\n")
    fileD.write("%s\n" % address.get("1.0", END))
    depot.set("")
    description.delete(0, END)
    description.delete(0, END)
    address.delete("1.0", END)
```

Bang!

OK, it says here I can recover by displaying an error message, then restarting from this line of code...

You can CATCH an exception.

← Exception handling code.

Creating exception handlers can really make life easy for your users. Instead of a flaky program that crashes or fails silently the first time something weird happens, you can write programs that *gracefully recover from errors*. Exception handlers **tidy up** when something goes wrong and can even let your user know that something strange happened.

That's what you need here: an exception handler that tells the user when there's a problem writing a delivery to the file.

How are exception handlers written in Python?

A piece of code that runs when an exception is thrown is called an exception handler.

Watch for exceptions with try/except

In order to recover from an error as it happens, you need to indicate the code that *might* throw an exception. In Python, you do this with `try` and `except`.

All you need to do is take the piece of potentially troublesome code and add the `try` and `except` labels:

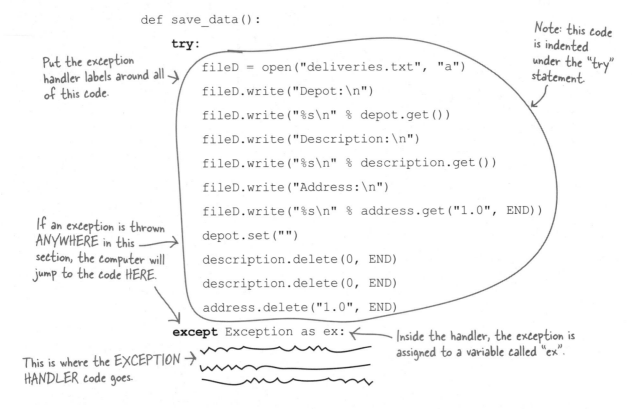

```
def save_data():

    try:

        fileD = open("deliveries.txt", "a")

        fileD.write("Depot:\n")

        fileD.write("%s\n" % depot.get())

        fileD.write("Description:\n")

        fileD.write("%s\n" % description.get())

        fileD.write("Address:\n")

        fileD.write("%s\n" % address.get("1.0", END))

        depot.set("")

        description.delete(0, END)

        description.delete(0, END)

        address.delete("1.0", END)

    except Exception as ex:
```

Put the exception handler labels around all of this code.

Note: this code is indented under the "try" statement.

If an exception is thrown ANYWHERE in this section, the computer will jump to the code HERE.

Inside the handler, the exception is assigned to a variable called "ex".

This is where the EXCEPTION HANDLER code goes.

If an exception is thrown *between* the `try` and `except` labels, the code that follows the `except` label runs. The code that threw the exception is *abandoned*. If no exception occurs, the code runs normally and the code that comes after the `except` label is ignored.

Notice that the `try`/`except` labels are wrapped around *all* of the function's code. If there's a problem opening the `deliveries.txt` file, you don't ever want to try writing to it. So, when trouble strikes, you should adandon ship and skip to the code that tries to recover from the error.

The code that then runs is the exception handler.

Exception Magnets

Assemble the code to handle an exception in the `save_data()` function. The exception handler needs to display the details of the exception in the title bar of the window. Note: remember to indent the code in the exception handler, in addition to the code in the `try` block.

```
fileD = open("deliveries.txt", "a")
fileD.write("Depot:\n")
fileD.write("%s\n" % depot.get())
fileD.write("Description:\n")
fileD.write("%s\n" % description.get())
fileD.write("Address:\n")
fileD.write("%s\n" % address.get("1.0", END))
depot.set("")
description.delete(0, END)
description.delete(0, END)
address.delete("1.0", END)
```

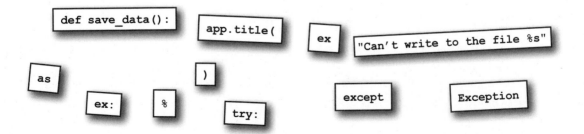

Exception Magnets Solution

You were asked to assemble the code to handle an exception in the save_data() function. The exception handler needs to display the details of the exception in the title bar of the window. You needed to remember to indent the code in the exception handler, in addition to the code in the try block.

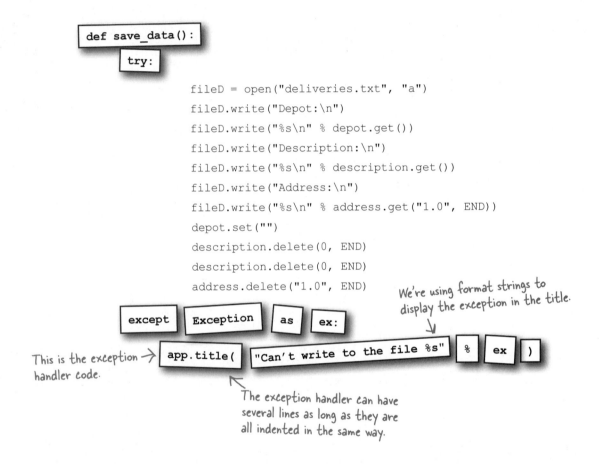

```
def save_data():
    try:
        fileD = open("deliveries.txt", "a")
        fileD.write("Depot:\n")
        fileD.write("%s\n" % depot.get())
        fileD.write("Description:\n")
        fileD.write("%s\n" % description.get())
        fileD.write("Address:\n")
        fileD.write("%s\n" % address.get("1.0", END))
        depot.set("")
        description.delete(0, END)
        description.delete(0, END)
        address.delete("1.0", END)
    except Exception as ex:
        app.title("Can't write to the file %s" % ex)
```

We're using format strings to display the exception in the title.

This is the exception → handler code.

The exception handler can have several lines as long as they are all indented in the same way.

Test Drive

Let's see if the code works. Make sure the `deliveries.txt` file is **read-only**. Then run the new version of the program in IDLE and try to record a delivery by clicking on the **Save** button.

Note: make sure
deliveries.txt is
set to read-only.

deliveries.txt

Clicking "Save"
causes the
title bar to
change, due to
the error.

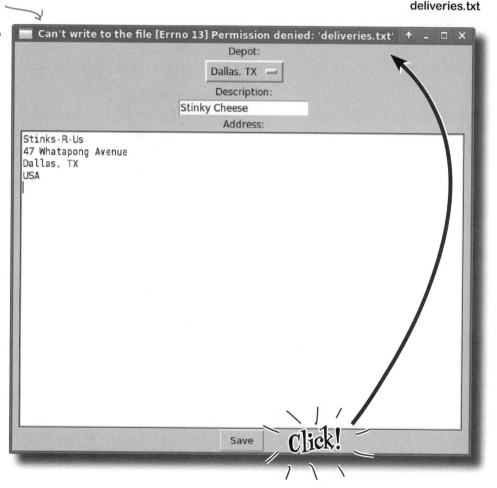

Sure enough, when you try to save the delivery details, the program catches the exception and the exception handler displays the error message in the window title.

Wonder what the people at Head-Ex will think of this?

There's an issue with the exception handler

You do a quick demo for the folks at Head-Ex and, even though the program works, it's not quite what they need.

I'm not sure the error message is really visible in the title bar. If there is an error, I really don't want to miss it.

The error message is more visible than when it was appearing in the *Python Shell*, but it isn't a whole lot more visible. Sure, you've proved that you can spot when an error happens and then run an exception handler in order to do something about the error. But you really need to do something that will **interrupt** the user and highlight the situation. You need something that will force the user to acknowledge the error before he continues doing something else.

A GUI message box might do the trick.

A message box <u>demands</u> attention

Most of the time, GUI programs put the user in charge. If the user chooses to click a button or edit a field, the computer lets them do just that in whatever order and at whatever time the user chooses. But sometimes, GUI programs need to stop the user and ask her a question, getting her to confirm or acknowledge something. That's where **message boxes** come in.

A *message box* is something that requires a response, which is why it's sometimes called a **dialog box**.

The simplest message box displays a message with a single **OK** button:

This icon shows it's a warning.

This is the message.

The user must click the "OK" button to continue, indicating that she acknowledges the message.

A message box always displays the message in a separate window, typically in front of your main GUI window. And it won't go away until you click it, dismissing it. That's why *message boxes* are the most commonly used way of displaying errors. The user *has* to read and respond to the error before continuing.

You should be sparing in how often you display message boxes, because if users see too many of them, they are likely to click them without reading the message. But, when used carefully, they keep your user informed and alert.

Creating message boxes in Python

All of the message box code is contained within a tkinter module called `messagebox`, so the first thing to do is import the module:

```
import tkinter.messagebox
```

Then, you're good to go. Within the `messagebox` module, there's a whole bunch of different dialogs to choose from. But all of them fall into two main categories.

Message boxes that <u>say</u> stuff

To display a simple message on the screen, you might display a message box like this:

The contents of the message.

```
tkinter.messagebox.showinfo("Delivery", "The cupcakes have arrived in Istanbul")
```

The title of the message box.

The icon in the window shows that this is just for information.

You need to click the OK button to close the dialog.

Message boxes that <u>ask</u> stuff

If you need a message box that asks the users a question, you will need to check the *return value* to see what they chose:

```
response = tkinter.messagebox.askyesnocancel("Gift?", "Gift wrap the package?")
```

A value is assigned to "response" after the user clicks one of the buttons.

When tkinter gets to this line, it will wait for the user to answer the question and then assign True (**yes**), False (**no**), or None (**cancel**) to the `response` variable.

Let's see what other message boxes are available.

These are the message boxes available in tkinter. Think carefully about each of the following examples. We know which we'd use at *Head First Labs*. Which type of box on the left would you choose for each of the messages on the right? Connect the messages to the boxes with lines.

showinfo   "OK to fire boosters?"

showwarning   "Your tartan clogs have arrived."

showerror   "Seriously, I think he's just ignoring the phone."

askquestion   "Danger, Will Robinson!"

askokcancel   "Do you want fries with that?"

askyesnocancel   "Dude, the printer's busted."

askretrycancel   "So, you want Nutella on your bacon and jelly sandwich?"

WHO DOES WHAT?
SOLUTION

These are the message boxes available in tkinter. You were to think
carefully about each of the following examples, then indicate which
type of box on the left you would choose for each of the messages on
the right. You were to connect the messages to the boxes with lines.

showinfo

showwarning

showerror

askquestion

askokcancel

askyesnocancel

askretrycancel

Are you REALLY sure you want to
continue and do this thing? It's your
last chance to change your mind.

"OK to fire boosters?"

This is pure information. Nothing
to worry about. Except the risk of
clashing with your velvet pixie hood.

"Your tartan clogs have arrived."

It didn't work last time, but if you like, you can try again.

"Seriously, I think he's just ignoring the phone."

OK, so there's nothing actually
broken YET, but BE CAREFUL

"Danger, Will Robinson!"

You are going to continue, but
do you want this extra option?

"Do you want fries with that?"

Stuff's broken. You need to know.

"Dude, the printer's busted."

Do you want this additional option, or would
you like to forget about the whole thing?

"So, you want Nutella on your bacon and jelly sandwich?"

Did your answers match ours? They might not. Selecting which type of message box to use
depends a lot upon the particular program you're writing and how serious you think a decision is.

Sharpen your pencil

The folks at Head-Ex want your program to display this message box if there's a problem saving a record to the `deliveries.txt` file:

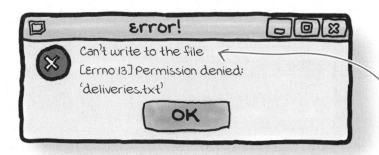

Complete the missing lines in this section of your program to create the message box.

Hint: You need to include a newline in the message box text.

```python
from tkinter import *

.........................................................................................

def save_data():
    try:
        fileD = open("deliveries.txt", "a")
        fileD.write("Depot:\n")
        fileD.write("%s\n" % depot.get())
        fileD.write("Description:\n")
        fileD.write("%s\n" % description.get())
        fileD.write("Address:\n")
        fileD.write("%s\n" % address.get("1.0", END))
        depot.set("")
        description.delete(0, END)
        description.delete(0, END)
        address.delete("1.0", END)
    except Exception as ex:

.........................................................................................
```

Sharpen your pencil
Solution

The folks at Head-Ex want your program to display this message box if there's a problem saving a record to the `deliveries.txt` file:

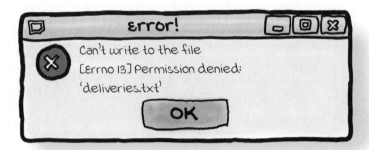

Complete the missing lines in this section of your program to create the message box.

Hint: You need to include a newline in the message box text.

```
from tkinter import *
```

Remember to import the necessary module. → `import tkinter.messagebox` ....

```
def save_data():
    try:
        fileD=open("deliveries.txt", "a")
        fileD.write("Depot\n")
        fileD.write("%s\n" % depot.get())
        fileD.write("Description\n")
        fileD.write("%s\n" % description.get())
        fileD.write("Address\n")
        fileD.write("%s\n" % address.get("1.0", END))
        depot.set("")
        description.delete(0, END)
        description.delete(0, END)
        address.delete("1.0", END)
    except Exception as ex:
```
.... `tkinter.messagebox.showerror("Error!", "Can't write to the file\n %s" % ex)` ....

You should use the showerror() function so that the dialog box gets the correct error icon.

TEST DRIVE

Now what happens if you try to save a record when the `deliveries.txt` file is read-only?

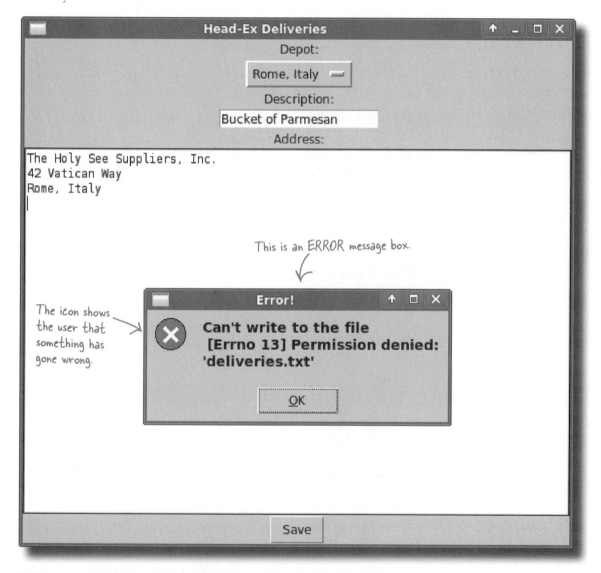

This is an ERROR message box.

The icon shows the user that something has gone wrong.

Great! The exception handler displays an error message with an icon that really alerts the user to the problem. Let's check back with Head-Ex to see if they like it.

That's exactly what we need. And not a moment too soon. We just had a delivery of durian, the world's stinkiest fruit. There's no way we want to leave THAT delivery too long in the stock room!

The error message box was exactly what Head-Ex needed.

By catching exceptions and displaying important information in message boxes, you can greatly improve the experience of your users when things go wrong.

Great work!

Your Programming Toolbox

You've got Chapter 8.5 under your belt. Let's look back at what you've learned in this chapter:

Programming Tools

✳ Some errors don't crash your program — they throw exceptions instead.

✳ You can run code when there's an exception — this is called "catching the exception."

✳ Code that runs because of an exception is called an exception handler.

✳ GUI message boxes display information and ask questions.

✳ Message boxes are also known as "dialog boxes."

✳ Message boxes require the user to respond, even if it is just to click an OK button.

Python Tools

✳ You can catch exceptions by using a try/except block.

✳ "except Exception as ex" will assign the exception message to a variable called "ex".

✳ You can display the exception error message by formatting it as a string.

✳ To display message boxes, you need to import the "tkinter.messagebox" module.

✳ Message boxes that display information are all called "show...()".

✳ Message boxes that ask questions are all called "ask...()".

✳ Message boxes return True if the response was OK, Yes, or Retry.

✳ Message boxes return False if the response was No.

✳ Message boxes return None if the response was Cancel.

9 graphical interface elements

Selecting the * *right tool*

> Oh, how lovely.

> Yikes! I was sure the salesman said the box contained an Ultimate GUI Toolkit™.

It's easy to make your programs more effective for your users.

And when it comes to GUI applications, there's a world of difference between a *working* interface and one that's both **useful** and **effective**. Selecting the right tool for the right job is a skill that comes with experience, and the best way to get that experience is to use the tools available to you. In this chapter, you'll continue to expand your GUI application building skills. There's a bunch of truly useful widgets waiting to be experienced. So, turn the page and let's get going.

Time to mix it up

Your best friend is an ultra hip DJ with a problem: his vinyl collection is now so *large* that he can't carry it all around from club to club anymore. He's decided to digitize his entire collection, put it on his laptop, and mix his sounds from there. His problem is that commercial mixing software *costs a fortune* and he doesn't like any of the free alternatives. He has his own ideas for the mixing software he wants.

What with spending all his time mixing music, he's never learned how to program his computer... and that's where you come in. If you help him to write the software he needs, he promises to showcase your work at the upcoming *World Music Mixing Expo*.

Let's build the mixing software bit-by-bit based on the DJ's requirements.

I'm dumping vinyl and going digital. Can you help me write my software? I need to be able to start and stop a track.

All of this has to go.

Code Magnets

A couple of buttons on a GUI ought to do it. Here's the code to a small tkinter program that starts and stops a sound file. Rearrange the code magnets to make the program:

```
from tkinter import *
import pygame.mixer
```

```
track = mixer.Sound(sound_file)
```

```
def track_start():
    track.play(loops = -1)
```

```
stop_button = Button(app, command = track_stop, text = "Stop")
stop_button.pack(side = RIGHT)
```

```
app.mainloop()
```

```
start_button = Button(app, command = track_start, text = "Start")
start_button.pack(side = LEFT)
```

```
def track_stop():
    track.stop()
```

```
mixer = pygame.mixer
mixer.init()
```

```
app = Tk()
app.title("Head First Mix")
app.geometry('250x100+200+100')
```

```
sound_file = "50459_M_RED_Nephlimizer.wav"
```

Code Magnets Solution

A couple of buttons on a GUI ought to do it. Here's the code to a small tkinter program that starts and stops a sound file. You were asked to rearrange the code magnets to make the program:

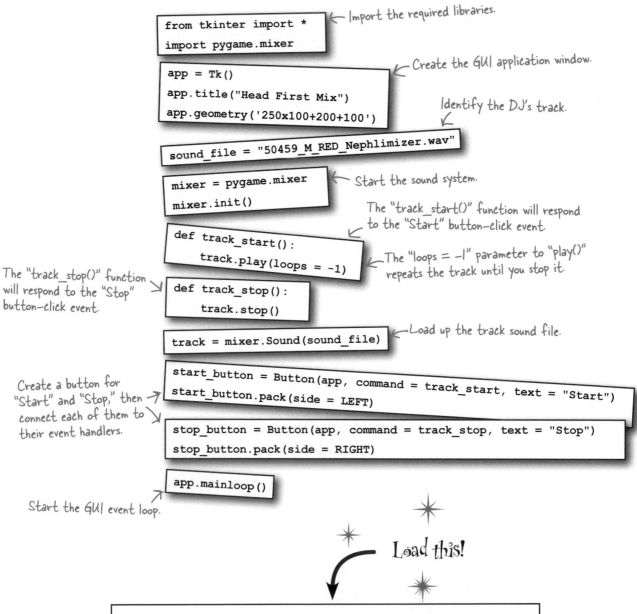

```python
from tkinter import *
import pygame.mixer
```
← Import the required libraries.

```python
app = Tk()
app.title("Head First Mix")
app.geometry('250x100+200+100')
```
← Create the GUI application window.

Identify the DJ's track.

```python
sound_file = "50459_M_RED_Nephlimizer.wav"
```

```python
mixer = pygame.mixer
mixer.init()
```
← Start the sound system.

The "track_start()" function will respond to the "Start" button-click event.

```python
def track_start():
    track.play(loops = -1)
```
← The "loops = –1" parameter to "play()" repeats the track until you stop it.

The "track_stop()" function will respond to the "Stop" button-click event.

```python
def track_stop():
    track.stop()
```

```python
track = mixer.Sound(sound_file)
```
← Load up the track sound file.

Create a button for "Start" and "Stop," then connect each of them to their event handlers.

```python
start_button = Button(app, command = track_start, text = "Start")
start_button.pack(side = LEFT)
```

```python
stop_button = Button(app, command = track_stop, text = "Stop")
stop_button.pack(side = RIGHT)
```

```python
app.mainloop()
```
Start the GUI event loop.

Load this!

Download the sound tracks for this chapter from the *Head First Programming* website. Be sure to put the sound files in the same directory/folder as your code.

Enter the code from the previous page into IDLE, save it as hfmix.pyw, and press F5 to try it out.

The first version of the DJ's program entered in IDLE.

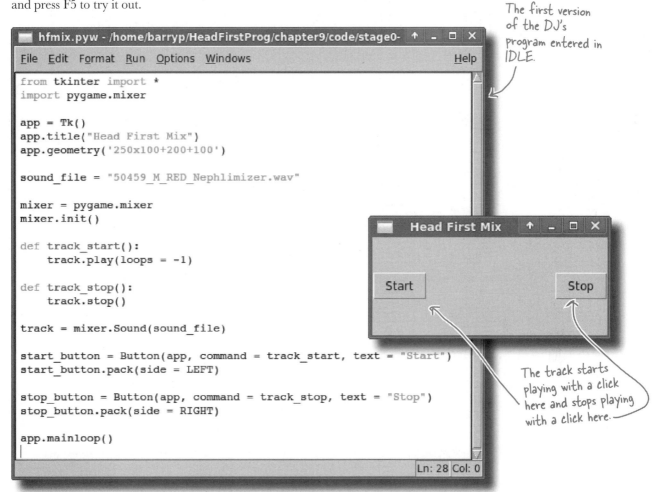

```
hfmix.pyw - /home/barryp/HeadFirstProg/chapter9/code/stage0-
File   Edit   Format   Run   Options   Windows                    Help

from tkinter import *
import pygame.mixer

app = Tk()
app.title("Head First Mix")
app.geometry('250x100+200+100')

sound_file = "50459_M_RED_Nephlimizer.wav"

mixer = pygame.mixer
mixer.init()

def track_start():
    track.play(loops = -1)

def track_stop():
    track.stop()

track = mixer.Sound(sound_file)

start_button = Button(app, command = track_start, text = "Start")
start_button.pack(side = LEFT)

stop_button = Button(app, command = track_stop, text = "Stop")
stop_button.pack(side = RIGHT)

app.mainloop()

                                                    Ln: 28 Col: 0
```

The track starts playing with a click here and stops playing with a click here.

You already know how to display buttons on a GUI and associate them with event-handling code. What's new in this code is the loops = -1 bit, which arranges to play the sound repeatedly. That is, the track *loops*.

That was almost too easy!

That's not a bad start...

The music just kept on playing...

In his haste to show off your program to his DJ rivals, your friend fired up the program *as is*. He didn't realize that the track you included by default is pretty *bad*. In a panic, he clicked the window's close box before pressing Stop, and the awful track *just kept right on playing*. His rivals haven't had such a good laugh in ages...

Not all events are generated by button clicks

Your GUI program processes lots of events, not just the events generated by your user when, for instance, buttons are clicked.

Your operating system can send events to your GUI program, too. Some of these events are commonly handled by the graphical programming technology you are working with. For most of the operating system's events, tkinter very kindly handles them for you. When you click the close box on your GUI, this generates a **Window Manager** event for your code to handle. If your code doesn't handle a Window Manager event, tkinter handles it for you in a default way, too.

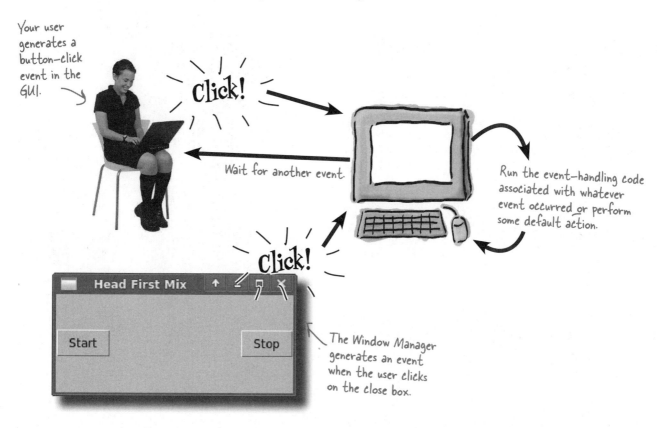

Your user generates a button-click event in the GUI.

Click!

Wait for another event.

Run the event-handling code associated with whatever event occurred or perform some default action.

Click!

Head First Mix

Start   Stop

The Window Manager generates an event when the user clicks on the close box.

If the default event handling *isn't* what you want, you have to **capture** the event before it gets to tkinter and is handled in the default way. At the moment, the click on the close box is being handled for you by tkinter and the default behavior is to *close the window.*

Let's take control of this default behavior.

Frank: What's up now?

Joe: Well, it looks like I have to worry about lots of other GUI events, not just my own.

Jim: Yeah. It appears the operating system *and* this Window Manager thing can give the GUI application work to do.

Frank: Yes, that's right. All that interactive loveliness comes at a cost.

Joe: Cost?!? You mean we have to pay?

Frank: No, not *that* sort of cost. You sometimes need to write a little extra code to interact with the Window Manager when and where necessary... that's what I mean by "cost."

Joe: Phew! So... what's a Window Manager, anyway?

Frank: It's something built into every GUI application that handles the management of your application's windows. Python's GUI, tkinter, has a Window Manager, as do all the other GUI toolkits.

Joe: So, how do I work with the events generated by the Window Manager?

Frank: You create a function with the code you want to run and then connect the function to the event.

Joe: OK, I get that. But which event do I connect up to? It's not like the Window Manager has a button to click on, is it?

Jim: That's a good question... Frank?

Frank: Well spotted. What happens with the Window Manager is that there's a set of protocol properties that you can interact with as and when required.

Joe: Protocol *what?* Properties?

Jim: Yeah, you've lost me there, Frank.

Frank: Yes, *protocol properties*... they really are not as scary as they sound. Remember: with GUIs, *it's all just code*.

Jim & Joe: Where have we heard *that* before... ?

Frank: Here, let me show you what I mean...

> You see, GUIs might look nice and easy, but they are actually a pretty complicated beast under the hood. There's lots of different events to worry about.

Joe

Frank

Jim

Study the three tkinter properties presented below and see if you can match up the properties to the correct description:

`WM_TAKE_FOCUS`

A message sent to your main window when the operating system is shutting down

`WM_SAVE_YOURSELF`

A message sent to your main window when the close box has been clicked

`WM_DELETE_WINDOW`

A message sent to your main window when the window has been selected after a mouse click

Which of these protocol messages do you think you need to capture?

Geek Bits

The tkinter library provides a mechanism to react to an event that is associated with the GUI window. These are known as Window Manager protocol properties. Think of the event as a *protocol event.*

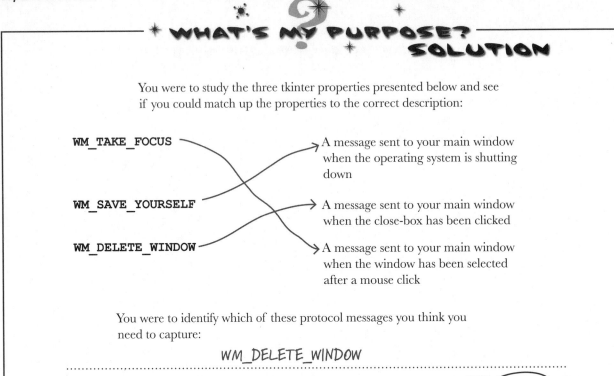

✦ WHAT'S MY PURPOSE? ❓ SOLUTION

You were to study the three tkinter properties presented below and see if you could match up the properties to the correct description:

WM_TAKE_FOCUS ——————→ A message sent to your main window when the operating system is shutting down

WM_SAVE_YOURSELF ——————→ A message sent to your main window when the close-box has been clicked

WM_DELETE_WINDOW ——————→ A message sent to your main window when the window has been selected after a mouse click

You were to identify which of these protocol messages you think you need to capture:

WM_DELETE_WINDOW

OK... here comes a click on the close box. What's my protocol? Ah, yes... it hasn't been captured, so I'll just execute the default behavior and close that sucker!

Controlling the Window Manager

To **capture** the event *before* it gets to tkinter, call your app's `protocol()` method and identify the function that should be called *instead of* executing the default behavior:

You'll have to create the "shutdown" function.

↓

Be sure to call "protocol()" BEFORE "mainloop()".

→
```
app.protocol("WM_DELETE_WINDOW", shutdown)
```
←

Associate the event-handling function with the property.

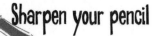 Sharpen your pencil

Now that you know about window manager properties and how to capture them, write the code for the `shutdown()` function:

Here's the code so far.

```
from tkinter import *
import pygame.mixer

app = Tk()
app.title("Head First Mix")
app.geometry('250x100+200+100')

sound_file = "50459_M_RED_Nephlimizer.wav"

mixer = pygame.mixer
mixer.init()

def track_start():
    track.play(loops = -1)

def track_stop():
    track.stop()
```

Put the "shutdown" function here.
```
..................................................................................
..................................................................................
..................................................................................
```

```
track = mixer.Sound(sound_file)

start_button = Button(app, command = track_start, text = "Start")
start_button.pack(side = LEFT)
stop_button = Button(app, command = track_stop, text = "Stop")
stop_button.pack(side = RIGHT)
```

What needs to go here?
```
..................................................................................
app.mainloop()
```

Sharpen your pencil
Solution

Now that you know about window manager properties and how to capture them, you were asked to write the code for the `shutdown()` function:

```python
from tkinter import *
import pygame.mixer

app = Tk()
app.title("Head First Mix")
app.geometry('250x100+200+100')

sound_file = "50459_M_RED_Nephlimizer.wav"

mixer = pygame.mixer
mixer.init()

def track_start():
    track.play(loops = -1)

def track_stop():
    track.stop()

def shutdown():
    track.stop()
```

Simply arrange for the track to stop playing when the window closes.

```python
track = mixer.Sound(sound_file)

start_button = Button(app, command = track_start, text = "Start")
start_button.pack(side = LEFT)
stop_button = Button(app, command = track_stop, text = "Stop")
stop_button.pack(side = RIGHT)
```

Call "app.protocol()" before the call to "app.mainloop()".

```python
app.protocol("WM_DELETE_WINDOW", shutdown)

app.mainloop()
```

TEST DRIVE

With the changes made to your program in IDLE, press F5 to see how things perform now.

No matter how often you click the close box, the window won't go away...

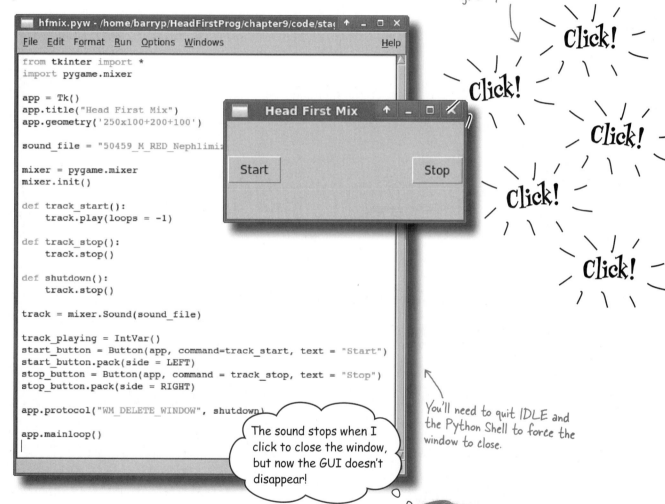

```
hfmix.pyw - /home/barryp/HeadFirstProg/chapter9/code/sta

File  Edit  Format  Run  Options  Windows                    Help

from tkinter import *
import pygame.mixer

app = Tk()
app.title("Head First Mix")
app.geometry('250x100+200+100')

sound_file = "50459_M_RED_Nephlimiz

mixer = pygame.mixer
mixer.init()

def track_start():
    track.play(loops = -1)

def track_stop():
    track.stop()

def shutdown():
    track.stop()

track = mixer.Sound(sound_file)

track_playing = IntVar()
start_button = Button(app, command=track_start, text = "Start")
start_button.pack(side = LEFT)
stop_button = Button(app, command = track_stop, text = "Stop")
stop_button.pack(side = RIGHT)

app.protocol("WM_DELETE_WINDOW", shutdown)

app.mainloop()
```

Click! Click! Click! Click! Click!

The sound stops when I click to close the window, but now the GUI doesn't disappear!

You'll need to quit IDLE and the Python Shell to force the window to close.

What gives? You've solved one problem, but created *another*. When the DJ clicks on the close box, the track stops playing, which *is* what you wanted. But now, the window won't close.

This can't be good, can it?

Capturing the protocol event isn't enough

Your code captures the protocol event and *redefines its behavior*. But, what about the behavior that used to execute *by default*?

Take a look at this small example program, which redefines the close-box protocol to check with the user before actually destroying the window:

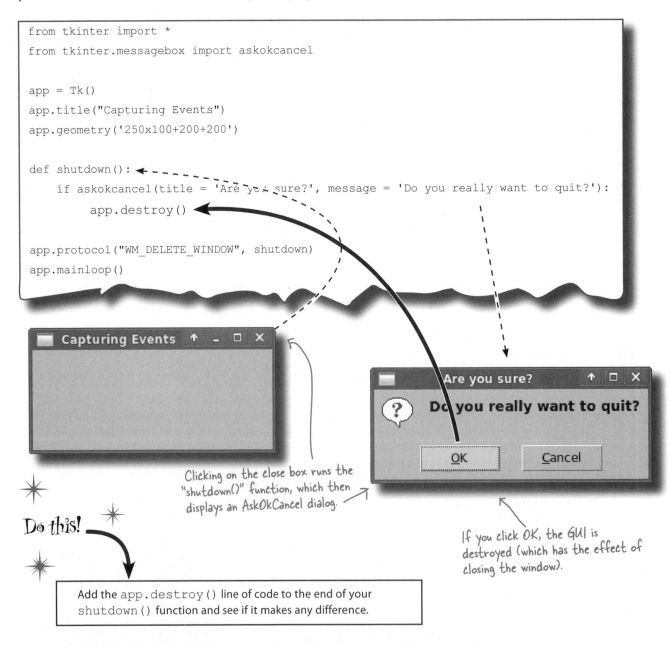

```
from tkinter import *
from tkinter.messagebox import askokcancel

app = Tk()
app.title("Capturing Events")
app.geometry('250x100+200+200')

def shutdown():
    if askokcancel(title = 'Are you sure?', message = 'Do you really want to quit?'):
        app.destroy()

app.protocol("WM_DELETE_WINDOW", shutdown)
app.mainloop()
```

Clicking on the close box runs the "shutdown()" function, which then displays an AskOkCancel dialog.

If you click OK, the GUI is destroyed (which has the effect of closing the window).

Do this!

Add the `app.destroy()` line of code to the end of your `shutdown()` function and see if it makes any difference.

Test Drive

You've added in the line of code that terminates (destroys) your GUI application. Now, press F5 to see what happens.

```
hfmix.pyw - /home/barryp/HeadFirstProg/chapter9/code/stage

File   Edit   Format   Run   Options   Windows                    Help

from tkinter import *
import pygame.mixer

app = Tk()
app.title("Head First Mix")
app.geometry('250x100+200+100')

sound_file = "50459_M_RED_Nephlimizer.wav"

mixer = pygame.mixer
mixer.init()

def track_start():
    track.play(loops = -1)

def track_stop():
    track.stop()

def shutdown():
    track.stop()
    app.destroy()

track = mixer.Sound(sound_file)

track_playing = IntVar()
start_button = Button(app, command=track_start, text = "Start")
start_button.pack(side = LEFT)
stop_button = Button(app, command = track_stop, text = "Stop")
stop_button.pack(side = RIGHT)

app.protocol("WM_DELETE_WINDOW", shutdown)

app.mainloop()

                                                    Ln: 34  Col: 0
```

When you click on the close box now, the GUI application disappears. Which helps explain why you can't see it on this page anymore!

This extra line of code makes all the difference.

That's great! Let's see my rivals scoff now...

Your GUI is not only doing what the DJ wants; it's behaving itself, too. By redefining the protocol event associated with the click on the close box, you are able to stop the track... eh... in its tracks. You also ensure that the default behavior associated with the click is performed by arranging to destroy the GUI application.

That's great!

Two buttons, or not two buttons?
That is the question...

The DJ is happy with the program so far. However, he thinks it would work better if he had just one button instead of two. He's convinced this would be easier to use, because he wouldn't have to move his mouse around the screen quite so much.

> Speed's important, dude. Can't I just press the button to start the track, then press it again to stop it?

2 buttons or not 2 buttons? ↑ – □ ✕

Start/Stop

Will the next click start or stop whatever this button does?

It *is* possible to use a single button here but, without changing the physical appearance of the button each time it's clicked, a user can't possibly know what *state* the button is currently in, even though the DJ does have ears *in this instance*. But, in general, using a button to switch between two states is *not* regarded as best practice in GUI design.

What your DJ friend actually wants is some sort of **visual toggle**... something that can be flipped between one of two states: on/off, open/close, flip/flop, and so on. You need to use a *different* graphical interface element.

Is there a GUI visual toggle you can use here?

Take a look at the following window that appears when you ask a full-featured web browser to display its preferences. Grab a pencil and draw a circle around any graphical interface elements you haven't worked with yet.

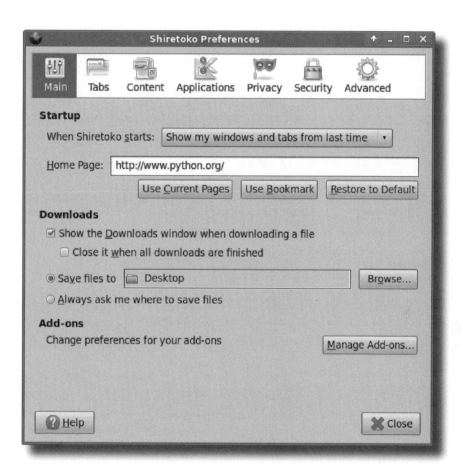

From the elements that you have circled, identify one that might be of use to you in your program. Which would work best as an on/off toggle?

Write your answer here. ↘

....

Exercise Solution

Take a look at the following window that appears when you ask a full-featured web browser to display its preferences. You were to grab a pencil and draw a circle around any graphical interface element you haven't worked with yet.

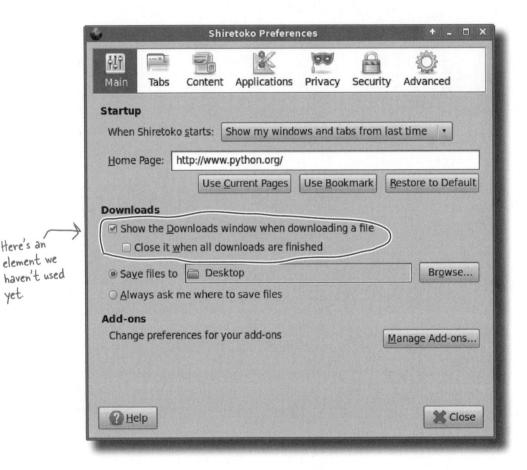

Here's an element we haven't used yet.

From the elements that you have circled, identify one that might be of use to you in your program. You were asked to identify an element that would work best as an on/off toggle:

The checkbox is either on or off. → The checkbox

The checkbox is an on/off, flip/flop toggle

The great thing about the checkbox graphical interface element is that it can be in only one of two states, either *on* or *off*. Depending on the current state of the checkbox, an object can be set to either 1 for "on" or 0 for "off."

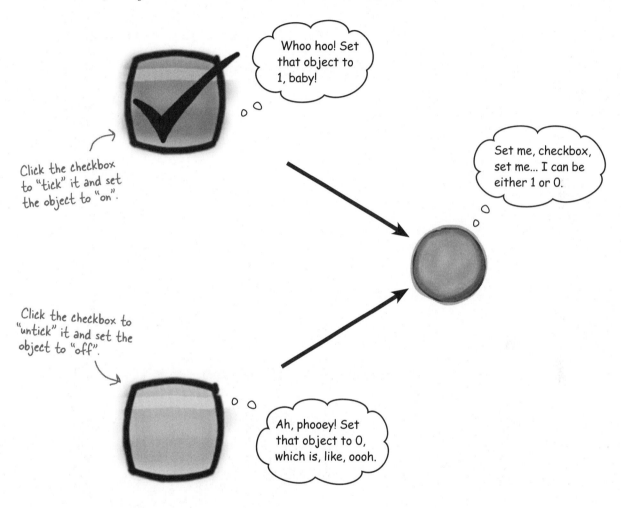

Whoo hoo! Set that object to 1, baby!

Click the checkbox to "tick" it and set the object to "on".

Set me, checkbox, set me... I can be either 1 or 0.

Click the checkbox to "untick" it and set the object to "off".

Ah, phooey! Set that object to 0, which is, like, oooh.

In tkinter, checkboxes are created using Checkbutton(), and they can be associated with a tkinter IntVar, first introduced in Chapter 7. The tkinter Checkbutton() is either on or off and sets the associated IntVar to either 1 or 0, which is perfect for what you need.

Let's look at using a checkbox in tkinter.

Working with checkboxes in tkinter

The tkinter `Checkbutton` needs three things: an `IntVar` to hold its current value, an event-handler function to run when it's ticked, and a descriptive label to say what it does. Take a look at this example code:

```
flipper = IntVar()
```
← Create an "IntVar" to hold a value that is either 1 or 0, depending on whether the checkbox is ticked.

The "flip_it()" function is the Checkbutton's event handler. ↘

```
def flip_it():
    if flipper.get() == 1:
        print("Cool. I'm all ON, man!")
    else:
        print("Phooey. I'm OFF.")
```

The Checkbutton is → associated with the "IntVar", links to the event handler, and has a descriptive label, too.

```
Checkbutton(app, variable = flipper,
                 command  = flip_it,
                 text     = "Flip it?").pack()
```

Using the get() method

If you look closely at the code for the `flip_it()` event handler, you'll notice that the message displayed on screen is controlled by whatever value is returned from the call to `flipper.get()`. The `get()` method is part of every `IntVar` object, and it lets you easily determine, in this case, the current value associated with the `flipper` variable.

But, what *sets* the value?

The `Checkbutton` automatically sets the value of `flipper` as a result of the click on the checkbox. Tick the box and the value is set to 1. Untick the box and the value is set to 0.

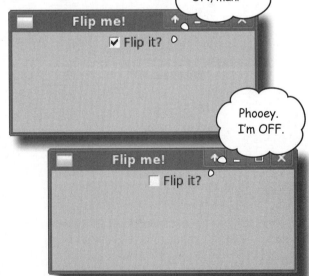

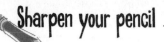
Sharpen your pencil

1 Here's your code from earlier. Use your pencil to put a line through the code you don't need anymore:

```python
from tkinter import *
import pygame.mixer

app = Tk()
app.title("Head First Mix")
app.geometry('250x100+200+100')

sound_file = "50459_M_RED_Nephlimizer.wav"

mixer = pygame.mixer
mixer.init()

def track_start():
    track.play(loops = -1)

def track_stop():
    track.stop()

def shutdown():
    track.stop()
    app.destroy()

track = mixer.Sound(sound_file)

start_button = Button(app, command = track_start, text = "Start")
start_button.pack(side = LEFT)
stop_button = Button(app, command = track_stop, text = "Stop")
stop_button.pack(side = RIGHT)

app.protocol("WM_DELETE_WINDOW", shutdown)
app.mainloop()
```

2 Write the code you need to implement the checkbox here, based on the sample code from the previous page. Give your `IntVar` the name `track_playing`. Use `track_toggle` as your function name, and call the checkbox `track_button`:

....

....

....

....

....

....

....

....

....

....

Sharpen your pencil
Solution

1 Here's your code from earlier. You were to use your pencil to put a line through the code you don't need anymore:

```python
from tkinter import *
import pygame.mixer

app = Tk()
app.title("Head First Mix")
app.geometry('250x100+200+100')

sound_file = "50459_M_RED_Nephlimizer.wav"

mixer = pygame.mixer
mixer.init()

def track_start():
    track.play(loops = -1)

def track_stop():
    track.stop()

def shutdown():
    track.stop()
    app.destroy()

track = mixer.Sound(sound_file)

start_button = Button(app, command = track_start, text = "Start")
start_button.pack(side = LEFT)
stop_button = Button(app, command = track_stop, text = "Stop")
stop_button.pack(side = RIGHT)

app.protocol("WM_DELETE_WINDOW", shutdown)
app.mainloop()
```

The functions that start and stop the track are no longer needed.

You can also get rid of the two buttons, since they aren't needed either.

2 Write the code you need to implement the checkbox here. You were asked to give your `IntVar` the name `track_playing`, use `track_toggle` as your function name, and call the checkbox `track_button`:

The "track_toggle" function either plays or stops the track, based on the state of the checkbox.

```python
def track_toggle():
    if track_playing.get() == 1:
        track.play(loops = -1)
    else:
        track.stop()
track_playing = IntVar()
track_button = Checkbutton(app, variable = track_playing,
                                command = track_toggle,
                                text     = sound_file)
track_button.pack()
```

All of this code needs to be added to your program BEFORE the call to "app.mainloop()".

Use the name of the sound file as the text associated with the checkbox.

Test Drive

With your program amended to include the checkbox code, let's run the latest version of the DJ's program in IDLE and see if the checkbox works as advertised.

```
hfmix.pyw - /home/barryp/HeadFirstProg/chapter9/co    ↑  _  □  ×
File  Edit  Format  Run  Options  Windows                    Help

from tkinter import *
import pygame.mixer

app = Tk()
app.title("Head First Mix")
app.geometry('250x100+200+100')

sound_file = "50459_M_RED_Nephlimizer.wav"

mixer = pygame.mixer
mixer.init()

def track_toggle():
    if track_playing.get() == 1:
        track.play(loops = -1)
    else:
        track.stop()

track = mixer.Sound(sound_file)

track_playing = IntVar()

track_button = Checkbutton(app, variable = track_playing,
                                command  = track_toggle,
                                text     = sound_file)
track_button.pack()

def shutdown():
    track.stop()
    app.destroy()

app.protocol("WM_DELETE_WINDOW", shutdown)
app.mainloop()
|
                                                      Ln: 34  Col: 0
```

Sweet! Toggle the sound on and off by simply clicking on the checkbox.

Creating the program bit by bit is working out. Each time your DJ friend needs something new, you incrementally improve the program in order to provide the functionalilty he needs. Of course, there's *always* something new.

Will this guy ever be satisfied?!?

Man, that's so easy to use! Let's adjust the volume, too, while the sound is playing...

Pump up the volume!

To make the program more useful, the DJ wants to be able to dynamically and interactively control the volume of the track as it plays. Basically, as the track plays, the DJ wants to fiddle with the volume.

Louder!

Softer, softer, softer...

In the physical world, most devices that have a volume control provide either a large, circular knob or a slider on a scale:

The control might look like this, a slider that can be moved from left (down) to right (up)...

...or the control might look like this. Turn it up to the right, down to the left..

Because a slider is much easier to manipulate with a click and drag of a mouse than a knob, the *slider on a scale* is used in lots of modern GUIs. It's the *classic choice* for showing a volume control.

Look closely at the slider. What do you need to model?

Model a slider on a scale

There's quite a bit going on with a slider on a scale. It's a *simple* control that everyone's familiar with, but the simplicity masks quite a bit of *complexity*. The devil is most definitely in the details:

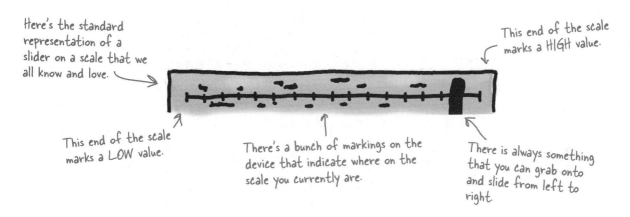

Here's the standard representation of a slider on a scale that we all know and love.

This end of the scale marks a HIGH value.

This end of the scale marks a LOW value.

There's a bunch of markings on the device that indicate where on the scale you currently are.

There is always something that you can grab onto and slide from left to right.

Sharpen your pencil

Look at the volume control shown above and identify four key characteristics of the volume control.

Write your four answers here.

1. ....

....

2. ....

....

3. ....

....

4. ....

....

Sharpen your pencil
Solution

You were to look at the volume control on the previous page and identify four key characteristics of the volume control.

1. There's a scale that goes from a low value to a high value.

2. The scale has a fixed set of intervals.

3. The volume control "slider" moves from left to right.

4. Moving the "slider" dynamically adjusts the volume based on its current position on the scale.

Start with the volume

Before you start worrying about creating the appropriate GUI interface element to actually model the slider, you first need to know how to adjust the volume of a track.

Once you know how to adjust the volume, you can then start to worry about linking the volume to the slider, with the current position of the slider dictating the current volume setting.

Then you can allow your user to *move the slider* which has the effect of dynamically and interactively adjusting the volume.

Sounds easy, eh?

Use pygame to set the volume

Turns out pygame has this functionality built right into its library code via the `set_volume()` method.

Take a look at this small example program:

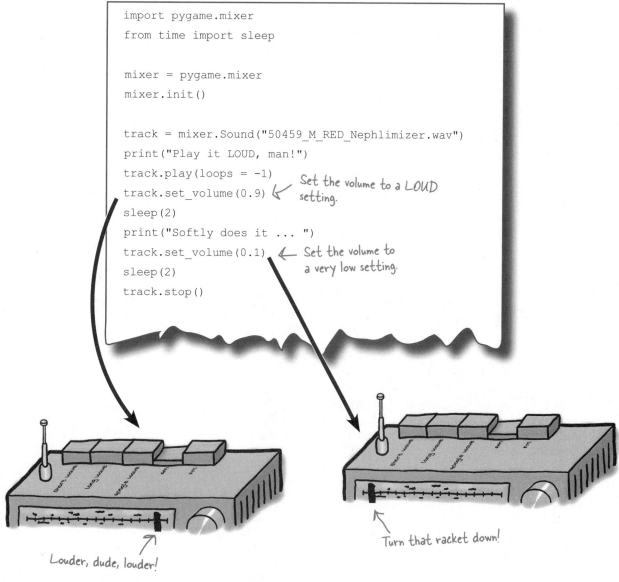

```
import pygame.mixer
from time import sleep

mixer = pygame.mixer
mixer.init()

track = mixer.Sound("50459_M_RED_Nephlimizer.wav")
print("Play it LOUD, man!")
track.play(loops = -1)
track.set_volume(0.9)
sleep(2)
print("Softly does it ... ")
track.set_volume(0.1)
sleep(2)
track.stop()
```

Set the volume to a LOUD setting.

Set the volume to a very low setting.

Louder, dude, louder!

Turn that racket down!

When you set the track's volume to a high value using `set_volume()`, it's the equivalent of *cranking up the volume* by moving the slider to the right. When you set it to a low value, that's like moving the slider to the left.

Use tkinter for everything else

The tkinter library has a graphical interface element called `Scale` that lives
to help you create a slider. Take a look at this example code and let's see how
it works:

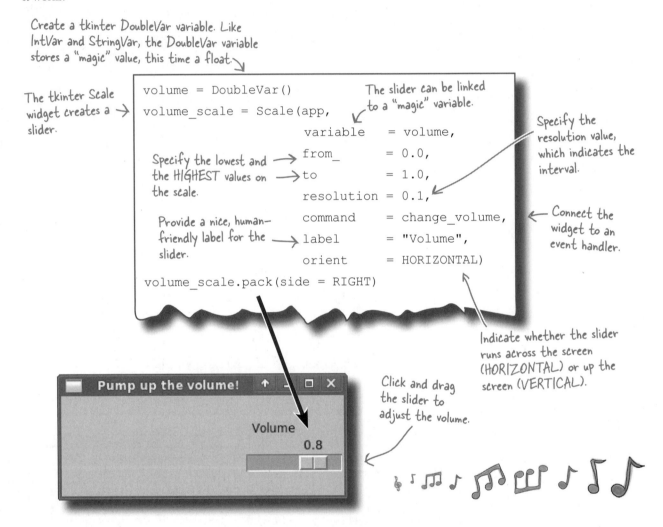

Create a tkinter DoubleVar variable. Like
IntVar and StringVar, the DoubleVar variable
stores a "magic" value, this time a float.

The tkinter Scale
widget creates a →
slider.

```
volume = DoubleVar()
volume_scale = Scale(app,
                          variable   = volume,
                          from_      = 0.0,
                          to         = 1.0,
                          resolution = 0.1,
                          command    = change_volume,
                          label      = "Volume",
                          orient     = HORIZONTAL)
volume_scale.pack(side = RIGHT)
```

The slider can be linked
to a "magic" variable.

Specify the lowest and →
the HIGHEST values on →
the scale.

Specify the
resolution value,
which indicates the
interval.

Provide a nice, human–
friendly label for the →
slider.

← Connect the
widget to an
event handler.

Indicate whether the slider
runs across the screen
(HORIZONTAL) or up the
screen (VERTICAL).

Pump up the volume!

Volume

0.8

Click and drag
the slider to
adjust the volume.

The `Scale()` element is your most complex tkinter widget yet. But, despite
this, it is not hard to work out what's going on here. The graphical interface
element is linked to a tkinter DoubleVar (called `variable`), the lowest/
highest slider values are provided (`to` and `from_`), and an interval between
them (`resolution`) is specified. The event handler is associated with an
event handler (`command`), a descriptive label is supplied (`label`), and, finally,
the orientation of the slider is specified (`orient`). There's a lot going on
here, but none of it is that hard to understand.

there are no
Dumb Questions

Q: The Scale() code on the previous page has a variable called from_, that is, the word "from" together with a trailing underscore. Was that a typo?

A: No, it wasn't a tyop, eh, typo. The reason for the underscore has to do with the fact that Python uses "from" as a *reserved word*. These are words that Python uses for its own **special purposes**, which means you cannot name one of your variables after a reserved word. As using the word "from" makes a lot of sense when taking about a scale, the authors of tkinter decided to tack on the underscore so that the meaning of the variable would be clear, while allowing for the variable name not to clash with a reserved word.

Q: Are there other reserved words?

A: Yes, a few. And every programming language has its own list. In Python, words like "while", "for", "if", "def", "class", and "pass" are all reserved words.

Q: What happens if I use one anyway?

A: Python will most likely complain with a syntax error.

Q: Where can I find a list?

A: Any good Python reference book will contain a list, and it's also included as part of the Python documentation that's installed with Python on your computer and available on the web at the main Python website.

Q: How do I know which graphical interface element to use and when?

A: This is really a matter of experience. However, a lot of platforms go to great lengths to specify exactly when each of the elements should be used and for what purpose. Of them all, the Macintosh is the leader of the pack. Apple's engineers have worked hard to strictly enforce consistent usage of the Mac GUI among programmers.

Q: So, it's a case of anything goes with the other operating systems?

A: No. That's not what we are saying. The Apple folks are very strict with their rules and regulations, and the others are less so. But there are still standards that you should try as much as possible to adhere to. One of the reasons for using a GUI is that your users will expect your program to work in a standard way. This makes your program immediately familiar to new users and lets them become productive with your program more quickly.

Q: So there are no badly designed GUI apps?

A: No. There are plenty of howlers out there... and they tend to be harder to use than necessary, due to the fact that the programmers responsible for creating them did not conform to established interface standards and practices. When it comes to GUI programs, *conformance is a good thing.*

Q: So does tkinter work well on all platforms?

A: The latest version of tkinter (which comes with Python 3) is pretty good. If you run your tkinter program on a Mac, it looks like a Mac OS X program, whereas on Windows it looks like a Windows application, and on Linux it takes on the look and feel of the graphical environment you happen to be using (there are a few choices on Linux).

Q: Other than tkinter, what other graphical toolkits does Python support, and should I learn any of them?

A: Python supports lots of other toolkits on lots of operating systems. For now, tkinter is all you really need, and you shouldn't worry about the other choices until you are in a situation where learning how to use them becomes a necessity.

Long Exercise

Take the pygame and tkinter code and combine it to support a volume control. Then, complete the next version of your program.

```python
from tkinter import *
import pygame.mixer
app = Tk()
app.title("Head First Mix")
app.geometry('250x100+200+100')


sound_file = "50459_M_RED_Nephlimizer.wav"


mixer = pygame.mixer
mixer.init()


def track_toggle():
    if track_playing.get() == 1:
        track.play(loops = -1)
    else:
        track.stop()
```

Add a function here to adjust the volume that the track currently plays at.

....

....

....

....

....

....

....

....

```
track = mixer.Sound(sound_file)
track_playing = IntVar()
track_button = Checkbutton(app, variable = track_playing,
                                command  = track_toggle,
                                text     = sound_file)
track_button.pack(side = LEFT)
```

....

....

Add the code
that implements
the volume
control here. → ....

....

....

....

....

....

....

....

```
def shutdown():
    track.stop()
    app.destroy()


app.protocol("WM_DELETE_WINDOW", shutdown)
app.mainloop()
```

LONG EXERCISE SOLUTION

You were to take the pygame and tkinter code and combine it to support a volume control, then complete the next version of your program.

```
from tkinter import *
import pygame.mixer
app = Tk()
app.title("Head First Mix")
app.geometry('250x100+200+100')

sound_file = "50459_M_RED_Nephlimizer.wav"


mixer = pygame.mixer
mixer.init()


def track_toggle():
    if track_playing.get() == 1:
        track.play(loops = -1)
    else:
        track.stop()
```

Things are starting to get crowded on the GUI, so let's have tkinter automatically decide on the geometry for us. Remove the "app. geometry()" call from the code.

Put the pygame code here.

```
def change_volume(v):
    track.set_volume(volume.get())
```

```
        track = mixer.Sound(sound_file)
        track_playing = IntVar()
        track_button = Checkbutton(app, variable = track_playing,
                                        command  = track_toggle,
                                        text     = sound_file)
        track_button.pack(side = LEFT)
```

Put the tkinter ——→
code here.

```
        volume = DoubleVar()

        volume.set(track.get_volume())

        volume_scale = Scale(variable  = volume,

                        from_      = 0.0,

                        to         = 1.0,

                        resolution = 0.1,

                        command    = change_volume,

                        label      = "Volume",

                        orient     = HORIZONTAL)

        volume_scale.pack(side = RIGHT)
```

```
    def shutdown():
        track.stop()
        app.destroy()


    app.protocol("WM_DELETE_WINDOW", shutdown)
    app.mainloop()
```

Test Drive

Let's take the latest version of the program for a spin in IDLE. In addition to turning the sound on and off with the checkbox, you should be able to dynamically and interactively adjust the volume with the slider.

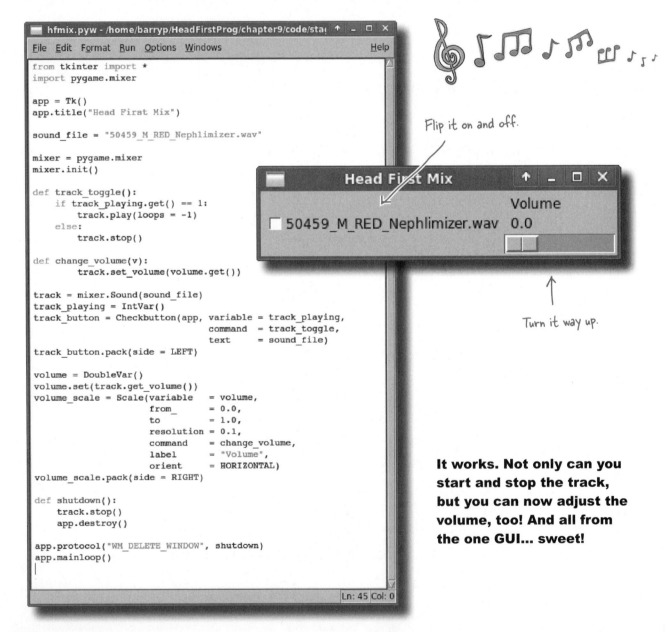

```
from tkinter import *
import pygame.mixer

app = Tk()
app.title("Head First Mix")

sound_file = "50459_M_RED_Nephlimizer.wav"

mixer = pygame.mixer
mixer.init()

def track_toggle():
    if track_playing.get() == 1:
        track.play(loops = -1)
    else:
        track.stop()

def change_volume(v):
        track.set_volume(volume.get())

track = mixer.Sound(sound_file)
track_playing = IntVar()
track_button = Checkbutton(app, variable = track_playing,
                                command  = track_toggle,
                                text     = sound_file)

track_button.pack(side = LEFT)

volume = DoubleVar()
volume.set(track.get_volume())
volume_scale = Scale(variable   = volume,
                     from_      = 0.0,
                     to         = 1.0,
                     resolution = 0.1,
                     command    = change_volume,
                     label      = "Volume",
                     orient     = HORIZONTAL)
volume_scale.pack(side = RIGHT)

def shutdown():
    track.stop()
    app.destroy()

app.protocol("WM_DELETE_WINDOW", shutdown)
app.mainloop()
```

hfmix.pyw - /home/barryp/HeadFirstProg/chapter9/code/sta

File Edit Format Run Options Windows   Help

Ln: 45 Col: 0

Flip it on and off.

Head First Mix

☐ 50459_M_RED_Nephlimizer.wav   Volume
0.0

Turn it way up.

It works. Not only can you start and stop the track, but you can now adjust the volume, too! And all from the one GUI... sweet!

The DJ is over the moon!

Your code has shown the DJ that his idea for the Ultimate Music Mixing program is not as far-fetched as everyone once thought. With his idea, talent, good looks, and—above all else—modesty, *together with* your **coding skills**, the world's the limit for what you can accomplish together. The World Music Mixing Expo is next month, and the DJ can't wait to show off your *completed software*.

Your Programming Toolbox

**You've got Chapter 9 under your belt.
Let's look back at what you've learned
in this chapter:**

Programming Tools

* The Window Manager manages the windows created by your GUI.

* GUI events can be generated by the operating system, the Window Manager, and your user.

* If you redefine some default functionality, be sure to code the default behavior into your code (if required).

* A checkbox lets you indicate whether something is set to ON or OFF.

* A scale/slider lets you implement a volume control.

* Be sure to look at other GUI programs when looking for inspiration and ideas for your own programs.

* Reserved words are names that have special meaning in a programming language and which cannot be used as variable names.

Python Tools

* app.destroy() – used to terminate a tkinter GUI application

* DoubleVar() – like IntVar and StringVar, but used to hold a floating-point number

* Checkbutton() – a tkinter widget for creating checkboxes

* Scale() – a tkinter widget for creating scales/sliders

10 custom widgets and classes

✳ *With an object in mind* ✳

Since we learned about custom widgets and object orientation, we've become a real class act.

Requirements can be complex, but programs don't have to be.

By using *object orientation*, you can give your programs **great power** without writing lots of extra code. Keep reading, and you'll create **custom widgets** that do exactly what *you* want and give you the power to take **your programming skills to the next level**.

The DJ wants to play more than one track

The *World Music Mixing Expo* is only a few weeks away. Your DJ friend is thrilled with the work you've done, but now he has a few extra requirements.

Just playing *one track* isn't enough. To be useful, the program needs to be able to *mix* several tracks together at the same time. Each track needs its own graphical interface elements (or *widgets*).

> I can fade a track in and out, but that's not enough. I need to be able to mix several tracks together.

How will you create the widgets for each track?

To play and control a single track, you created two **widgets** on the GUI: a *check button* to start and stop the track and a *scale* to change the volume. Then you added **event-handling code** to hook those widgets up to the sound system.

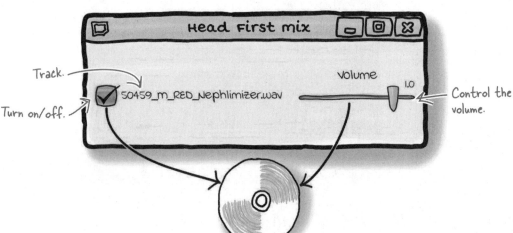

Track.

Turn on/off.

Head First mix

Volume

50459_m_RED_Nephlimizer.wav

1.0

Control the volume.

To play multiple tracks together, you just need *more of the same*. Each track will need its *own set of widgets* and its *own event handlers* to connect the widgets and the track together. Then, each set of widgets needs to be added to the same window in the GUI.

Let's generate the widgets and event handlers.

Create code for each track as a function

You *could* just copy and paste the code several times for each track. But duplicated code is a **bad idea**, because it can lead to all sorts of problems whenever you need to change how the code for each track works. Instead of *duplicating* code, you should always try to *reuse* it.

One way to reuse code is by creating a function that will generate the widgets and the event handlers *as needed*.

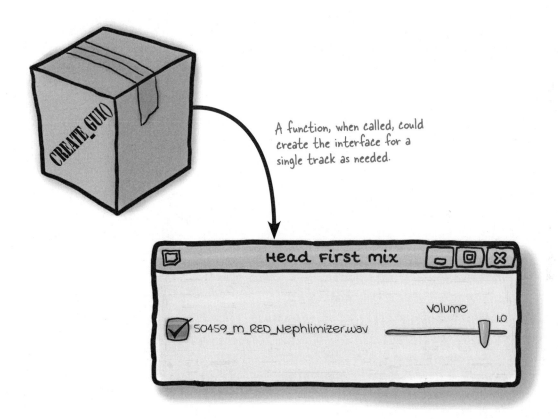

A function, when called, could create the interface for a single track as needed.

If you have a function that creates the widgets and event handlers for a *single* track, you could call it for *each* of the tracks, which would then quickly let you build the *entire interface*.

But what code would you need in such a function?

 **Long Exercise** —————————————————————————

Here is the code from the end of the previous chapter. Study it carefully, and then, in the space on the next page, write the code for your new function (based on the code below).

```python
from tkinter import *
import pygame.mixer

app = Tk()
app.title("Head First Mix")
sound_file = "50459_M_RED_Nephlimizer.wav"
mixer = pygame.mixer
mixer.init()
def track_toggle():
    if track_playing.get() == 1:
        track.play(loops = -1)
    else:
        track.stop()

def change_volume(v):
        track.set_volume(volume.get())

track = mixer.Sound(sound_file)
track_playing = IntVar()
track_button = Checkbutton(app, variable = track_playing,
                    command  = track_toggle, text = sound_file)
track_button.pack(side = LEFT)
volume = DoubleVar()
volume.set(track.get_volume())
volume_scale = Scale(variable = volume, from_ = 0.0, to = 1.0, resolution = 0.1,
                command = change_volume, label = "Volume", orient = HORIZONTAL)
volume_scale.pack(side = RIGHT)

def shutdown():
    track.stop()
    app.destroy()

app.protocol("WM_DELETE_WINDOW", shutdown)
app.mainloop()
```

Begin by importing the libraries you need.

Create the GUI application...

...and initialize the sound system.

The event-handler functions detail what happens when an event occurs.

Define the checkbox widget.

Define the slider widget.

Handle a click on the close box.

Start the event loop.

LONG EXERCISE SOLUTION

Here is the code from the end of the previous chapter. You were to study it carefully, and then, in the space on the next page, write the code for your new function (based on the code below).

```python
from tkinter import *
import pygame.mixer

app = Tk()
app.title("Head First Mix")
sound_file = "50459_M_RED_Nephlimizer.wav"
mixer = pygame.mixer
mixer.init()

def track_toggle():
    if track_playing.get() == 1:
        track.play(loops = -1)
    else:
        track.stop()

def change_volume(v):
        track.set_volume(volume.get())

track = mixer.Sound(sound_file)
track_playing = IntVar()
track_button = Checkbutton(app, variable = track_playing,
                                command  = track_toggle, text = sound_file)
track_button.pack(side = LEFT)
volume = DoubleVar()
volume.set(track.get_volume())
volume_scale = Scale(variable = volume, from_ = 0.0, to = 1.0, resolution = 0.1,
                        command = change_volume, label = "Volume", orient = HORIZONTAL)
volume_scale.pack(side = RIGHT)

def shutdown():
    track.stop()
    app.destroy()

app.protocol("WM_DELETE_WINDOW", shutdown)
app.mainloop()
```

Begin by importing the libraries you need to use in this module. →

```
from tkinter import *

import pygame

def create_gui(app, mixer, sound_file):

        def track_toggle():
                if track_playing.get() == 1:
                        track.play(loops = -1)
                else:
                        track.stop()


        def change_volume(v):
                track.set_volume(volume.get())


        track = mixer.Sound(sound_file)
        track_playing = IntVar()
        track_button = Checkbutton(app, variable = track_playing,
                                        command = track_toggle,
                                        text = sound_file)
        track_button.pack(side = LEFT)
        volume = DoubleVar()
        volume.set(track.get_volume())
        volume_scale = Scale(variable = volume, from_ = 0.0, to = 1.0,
                        resolution = 0.1, command = change_volume,
                        label = "Volume", orient = HORIZONTAL)
        volume_scale.pack(side = RIGHT)
```

Create a new function that contains the GUI-creating code from the current program.

All of this code is part of the function, so it needs to be indented.

The new function contains <u>other</u> functions

With all the code gathered together in a new function, the code for the
`create_gui()` function looks like this:

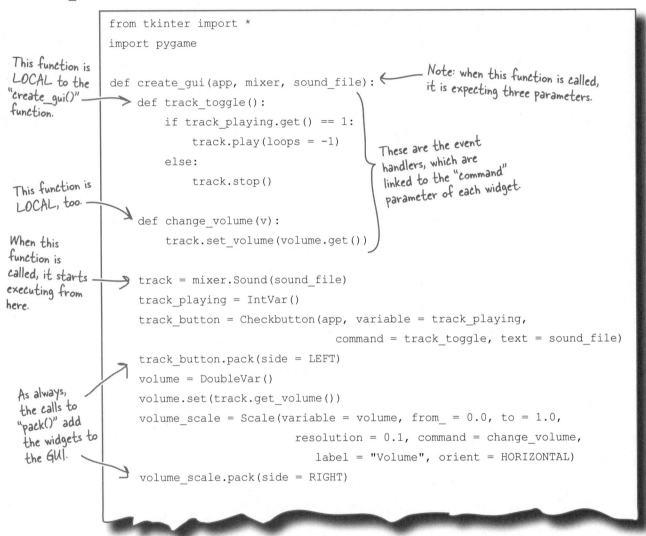

This function is LOCAL to the "create_gui()" function.

Note: when this function is called, it is expecting three parameters.

These are the event handlers, which are linked to the "command" parameter of each widget.

This function is LOCAL, too.

When this function is called, it starts executing from here.

As always, the calls to "pack()" add the widgets to the GUI.

```
from tkinter import *
import pygame


def create_gui(app, mixer, sound_file):
    def track_toggle():
        if track_playing.get() == 1:
            track.play(loops = -1)
        else:
            track.stop()


    def change_volume(v):
        track.set_volume(volume.get())

    track = mixer.Sound(sound_file)
    track_playing = IntVar()
    track_button = Checkbutton(app, variable = track_playing,
                                command = track_toggle, text = sound_file)
    track_button.pack(side = LEFT)
    volume = DoubleVar()
    volume.set(track.get_volume())
    volume_scale = Scale(variable = volume, from_ = 0.0, to = 1.0,
                            resolution = 0.1, command = change_volume,
                                label = "Volume", orient = HORIZONTAL)
    volume_scale.pack(side = RIGHT)
```

Do you notice anything strange? The new function actually has two *other
functions* inside it. Python (and several languages) lets you create **local
functions**. A *local function* is just a **function inside a function**.

Let's see why they're important for the DJ's program.

**A function-in-a-
function is called
a local function.**

Your new function needs to create widgets <u>and</u> event handlers

When you're wiring up the widgets in the interface, you need event handlers to respond to changes in the state of the widgets. If someone clicks the checkbox to play the track, the `track_toggle()` event handler gets called and switches the track on or off.

But if you are creating *several* checkoxes, you are going to need a *separate* event handler for *each* of them.

That's why you have *local functions* inside `create_gui()`. As well as creating new widgets for the interface, it also uses the local functions to create new event handlers.

Each widget needs its own event handler.

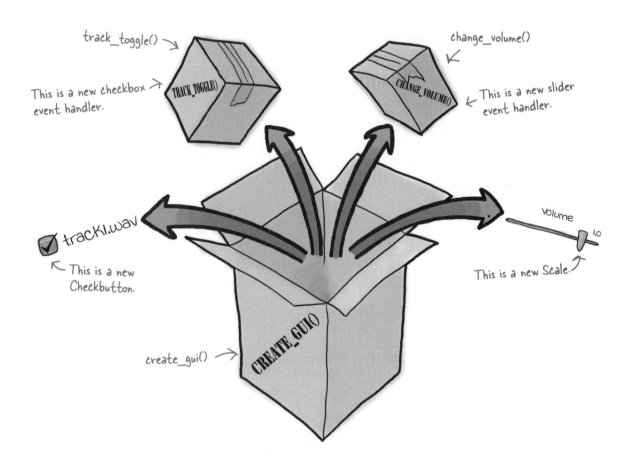

track_toggle()

This is a new checkbox event handler.

change_volume()

This is a new slider event handler.

trackl.wav

This is a new Checkbutton.

volume   1.0

This is a new Scale.

create_gui()

Now, let's update the program to use this new function.

Functions inside of functions inside of functions inside of functions... now, that's what I call complexity. Of course, everything's local, you know.

Jim

Frank

Joe

Frank: A function inside a function? Surely that's not legal?

Jim: Well... it depends on the programming language.

Joe: Don't tell me this is something that *only* works with Python?!?

Jim: No... there are lots of programming languages that allow you to put a function inside another function.

Frank: Name one (other than Python)!

Jim: Pascal.

Frank: Pasc... what?!?

Jim: Look, it really doesn't matter which programming language supports this feature. What is important is that we can do it.

Frank: And by "we" you mean "Python."

Jim: OK, yes. Python can do it.

Frank: That's all I was trying to say...

Joe: So, this is cool how?

Jim: Because it lets you localize functionality and handle complexity.

Joe: What?!?

Jim: Look: if a function gets big and complex, it can help to break the function down into a collection of smaller functions, just like we do when programs get big. We can keep the functionality local to the code that needs it *inside* the function. That way, we keep things as simple as we can

Joe: Even if the code itself is complex?

Frank: Like the GUI-building code we are working on now?

Jim: Yes.

Frank: OK. A function of functions it is, then. I'm all for keeping it simple, stupid. ;-)

Joe: Yes, I like KISS, too.

Jim: Yeah... their last album was really something special, wasn't it?

Frank & Joe: Eh?!?

Exercise

Begin by putting the `create_gui()` function in a separate module called `sound_panel.py`. Then, write a new version of the `hfmix.pyw` program that uses the `sound_panel.py` module:

Write your code here.

....

....

....

....

....

....

....

....

....

....

....

....

....

....

....

....

....

....

....

....

....

....

....

Exercise Solution

You were asked to begin by putting the `create_gui()` function in a separate module called `sound_panel.py`. Then, you were to write a new version of the `hfmix.pyw` program that uses the `sound_panel.py` module:

Import all the functions from the new module. →

```
from tkinter import *
from sound_panel import *
import pygame.mixer

app = Tk()
app.title("Head First Mix")



mixer = pygame.mixer
mixer.init()
```

By calling the new function TWICE, you create TWO sets of sound controls on the GUI. →

```
create_gui(app, mixer, "50459_M_RED_Nephlimizer.wav")
create_gui(app, mixer, "49119_M_RED_HardBouncer.wav")

def shutdown():
    track.stop()
    app.destroy()

app.protocol("WM_DELETE_WINDOW", shutdown)

app.mainloop()
```

TEST DRIVE

With the code typed into IDLE, take this latest version of the DJ's program for a quick spin by pressing F5.

These check buttons start and stop each of the tracks.

These scales control the volume.

The program has created a checkbox and a volume slider for each track. The program called the `create_gui()` function *twice*, creating *two* sets of widgets. Of course, you can call it as many times as you like and the `create_gui()` function will create the two widgets for each track.

When you click on the two checkboxes, the two tracks both play *at the same time*! You can start and stop each of them independently by selecting and deselecting the checkboxes. But more than that, the volume sliders *independently* change the volume of the tracks, allowing you to *mix* them together.

This is a **big deal**. The `create_gui()` function is not only creating the separate widgets and adding them to the interface, but it is also creating the *event handlers* that allow each pair of widgets to control each separate track. Here the program is controlling just two tracks, but if you added more calls to `create_gui()` in the code, there's no reason why you couldn't get the interface to work with as many tracks as you like.

Let's see what the DJ thinks.

The DJ is confused

The program does exactly what the DJ wants, right? Well, not quite.

> How am I supposed to know which volume scale is for which track?

The problem is that even though the program *technically* works, it has a *confusing* interface. All of the checkboxes are added on the **left** of the interface, and all of the volume controls are on the **right**.

There's nothing in the interface that indicates which **volume scale** goes with which **track**.

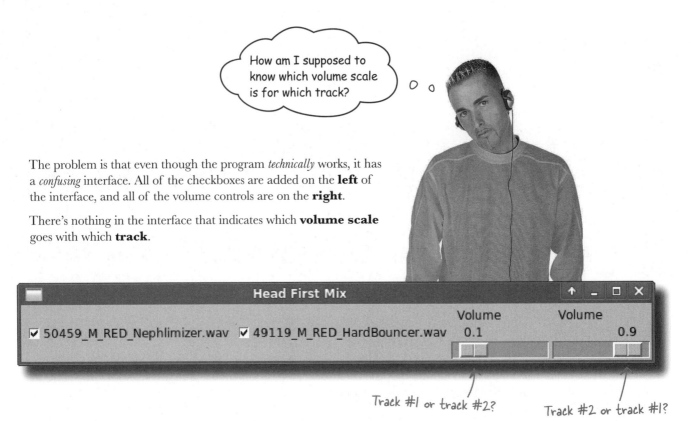

Track #1 or track #2?

Track #2 or track #1?

The checkboxes are labeled with the filename of the track, but the volume sliders aren't. Even though each volume slider is linked to a single track, there is nothing in the interface that tells the user *which track that is*.

So... what to do? You *could* just add labels to each volume slider. That would probably fix it, but adding more widgets, like labels, can make an interface more complex. And you want your interfaces (and your GUI code) to be **simple** and **clean**.

Fortunately, there is a way of rearranging the widgets in the interface to make it a *lot clearer*.

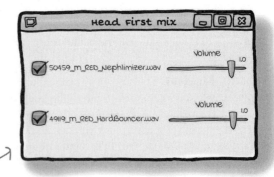

To avoid confusion, the GUI needs to look something like this.

Group widgets together

If the interface were laid out with the checkbox for a track **grouped** alongside the volume slider for the *same* track, it would look better.

Each track could then have a row of widgets associated with it. As long as you know which widgets belong to which track, you can load a lot more tracks at once without the checkboxes and sliders getting separated (and without your users getting confused).

The program currently uses a *function* to add the checkboxes and sliders to the interface one widget at a time. If you call the function several times, the computer creates two more widgets with each call. But the widgets are *not* grouped. So, how do you group widgets together in a GUI interface?

Create a new type of widget

What if you *don't* just hand the computer a set of instructions? What if you give it a brand new widget instead?

If you create a **new kind of widget** that groups a checkbox with a slider, you can add your new widget to the interface and then **guarantee** that the checkbox and slider stay together:

Add a checkbox
Add a slider. Add a checkbox...

The GUI packer

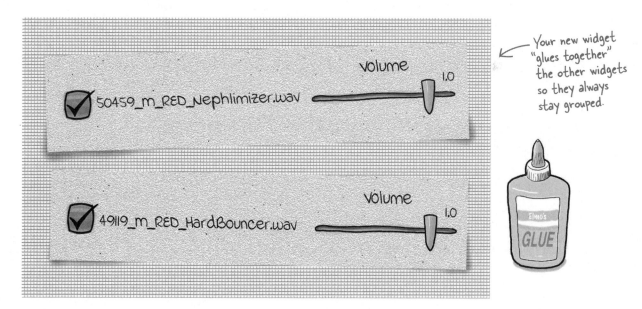

← Your new widget "glues together" the other widgets so they always stay grouped.

Your *new* widget becomes a new *building block* for your GUI interface.

So, how are new widgets created? And how do they work?

A frame widget contains other widgets

Most GUI libraries (including tkinter) let you create **custom widgets** from a set of other components, and tkinter includes a special kind of widget called a **frame**. A frame works just like a picture frame, in that it surrounds other things. It's rectangular and it can *contain* other widgets:

A frame is like... a frame.

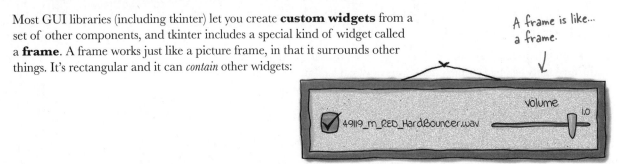

In tkinter, a frame is created using `Frame()`. If you can work out a way to *create a new type of frame* (called, say, `SoundPanel`) that contains the checkbox and the slider, then you could use code something like this in your program:

Create a new SoundPanel widget.

These are the same parameters you passed to the "create_gui()" method.

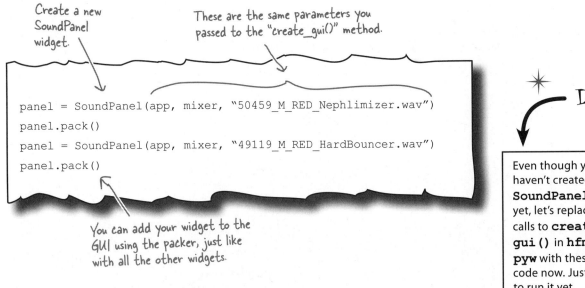

```
panel = SoundPanel(app, mixer, "50459_M_RED_Nephlimizer.wav")
panel.pack()
panel = SoundPanel(app, mixer, "49119_M_RED_HardBouncer.wav")
panel.pack()
```

You can add your widget to the GUI using the packer, just like with all the other widgets.

Do this!

Even though you haven't created the **SoundPanel** code yet, let's replace the calls to **create_gui()** in **hfmix.pyw** with these lines of code now. Just don't try to run it yet.

This look like a *great solution*. However, you still have a *big problem*.

This code uses an **entirely new type of object**, a whole new kind of widget that has *never* existed before. How do you tell the computer to create something like that, which is effectively a *custom GUI object*?

How do you convince the computer to create a new widget each time you call SoundPanel()?

Wouldn't it be dreamy if there were a way in code to create an entirely new kind of widget. But I know it's just a fantasy...

A class is a machine for creating objects

Object oriented programming (OOP) languages (like Python) let you create an entirely new kind of object using a *class*. A class is like a *template* that you use to create new objects.

Think of the class like a *cookie-cutter*, and think of the object as the cookie that is created *based on the class*. As all the cookies are created from the same cookie cutter, they all have the **same characteristics**, even though they are all *individual* cookies. When an individual object is created from a class, it's referred to as an *instance* of that class.

So, if you can arrange for SoundPanel() to be a class, you can create custom widgets as required:

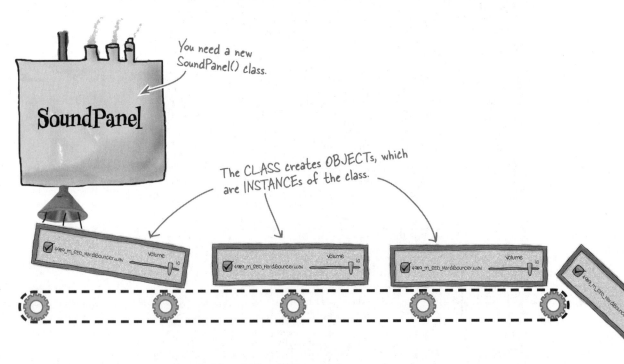

You need a new
SoundPanel() class.

The CLASS creates OBJECTs, which
are INSTANCEs of the class.

You need code that creates a new grouped widget in the GUI every time you make a call like this:

Use the class to create a new object.

```
panel = SoundPanel(app, mixer, "49119_M_RED_HardBouncer.wav")
```

Let's define a SoundPanel() class.

A class has methods that define behavior

The `SoundPanel()` class creates a new kind of tkinter `Frame()`, and you can specify this *relationship* using the code like this:

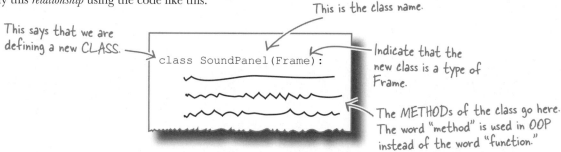

This says that we are defining a new CLASS.

This is the class name.

```
class SoundPanel(Frame):
```

Indicate that the new class is a type of Frame.

The METHODs of the class go here. The word "method" is used in OOP instead of the word "function."

As well as the *what* (it's a frame), you also have to worry about the *how*, which will define the behavior of your new widgets. To do this, you need to add **methods** inside the class. To understand how this works, imagine you have created an alarm button object from a class. The alarm button will need to know what to do when somebody hits it:

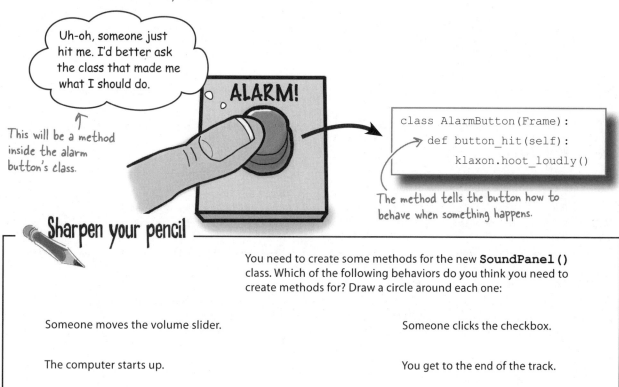

Uh-oh, someone just hit me. I'd better ask the class that made me what I should do.

This will be a method inside the alarm button's class.

```
class AlarmButton(Frame):
    def button_hit(self):
        klaxon.hoot_loudly()
```

The method tells the button how to behave when something happens.

Sharpen your pencil

You need to create some methods for the new **SoundPanel()** class. Which of the following behaviors do you think you need to create methods for? Draw a circle around each one:

Someone moves the volume slider.

The computer starts up.

Create the interface.

Someone clicks the checkbox.

You get to the end of the track.

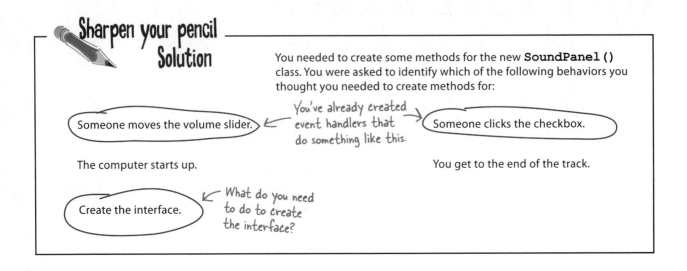

Sharpen your pencil
Solution

You needed to create some methods for the new **SoundPanel()** class. You were asked to identify which of the following behaviors you thought you needed to create methods for:

Someone moves the volume slider.

You've already created event handlers that do something like this.

Someone clicks the checkbox.

The computer starts up.

You get to the end of the track.

Create the interface.

What do you need to do to create the interface?

there are no Dumb Questions

Q: Why is there a method to create the widget?

A: There isn't a method to create the widget. But there is a method to create the interface. That method will run immediately after the widget is created.

Q: I don't get it. What's the difference between a widget and an object?

A: A widget is a particular type of object. It's an object that you can add to a graphical user interface.

Q: So there are some objects that are not widgets?

A: Absolutely. Most objects are used behind the scenes in programs. All of the numbers and strings you've used so far have actually been objects.

Q: So you can't always see objects on the screen then?

A: No, most objects run quietly in memory and they don't have any display at all.

Q: Is Python the only object oriented language?

A: Lots of languages—such as Java, C#, and Ruby—use objects to handle complexity.

Q: So learning object orientation is a good way of getting into other languages?

A: Yes, understanding object orientation gives you a insight into how other languages think.

But how does an object call a method?

To see in more detail *how* the new `SoundPanel` widgets use the methods in the `SoundPanel` *class*, let's look in more detail at just one of the methods. What happens if someone clicks on the checkbox within the widget?

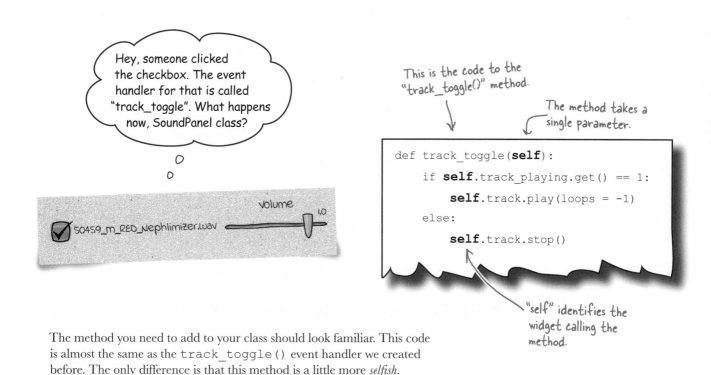

Hey, someone clicked the checkbox. The event handler for that is called "track_toggle". What happens now, SoundPanel class?

This is the code to the "track_toggle()" method.

The method takes a single parameter.

```python
def track_toggle(self):
    if self.track_playing.get() == 1:
        self.track.play(loops = -1)
    else:
        self.track.stop()
```

"self" identifies the widget calling the method.

The method you need to add to your class should look familiar. This code is almost the same as the `track_toggle()` event handler we created before. The only difference is that this method is a little more *selfish*.

self identifies the widget calling the method

The methods in the class are going to be used for **lots** of objects, so the code in the class needs some way to know which `SoundPanel` object it is working with at any point in time. It does that with the **self** variable.

The `self` variable is passed to each of the methods in the class *automatically* by Python and it identifies the current widget object being used. By adding "**self.**" to the front of the object's variable names in the class code, you make sure the code is using the data that belongs to the **current widget**.

Let's add some methods to the SoundPanel() class...

The SoundPanel class looks a lot like the create_gui() function

If you convert the original `change_volume()` function to a method and add it to the class, you end up with code that looks rather like the original `create_gui()` function:

Most of this code looks very similar to the "create_gui()" method, except for all those uses of "self".

```
from tkinter import *
import pygame.mixer

class SoundPanel(Frame):
    def track_toggle(self):
        if self.track_playing.get() == 1:
            self.track.play(loops = -1)
        else:
            self.track.stop()


    def change_volume(self):
        self.track.set_volume(self.volume.get())
```

In fact, the new `SoundPanel()` class can completely **replace** the code in the `sound_panel.py` file (as `create_gui()` is no longer needed).

But before you do that, there's still a little more code to write. The class needs to be told what to do when the brand new `SoundPanel()` is created. The class needs an **initializer** method that knows how to create instances of the class.

Some programming languages call these initializer methods CONSTRUCTORs, because they detail what happens when a new object is created or "constructed."

Let's create the initializer for the SoundPanel() class.

Code Magnets

We've started to create the initializer code for you, but there are still a few parts missing. See if you can work out where the missing code fragments fit. Here is the code that creates a `SoundPanel()` object. Position the code magnets properly to complete the method:

```
def __init__(self, app, mixer, sound_file):
    Frame.__init__(self, app)
```

Because SoundPanel() inherits from tkinter's Frame(), you need to be sure to initialize the Frame() BEFORE you initialize the SoundPanel().

```
    track_button = Checkbutton(              , variable =                                    ,

                              command = self.track_toggle, text = sound_file)
    track_button.pack(side = LEFT)



    self.volume.set(track.get_volume())
    volume_scale = Scale(          , variable = self.volume, from_ = 0.0, to = 1.0,

                         resolution = 0.1, command =                      ,

                         label = "Volume", orient = HORIZONTAL)
    volume_scale.pack(side = RIGHT)
```

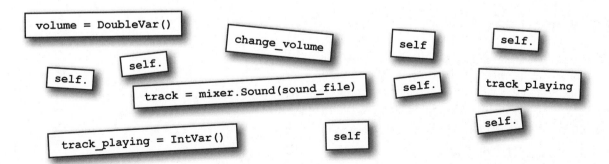

```
volume = DoubleVar()
```

```
change_volume
```

```
self
```

```
self.
```

```
self.
```

```
self.
```

```
track = mixer.Sound(sound_file)
```

```
self.
```

```
track_playing
```

```
self.
```

```
track_playing = IntVar()
```

```
self
```

Code Magnets Solution

We've started to create the initializer code for you, but there are still a few parts missing. See if you can work out where the missing code fragments fit. Here is the code that creates a SoundPanel() object. You were asked to position the code magnets properly to complete the method:

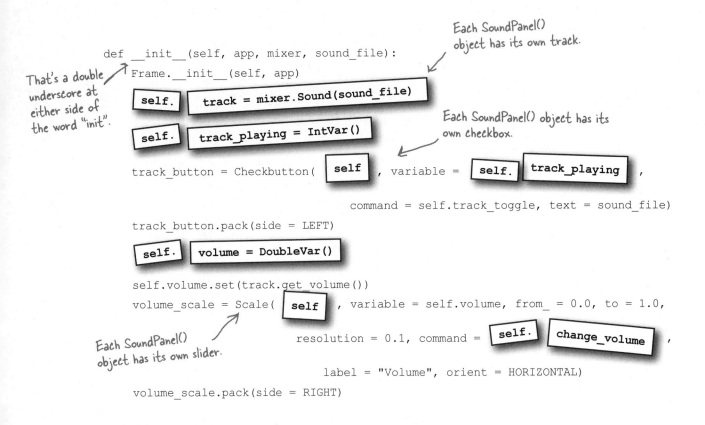

Each SoundPanel() object has its own track.

That's a double underscore at either side of the word "init".

Each SoundPanel() object has its own checkbox.

Each SoundPanel() object has its own slider.

```
def __init__(self, app, mixer, sound_file):
    Frame.__init__(self, app)
    self.track = mixer.Sound(sound_file)
    self.track_playing = IntVar()
    track_button = Checkbutton(self, variable = self.track_playing,
                               command = self.track_toggle, text = sound_file)
    track_button.pack(side = LEFT)
    self.volume = DoubleVar()
    self.volume.set(track.get_volume())
    volume_scale = Scale(self, variable = self.volume, from_ = 0.0, to = 1.0,
                         resolution = 0.1, command = self.change_volume,
                         label = "Volume", orient = HORIZONTAL)
    volume_scale.pack(side = RIGHT)
```

class = methods + data

The SoundPanel() class has *methods* that define the *behavior* that it implements. In addition to the methods, the class also has to detail the *data* that it holds. For the SoundPanel() class, this data is made up from three things: the track to play, its checkbox, and its associated slider.

The Class Exposed

This week's interview:
Life in senior object management.

Head First: Hello, Class. It's good of you to find the time to speak to us.

Class: I assure you the inestimable pleasure is all mine.

Head First: So, to begin...

Class: One moment... <hums>

Head First: I'm sorry. What's that?

Class: Apologies. Just checking my initializer. I always do it when I create.

Head First: Ah, yes. That's your constructor, isn't it? The method you use to create objects?

Class: Well, I'm aware that some people refer to it as a *constructor*, but I prefer **initializer**. I don't use it to create objects, you see. I just use it to configure them once they've been created.

Head First: You have a lot of methods?

Class: Oh, more than you can possibly imagine.

Head First: In the code we've just seen, the SoundPanel() class, there were only three methods, weren't there?

Class: Oh, dear boy, there were only three methods defined explicitly in the class. But SoundPanel() *inherited* many, many more methods from its parent class, dear old tkinter's Frame().

Head First: Frame() has a lot of methods, too?

Class: Too many to discuss, really. There are methods to paint components on the screen and details of what to do if things change size. Frame is a fearfully busy fellow. <beep beep> Excuse me. Hello? Yes? No, you need to stop playing track four. No, no, it's quite all right. Goodbye.

Head First: One of your objects?

Class: Yes. They keep me very busy, but I'd miss them if they didn't call.

Head First: I believe when someone calls an object method, the object always asks you to get involved?

Class: Yes. I'm in charge of the object's behavior. I do think it is so important to behave properly. Don't you?

Head First: Of course! Class, thank you.

Class: Love the tie, by the way.

Code Review

It's always good every once in a while to check back on the state of your code and make sure everything's looking spiffy. This is what your program should look like at this point. It's probably worth checking to make sure everything in your code looks like this:

hfmix.pyw

```python
from tkinter import *
from sound_panel import *
import pygame.mixer


app = Tk()
app.title("Head First Mix")



mixer = pygame.mixer
mixer.init()

panel = SoundPanel(app, mixer, "50459_M_RED_Nephlimizer.wav")
panel.pack()
panel = SoundPanel(app, mixer, "49119_M_RED_HardBouncer.wav")
panel.pack()

def shutdown():
    track.stop()
    app.destroy()

app.protocol("WM_DELETE_WINDOW", shutdown)

app.mainloop()
```

Did you remember to use SoundPanel() instead of create_gui()?

sound_panel.py

```python
from tkinter import *
import pygame.mixer

class SoundPanel(Frame):
    def __init__(self, app, mixer, sound_file):
        Frame.__init__(self, app)
        self.track = mixer.Sound(sound_file)
        self.track_playing = IntVar()
        track_button = Checkbutton(self, variable = self.track_playing,
                                   command = self.track_toggle, text = sound_file)
        track_button.pack(side = LEFT)
        self.volume = DoubleVar()
        self.volume.set(self.track.get_volume())
        volume_scale = Scale(self, variable = self.volume, from_ = 0.0, to = 1.0,
                             resolution = 0.1, command = self.change_volume,
                             label = "Volume", orient = HORIZONTAL)
        volume_scale.pack(side = RIGHT)

    def track_toggle(self):
        if self.track_playing.get() == 1:
            self.track.play(loops = -1)
        else:
            self.track.stop()

    def change_volume(self, v):
        self.track.set_volume(self.volume.get())
```

An initializer method comes first. Note that this method has to be called "__init__()" in Python in order to be called automatically when the object is created.

Test Drive

OK, so you're *finally* ready to start up your new **custom widget** code. This is what it looks like after you bring your code into IDLE and press F5:

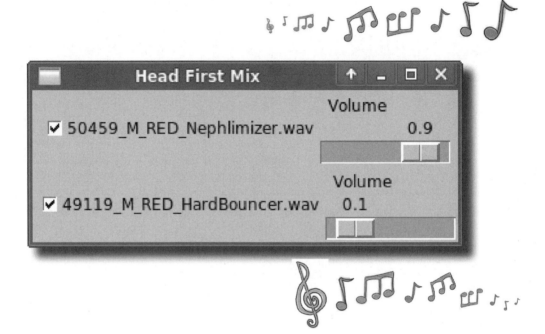

The checkboxes and volume scales are now **grouped together** on the same **widget** within the GUI. From now on, you will know that the widgets on your GUI will always stay together as the SoundPanel() class has grouped them for you.

Dude, that interface looks awesome! It's so easy to use!

there are no
Dumb Questions

Q: **I don't get it. What's this "self" thing again?**

A: "self" is a variable that refers to the calling object.

Q: **The calling object? What does that mean?**

A: Imagine you create a new method called `bleep()` in the `SoundPanel` class. An object called `panel` can use the `bleep()` method as needed, and when it does, it calls the `SoundPanel` class. The "self." bit ensures that the `bleep()` method associated with the `panel` object is called, not some other `bleep()` method associated with some other object.

Q: **So objects don't actually own their own methods?**

A: In some languages, such as Ruby, they can, but in most languages, no, objects don't own their own methods. The methods all belong to the class that created the object.

Q: **But why do I need to add "self." to the start of the variables?**

A: Because then you are changing data inside the current object referred to by "self.". You will be working with the object's own data, and not with data that belongs to the class.

Q: **Not all the variables had "self." at the beginning. Why is that?**

A: If you look at the code, the `volume_scale` variable does not begin with "self.". That's because the object does not need to keep track of the `volume_scale` variable once the initializer method has finished creating the object. `volume_scale` is a variable that is local to the initializer.

BULLET POINTS

- The SoundPanel widget is a type of frame.

- Objects get created by classes.

- A class has methods.

- The methods define the behavior of the object.

- When an object needs to know what to do, it calls a method in the class that created it.

- The methods in the class all have a `self` variable.

- The `self` variable points to the object that called the method.

- By *prefixing* variables with "`self.`", you can keep each object's values separate from each other.

The DJ has an entire directory of tracks

The DJ is so impressed by how usable your program is that he wants to try it out tonight for his **complete set**, prior to its official unveiling at the *World Music Mixing Expo*. The DJ needs to work with a lot more than two tracks. In fact, he has an entire directory full of loops.

Directory
full of loops.

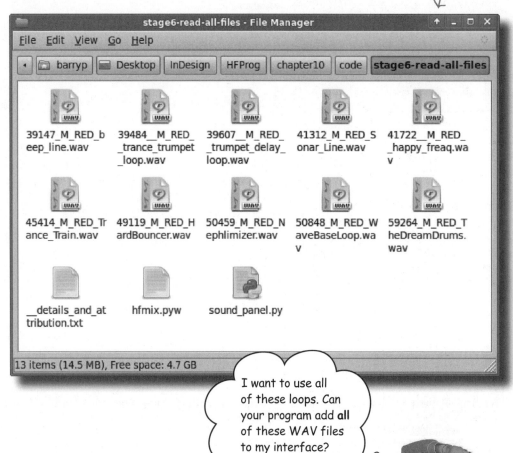

I want to use all of these loops. Can your program add **all** of these WAV files to my interface?

Now you *could* just change the code to add the extra files to the interface, but the DJ wants to be able to manage which tracks the program uses. So you will have to *find* all of the WAV files in the current directory and then *add* them to the interface *when the program starts*.

Let's get this thing to work.

Pool Puzzle

Your **job** is to take segments from the pool and place them into the blank lines in the code. You may **not** use the same segment more than once, and you won't need to use all the segments. Your **goal** is to complete the code in `hfmix.pyw` so that it reads *all* the tracks from the directory and then adds them to the GUI interface.

```python
from tkinter import *
from sound_panel import *
import pygame.mixer
import os

app = Tk()
app.title("Head First Mix")

mixer = pygame.mixer
mixer.init()
.................................................................................
.................................................................................
.................................................................................
.................................................................................
.................................................................................
.................................................................................
.................................................................................
.................................................................................

def shutdown():
        track.stop()

        app.destroy()

app.protocol("WM_DELETE_WINDOW", shutdown)
app.mainloop()
```

Note: each thing from the pool can be used only once!

```python
        panel.pack()

    for fname in dirList:
                        dirList = os.listdir(".")
panel = SoundPanel(app, mixer, fname)

        "50459_M_RED_Nephlimizer.wav"
                                if fname.endswith(".wav"):
```

Pool Puzzle Solution

Your **job** was to take segments from the pool and place them into the blank lines in the code. You could **not** use the same segment more than once, and you didn't need to use all the segments. Your **goal** was to complete the code in `hfmix.pyw` so that it reads *all* the tracks from the directory and then adds them to the GUI interface.

```
from tkinter import *
from sound_panel import *
import pygame.mixer
import os

app = Tk()
app.title("Head First Mix")

mixer = pygame.mixer
mixer.init()

dirList = os.listdir(".")
for fname in dirList:
    if fname.endswith(".wav"):
        panel = SoundPanel(app, mixer, fname)
        panel.pack()

def shutdown():
    track.stop()

    app.destroy()

app.protocol("WM_DELETE_WINDOW", shutdown)
app.mainloop()
```

You need to talk to the operating system, so import the "os" module.

Get the names of all the files in the current directory.

Take each of the filenames...

...and if it ends in ".wav"...

...create a SoundPanel() and add it to the GUI.

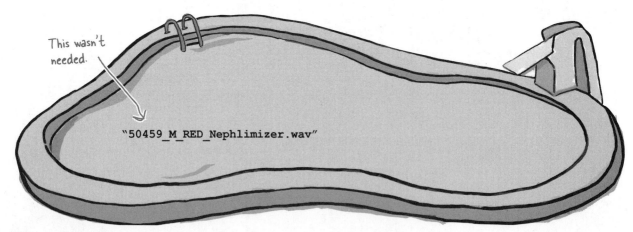

This wasn't needed.

"50459_M_RED_Nephlimizer.wav"

TEST DRIVE

With the code in IDLE and all the sound files in the directory, press F5. You should see something that looks a lot more powerful than the simple two-track mixer you had before:

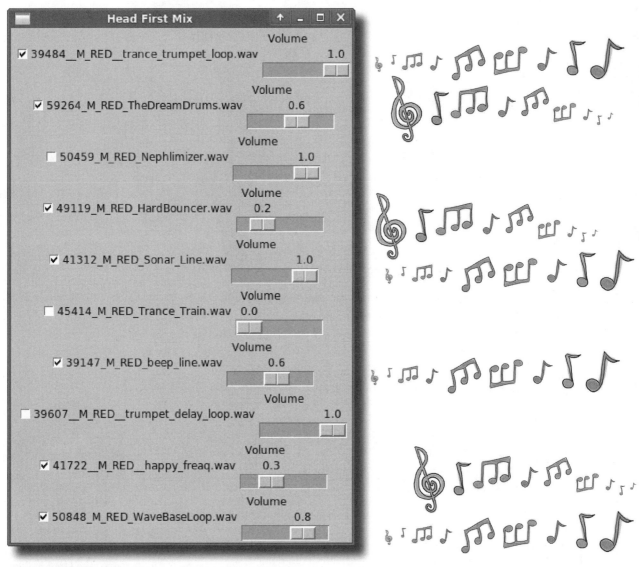

Every single track from the directory now appears on the interface and can be individually controlled. The program looks like it *finally* does everything the DJ wants. But the *real test* will be how it performs at World Music Mixing Expo...

It's party time!

The mixer program brought the house down!

The DJ took your program to the World Music Mixing Expo and rocked the house, with your name in lights! By using classes for the widgets and creating an object oriented program, you made your good program (and the DJ's performance) *great*.

Object orientation is meant to help you create **complex programs** with **very little code**. A lot of languages use object orientation, and not just for graphical user interfaces. You can use objects to build web applications or simulators or games. Any time you need to write an advanced program but don't want your code to turn into a tangled mess of spaghetti, object orientation can come to the rescue!

Congratulations!

You got to the end of the book! And what a great journey it's been. You've ruled with control statements. You've powered-up your programs with modular code. You've made graphical user interfaces that sing and, finally, you took your coding skills to the next level with object orientation.

Well done!

Your Programming Toolbox

You've got Chapter 10 under your belt. Let's look back at what you've learned in this chapter:

Programming Tools

* Local functions live inside other functions.

* Object orientation is a way of using software objects to handle complexity.

* Classes are machines to create objects; think of them like a "cookie cutter".

* Classes have methods that define their objects' behavior.

* Created objects are known as "instances" of some class.

* An initializer tells an object what to do once it's been created.

* Some languages call initializers "constructors."

* Not all objects are GUI objects.

* Widgets are a kind of object.

Python Tools

* Frame() – tkinter's frames are widgets that contain other widgets and help to keep the widgets together (grouped).

* class – a keyword that introduces a new class definition.

* __init__() – the name of the method that is called automatically on object creation.

* self – methods have a special variable called "self" that is set to the current object.

* Adding "self." to the start of a variable means it belongs to the current object.

Leaving town...

It's been great having you here in Codeville!

We're sad to see you leave, but there's nothing like taking what you've learned and putting it to use. You're just beginning your programming journey and we've put you in the driving seat. We're dying to hear how things go, so **_drop us a line_** at the Head First Labs web site, **www.headfirstlabs.com**, and let us know how programming is paying off for **YOU**!

appendix i: leftovers

The Top Ten Things (we didn't cover)

You can never have enough tools... especially when the job's not finished yet.

You've come a long way.

But learning how to program is an activity that never stops. The more you code, the more you'll need to learn **new ways to do certain things**. You'll need to master **new tools** and **new techniques**, too. There's just not enough room in this book to show you everything you might possibly need to know. So, here's our list of the top ten things we didn't cover that you might want to learn more about next.

#1: Doing things "The Python Way"

Throughout this book, we have very stubbornly resisted writing code in the most correct *Python Way*. "That's not how a Python programmer would do it," was a familiar refrain heard from the *Head First Programming* technical reviewers. Without fail, and with the greatest of respect to our reviewers, we generally *ignored* this advice.

You see, every programming language has its preferred, tried and true, agreed, and accepted way of doing certain things, collectively known as *programming idioms*. And Python is no exception. This is, of course, a **very good thing**, because the more programmers using a particular language who follow the standard way of doing something, the better. Except, that is, when writing a book like this: one designed from the get-go to teach **programming concepts**.

There are times when the idiom, although very smart, can be hard to understand and even harder to explain. So, when we had a choice between showing you how to do something in a *generic way* over showing you how to do it the Python way, we nearly always chose the former approach over the latter. This has the effect of making some of the code in this book positively repulsive to hardened Python programmers, something that is of little concern to us, as this book isn't for them (and they have lots of other books already).

This book is for *you*: the reader who wants to learn how to program regardless of the programming language chosen.

Having said all that, if you now want to learn more about *The Python Way*, start by scanning through the booklist and book reviews maintained on the main Python website:

http://wiki.python.org/moin/PythonBooks

Yes, that's supposed to be an "o".

Holy smokes! I can't believe they did it that way...

Python guru.

Learn lots about Python from Mark Lutz's classic, "Learning Python, 4th Edition," which now covers Python 3 and previous releases.

#2: Using Python 2

If you remember way back in the **Readme**, we stated we were using release 3 of Python in this book. Of course, there's much more to Python that just release 3, as the previous version of the language, release 2, is still *very, very popular*.

And rightly so. Python 2 has been around for nearly a decade and has an impressive collection of technologies built around it, including Google's *App Engine*, the *Django Web Framework*, Zope's *Content Management System*, and the *Twisted Networking Libraries* (to name just a few).

Despite all the Python 2 goodness out there, we still went with release 3 for this book and our reasoning was very simple: *better to go with the future than settle on the past*. The good folks that bring the world Python have stated that Python 3 is where all the cool, new stuff will happen with the language. Release 2 has entered what's known as *bug-fix mode only*: if something is found in 2 that is broken, it'll be fixed, but no new features will be added.

And here's the good news: there's not much difference between the code you've been writing for Python 3 and what you would write for release 2, should you find yourself in the position of needing to (perhaps as a result of needing to fix some existing Python 2 code or working with a technology that's based on Python 2).

Here are a few lines of Python 2 code that highlight some of the differences:

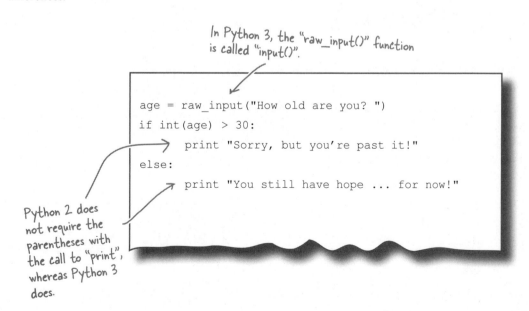

In Python 3, the "raw_input()" function is called "input()".

```
age = raw_input("How old are you? ")
if int(age) > 30:
    print "Sorry, but you're past it!"
else:
    print "You still have hope ... for now!"
```

Python 2 does not require the parentheses with the call to "print", whereas Python 3 does.

#3: Other programming languages

When it comes to teaching programming concepts, there's more than enough to cover without trying to cover multiple programming languages.

We like Python and hope over the course of this book that you've grown to like Python, too. However, if you want to explore or need to learn another programming language, there's lots of help out there. Simply going to your favorite search engine and typing in the name of your chosen programming language produces a torrent of sites offering to provide you with everything you need to know.

Two modern languages that are important are **Java** and **C#**. And guess what? If you have to learn these technologies, *Head First Labs* has you covered.

Very good, too

An absolute classic, now in its Second Edition

Having completed this book, you can now pick up either of these books and confidently work your way through them.

Of course, if you find yourself working in a Java or C# programming environment and missing Python, don't despair. Two active projects within the Python Community *integrate* Python with the above programming languages and are well worth checking out (search on the project name to learn more):

Run Python code within the Java Virtual Machine.

Integrate Python with C# and .NET.

#4: Automated testing techniques

And, no, before you ask, this has *nothing* to do with program-testing robots automatically testing your code for you (which, we agree, would be nice).

Automated testing *does* have everything to do with trying to make sure, as far as possible, that your code is **working properly**.

But, how is this possible?

The truth is, it's very hard to know for sure that your code is working perfectly 100% of the time. Programs and software systems are complex beasts. Over time, they grow, and it gets increasingly hard to know for sure if they are working quite the way you want them to.

To help, programmers test their code. When they are done, they test, test, then test some more. And just to be sure, they *test again*. In fact, programmers often *test to destruction*, which refers to attempting everything they know to try and break the program and make it misbehave. If testing finds a problem, the code is then fixed so that whatever it was isn't a problem anymore.

To help with the grunt work that testing sometimes is, Python comes with a handy built-in module called `unittest`. This module's sole purpose in life is to allow you *to write code that tests your code*. Trust us, this isn't as strange as it sounds. The `unittest` module provides a framework within which you can exercise your code to ensure it's working the way you want it to.

The idea is simple enough: as you write your code, you write a little *extra bit of code* based on `unittest` to check that your new code is working properly. If the test works (that is, it successfully demonstrates that your code is OK), you are then in a position to automate the testing of your code by reusing your `unittest` code.

For more details, check out the description of `unittest` in your favorite Python book or online in the official Python documentation.

And now that you know about `unittest`, you have no excuse *not* to use it to test *your* code.

Writing code to test code?!? Isn't that one of those chicken and egg things?

#5: Debugging

This is not as disgusting as it sounds.

Debugging is related to testing. It is the process of dealing with errors that aren't picked up during testing but, instead, blow up in your face when you run your code or—worse—blow up in the face of your user!

Tracking down where a problem is can sometimes feel like a bit of an art form, but there are some tried and true techniques that can make things easier for you. *Experience helps a lot.*

One of the most important things you can know about when it comes to debugging code is a thing called the **debugger**. This is a software tool that can be used by programmers to run code step by step or line by line. As the program runs, the debugger lets you **watch** what's going on and then potentially **see** when something goes wrong. If you can work out where in your code the problem lies, it makes it easier to fix, and the debugger is designed to help you do just that.

It is a rare programming technology indeed that comes *without* a debugger. Python's is called **pdb** and it can be accessed from within IDLE and within the Python Shell. Check the Python online documentation for more information on pdb.

The problem is not with the hardware; it's with your program. You'll have to DEBUG your code.

As mentioned at the top of the page: *debugging is related to testing*. Typically, you debug your code *after* it is up and running and (possibly) delivered to your user. You test your code as you write it and *before* you give your program to your users. The idea is that you only ever give a user your program when you're happy it works the way you want it to.

To be honest, though, there are no hard and fast rules here, and a lot of programmers blur the line between debugging and testing, treating it all as one activity.

#6: Command-line execution

Throughout the 10½ chapters of this book, you've consistently executed your code from within the IDLE programming environment. This has been great while developing and working on your code, but it's probably not *how* you want your users to run your programs. It turns out there's more than one way to do it when it comes to running your code. The method available to you (and your users) will vary depending on the operating system you're using.

Your operating system might have a *file association* already in place that allows you to double-click on a Python program and have it execute for you. If this is the case, feel free to double-click to your heart's content. If not, here's how to start Python from the command line on the "big 3" operating systems. Let's assume the program you're running is called `coffee_pos.py`:

On Windows, enter the "C:\Python31\python.exe" command together with the name of the program you want to execute.

```
Microsoft Windows XP [Version 5.1.2600]
(C) Copyright 1985-2001 Microsoft Corp.


C:\Documents and Settings\hfprog> C:\Python31\python.exe coffee_pos.py
1. DONUT
2. LATTE
3. FILTER
4. MUFFIN
5. Quit
Choose an option: █
```

```
File  Edit  Window  Help   Mac OS X and Linux

$ python3 coffee_pos.py

1. DONUT
2. LATTE
3. FILTER
4. MUFFIN
5. Quit
Choose an option: █
```

Simply enter "python3" together with the name of the program you want to run on the Mac OS X or Linux command line.

#7: Ooops... we could've covered more OOP

Chapter 10 introduced the important concept of *classes*, and throughout the book we've touched on *objects* in lots of different places. Doing justice to all the concepts of *object oriented programming* (OOP) would easily take an entire book all on its own.

The bit of OOP covered in Chapter 10 relates to the concept of **encapsulation**. This is the process of *bundling* data with methods into prebuilt *templates* that can be used to create *functionally identical objects* of a certain *type*.

Now... if your eyes glazed over reading that last line, don't worry; you are as normal as the rest of us. OOP is full of terminology like this. As well as encapsulation, there's **inheritance** and **polymorphism**, too.

Discussing all the ins and outs of OOP is something that takes a little time and it is *not* something that we are going to try and do on just one page!

That said, OOP really comes into its own when your programs get very large and turn into **software systems**. When systems start to scale (get really, really big), the importance of proper design takes center stage, and OOP can help here—big time. Again, there's help from those lovely people at *Head First Labs*.

This book assumes you already know a little bit about Java, so consider reading Head First Java first.

↓

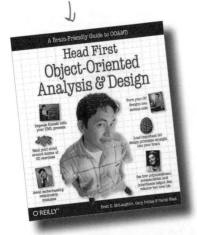

Encapsulation?!?
Polymorphism?!?
Inheritance?!?
Could they not have chosen such intimidating terms?

#8: Algorithms

There are plenty of great books that believe it's impossible to learn about programming without also learning about *algorithms*.

The word "algorithm" is used to describe a precise and established way of solving a particular problem in any programming language. It's often useful to think of an algorithm as a *recipe*.

In the good ol' days, it was certainly true that every programmer had to have a good grasp of algorithms in order to get anything of any worth done. But, luckily for you, this is no longer the case.

Nowadays, with programming technologies such as Python (and Ruby, Perl, Java, and C#), this is less of an issue because modern programming languages just do so much for you.

For instance, if you need to sort something in Python, you either call the `sort()` method on a object or use the built-in `sorted()` function, and the thing you are working with is duly sorted. You are probably less concerned (and rightly so) with how the sort *actually occurred*—that is, with the details of the algorithm used to sort your data. Was it the *quicksort* algorithm or the *bubblesort*? Maybe it was *timsort* or something else entirely? Maybe you don't care, because calling `sort()` or using `sorted()` orders your data in the way you desire and frees you to move onto some other problem that needs solving.

You could take the time to write a really cool sort function and learn lots about algorithms in the process but, let's face it, *life is far too short*.

If you want to write your own programming language, you'll need to learn lots about algorithms. If all you want to do is use an existing programming language (like Python), you can worry less about algorithms and more about writing code, which is precisely how it should be (in our opinion).

#9: ~~Advanced~~ ^Scary^ programming topics

There are a bunch of *advanced* programming topics that were never likely to make it into a book like this. Here is a list of six such topics (all supported by Python 3).

Threads are a programming technology that allows you to break your program into *discrete coded chunks* that can then be executed in parallel or concurrently. Each chunk is known as a *thread*. Using threads can result in some beautiful coding designs, which can make the solving of a certain class of problem almost trivial. Under certain circumstances and restrictions, it is possible to have threads communicate with each other and share data, which, although possible, is hard to get right and can lead to some rather tricky and hard-to-track-down bugs. If you think you need threads, approach with *extreme caution* and be prepared to have your brain expanded in ways that you never thought possible.

Recursion is a programming technique that allows you to create a function that is capable of *calling itself* in order to get its work done. There are certain types of mathematical problems that are well-suited to a recursive solution, but not much else.

Metaprogramming refers to writing programs that can write other programs or manipulate themselves (sounds icky, and it can be). It is not for the faint of heart.

Functional programming (typified by languages such as **Lisp**) is a technique that treats computation as a series of function calls that specify *what* is required of the program, as opposed to a *procedural program*, which details the steps that are required in order to solve a problem.

Regular expressions are a technology that allows you to specify concisely what it is you are looking for in your data. Having written a regular expression (or **regex**), Python can then go and get it for you. Every programmer should know how to take advantage of regexes. The trouble is, they look so very strange at first that most coders recoil in disgust. This is a pity, as we think regexes are super cool and *well-worth learning*.

Unicode is an industry standard that allows you to consistently represent and work with text written in most of the world's languages or "writing systems." If you are working with text originating from somewhere other than the place where they speak your language, then you'll want to know a bit about the Unicode character encoding system.

If you find yourself needing any of this stuff, best to start on the Internet and do some background reading on the topic before buying a book with your hard-earned cash. The **Wikipedia** entries for each of these six topics are good starting points.

You mean I won't have to read all these right now?

#10: Other IDEs, shells, and text editors

It might be hard for you to fathom, but there is life beyond IDLE. There's life beyond the Python Shell, too. Both IDLE and the Python Shell are great learning tools, but sooner or later, you might find yourself wanting *more*.

iPython is a bit like the Python Shell *on steroids*, and a lot of Python programmers swear by it. It has a lot of extra features over and above those in the normal shell that are designed to make the Python programmer's life easier. It is well-worth looking into.

When it comes to full-blown programming environments, there are many choices. Search the Internet for "Python IDE" to see a complete list. A few that come up more than most include: **Komodo**, **Eclipse,** and **Eric**. It's worth taking a look at each, and then deciding if one of them (or something else entirely) is just right for you.

IDLE and the Python Shell may satisfy your needs. But, if you are looking for *more* from your programming tool, there's lots of choices out there.

As for text editors... well, there are lots of choices, too. Some people prefer **Emacs**, while others prefer **vi**. The *Head First Labs* advice is to try out a few editors before picking the one that *best suits your needs*.

Index

Symbols

: (colon)
    in if/else branches, 22
    in index of string, 43
    in while loops, 29

{} (curly brackets), creating hashes, 153

= (equal sign), assignment operator, 4, 35

== (equal sign, double), equal to operator, 4, 15

!= (exclamation point, equal sign), not equal to operator, 30

() (parentheses)
    in format strings, 182
    in function definition, 82

% (percentage symbol), preceding format strings, 180–182

. (period), in library function request, 69

+ (plus sign), addition operator, 58

 # (pound sign), preceding comments, 95, 205

> (right angle bracket), greater than operator, 62, 75

[] (square brackets)
    creating arrays, 132, 134
    enclosing index of array, 132
    enclosing index of string, 42
    enclosing key for hash, 153

A

abstraction, 93

addition operator (+), 58

algorithms, 393

append

append() method, arrays, 132, 144

arguments (parameters), 96–98, 101, 111

arrays (lists), 130–134, 144, 285
    adding items to, 138
    counting occurrences of values in, 138
    creating, 132, 134
    extending, 132, 138
    index (offset value) for, 132
    methods for, 138
    multi-dimensional arrays, 152
    removing items from, 138
    reversing order of, 138, 140
    searching, 138
    sorting, 136–140, 144

askokcancel message boxes, 306

askquestion message boxes, 306

askretrycancel message boxes, 306

askyesnocancel message boxes, 304, 306

assignment
    of multiple values, 122–124
    of single values, 4, 35

assignment operator (=), 4, 35

associative arrays. (*see* hashes)

automated testing, 389

B

Bates, Bert (Head First Java), 388

Beighley, Lynn (Head First SQL), 170

bloated code, 81

books

Head First C# (Stellman, Greene), 388

Head First Java (Sierra, Bates), 388

Head First Object-Oriented Analysis & Design (McLaughlin, Pollice, West), 392

Head First SQL (Beighley), 170

Learning Python, 4th Edition (Lutz), 386

brackets, curly ({}), creating hashes, 153, 175

brackets, square ([])
    creating arrays, 132, 134
    enclosing index of array, 132
    enclosing index of string, 42
    enclosing key for hash, 153

branches, 14, 15–21, 24

break statement, 255

Button() widget, 255
    connecting code to, 239–244, 245
    creating, 234–236

C

C# language
    compared to Python, 9
    learning, 388

characters. (*see* strings)

Checkbutton() widget, 331–335, 348

classes, 366, 372–373, 383. (*see also* methods; objects)
    constructors for, 370–373, 383
    data for, 372
    defining, 367–368

clock() function, time library, 70

close() method, files, 116, 144

code
    bloated, 81

command-line execution of, 391

comments in, 95, 205

debugging, 390

duplicating, 80–81

indents in, 21, 22

paths in, 13, 20–21

pseudo-code, 127

Python practices for, 386

reusing with functions, 81–82, 351–360

reusing with modules, 192–199, 200–202, 205–211, 214

running from IDLE, 7–8

saving, 7

testing, 389

white space in, 22

code examples. (*see* examples)

coffee examples. (*see* health club example; Starbuzz Coffee example)

collection variables. (*see* data structures)

colon (:)
    in if/else branches, 22
    in index of string, 43
    in while loops, 29

combo boxes, 248

command-line execution, 391

comments, 95, 205

conditionals, 35
    in branches, 14–15
    in while loops, 29

constructors (initializer methods), 370–373, 383

control variables, 278

controller, 277, 292

count() method, arrays, 138

crashes, 296

curly brackets ({}), creating hashes, 153, 175

D

data entry widgets
    Checkbutton() widget, 331–335, 348
    Entry() widget, 261–262, 266–267, 269, 292
    model for, 276–278, 285, 292
    OptionMenu() widget, 284–290, 292
    populating dynamically, 288–290, 292
    RadioButton() widget, 272–273, 275–280, 292
    restricting input to, 271–273
    Scale() widget, 336–338, 340–345, 348
    Text() widget, 261, 263, 266–267, 269, 292

data storage, 129–130

data structures, 131, 150. (*see also* arrays; hashes)
    list of, 152
    returning from functions, 164–167

database, 170–172, 175

datatypes, converting, 4, 9, 64–65, 75

date and time functions, 68–73

daylight() function, time library, 70

debugging, 390

decision points. (*see* branches)

decode() method, 49

def keyword, 82, 111

delete() method, data entry widgets, 262, 263, 267, 269

delivery company example, 258–291
    dynamic depot options for, 283–291
    errors in delivery tracking, handling, 294–310
    GUI for delivery system, 258–268
    user input, controlling, 271–281

destroy() method, apps, 326, 348

dialog boxes, 248. (*see also* message boxes)

dictionaries. (*see* hashes)

directories, reading files in, 378–381

disk storage, 129

DJ example. (*see* mixing software example)

Don't Repeat Yourself (DRY), 88

DoubleVar() variable, 340, 345, 348

drop down lists, 248. (*see also* OptionMenu() widget)

DRY (Don't Repeat Yourself), 88

E

Eclipse IDE, 395

editors, 5, 395. (*see also* IDLE)

Emacs editor, 395

encapsulation, 392

endswith() method, strings, 56

Entry() widget, 261, 269, 292
    creating, 266–267
    methods for, 262

equal sign (=), assignment operator, 4

equal sign, double (==), equal to operator, 4, 15

Eric IDE, 395

errors, 311. (*see also* debugging; testing)
    crashes resulting from, 296
    displayed in Shell instead of GUI, 295
    displaying in message boxes, 303–309
    exceptions, 296–300, 311
    TypeError message, 63–64
    ValueError message, 119–120

event loop, 233–234, 255

events
    handlers for, 239, 244–245, 255
    from operating system, 319, 348
    from Window Manager, 319–324, 326–327

examples
    delivery company example, 258–291
    game show example, 216–254

guessing game, 3–34

health club example, 178–213

mixing software example, 314–347, 350–382

Starbuzz Coffee, 38–74, 78–110

storeroom example, 294–310

Surf-A-Thon example, 114–143, 146–174

except statement, 298–300, 311

exceptions, 296–300, 311

exclamation point, equal sign (!=), not equal to operator, 30

extend() method, arrays, 138

F

false value, 14

File menu

New Window option, 6

Save option, 7

files

handles for, 116

permissions for, 295

reading all files in directory, 378–381

reading from, 116–118, 166

find() method, strings, 56–58

float() function, 64–65, 118

for loop, 116–118, 154–156

format strings, 180–184, 186, 214

formatted data, 179

FQNs (fully qualified names), 207–211, 213, 214

Frame() widget, 364, 373, 383

fully qualified names (FQNs), 207–211, 213, 214

functional programming, 394

functions, 82. (*see also* reusing code; specific functions)

calling, 82, 84

creating (defining), 82, 111

local functions, 356–358, 383

parameters for, 96–98, 101, 111

returning data structures from, 164–167, 170–172

returning values from, 87–88, 111

with same name in different modules, 206–211, 213

scope of variables in, 104–108

G

game show example, 216–254

answers, displaying in GUI, 246–254

answers, sound effects for, 216–228

answers, tallying, 216–218, 226–228

GUI for, 230–245

get() method

data entry widgets, 262, 263, 269, 278

IntVar() variable, 332, 334

get_busy() method, channels, 221

global variables, 108–109, 244

gmtime() function, time library, 70

graphical user interface. (*see* GUI)

greater than operator (>), 62, 75

Greene, Jennifer (Head First C#), 388

grouping widgets, 363–364

guessing game example, 3–34

guesses, determining if correct, 3–8

guesses, higher or lower hints for, 10–25

multiple guesses, allowing, 26–34

GUI (graphical user interface), 215, 230–232. (*see also* widgets)

displaying messages in, 246–254, 303–309, 311

errors not displayed in, 295

event loop for, 233–234

guidelines for, 341

positioning widgets in, 235–238

H

hash mark (#), preceding comments, 95, 205

hashes (dictionaries), 152, 175
    adding data to, 153, 156, 161–162
    creating, 153, 175
    iterating through data, 154–156
    keys of, restrictions on, 156
    returning from functions, 164–167, 170–172
    sorting, 158

Head First C# (Stellman, Greene), 388

Head First Java (Sierra, Bates), 388

Head First Object-Oriented Analysis & Design
    (McLaughlin, Pollice, West), 392

Head First SQL (Beighley), 170

health club example, 178–213
    file format changes, 187–199
    multiple price discounts, 204–213
    price discount, 200–203
    transactions, recording in file, 179–186

Help menu, 22

HTML, as strings, 49

I

IDE (Integrated Development Environment), 5, 9, 395

IDLE, 5, 9, 22

if/else branches, 4, 15–21, 24

import statement, 49, 69

importing
    libraries, 49, 69, 221, 226
    modules, 193, 199, 202, 211, 214

indents in code, 21, 22

index (offset value)
    for arrays, 132
    for strings, 42

index() method, arrays, 138

inheritance, 392

__init__() method, 372, 375, 383

initializer methods (constructors), 370–373, 383

input() function, 4, 35, 387

insert() method
    arrays, 138
    data entry widgets, 262, 263, 269

int() function, 4, 9, 35

Integrated Development Environment (IDE), 5, 9, 395

internationalization, format strings for, 186

interpreter, 5. (*see also* IDLE)

IntVar() variable, 249, 253, 255

iPython shell, 395

IronPython project, 388

items() method, hashes, 154, 175

iteration. (*see* loops)

J

Java language
    compared to Python, 9
    learning, 388

Jython project, 388

K

keys() method, hashes, 154, 175

key-value lists. (*see* hashes)

Komodo IDE, 395

L

Label() widget, 248–253, 255

labels for values. (*see* variables)

Learning Python, 4th Edition (Lutz), 386

libraries, 75. (*see also* pygame library)
    importing, 49, 69, 221, 226
    third-party libraries (packages), 220, 223
    time library, 68–73
    tkinter library, 233–236, 238, 255, 341

linked lists, 152

listdir() function, 380

lists. (*see* arrays)

local functions, 356–358, 383

local variables, 105, 106, 111

localtime() function, time library, 70

loops, 28, 35
    delaying iterations of, 67–73
    event loop, 233–234, 255
    for loop, 116–118, 154–156
    while loop, 29–33, 61–65

lower() method, strings, 56

Lutz, Mark (Learning Python, 4th Edition), 386

M

mainloop() method, tkinter, 234, 253

mappings. (*see* hashes)

McLaughlin, Brett D. (Head First Object-Oriented Analysis & Design), 392

memory, 129–130

menus, 248

message boxes, 303–309, 311

messages
    error messages. (*see* errors)
    protocol messages, 322
    sending to Twitter, 93–98, 101

metaprogramming, 394

methods, 377, 383. (*see also* specific methods)
    calling, 369–372
    defining, 367–368

mixing software example, 314–347, 350–382
    multiple tracks, controlling, 350–376
    multiple tracks, reading from directory, 378–382
    toggle for starting and stopping, 328–335
    tracks, starting and stopping, 314–327
    volume control, 336–347

model for data entry widgets, 276–278, 285, 292

Model View Controller (MVC), 277

modular code, 192–199, 200–202, 205–211, 214. (*see also* reusing code)

module. (*see* code)

multi-dimensional arrays, 152

multiple assignment, 122–124

MVC (Model View Controller), 277

N

\n, newline in format strings, 182

New Window option, File menu, 6

not equal to operator (!=), 30

O

object API, 292

object-oriented languages, 368, 383

object-oriented programming (OOP), 392

objects, 366, 368, 377, 383. (*see also* classes; methods)

offset value (index) of strings, 42

OOP (object-oriented programming), 392

open() function, 116, 144

OptionMenu() widget, 284–290, 292

Options menu, 22

ordered lists. (*see also* sorting data)

P

pack() method, tkinter, 235–236, 238, 264, 269

packages (third-party libraries), 220, 223

parameters for functions, 96–98, 101, 111

parentheses (())
  in format strings, 182
  in function definition, 82

pass statement, 221, 255

paths in code, 13, 20–21

pdb debugger, 390

percentage symbol (%), preceding format strings, 180–182

period (.), in library function request, 69

permissions for files, 295

play() method, sounds, 221

plus sign (+), addition operator, 58

point-of-sale (POS) system, 178. (*see also* health club example)

Pollice, Gary (Head First Object-Oriented Analysis & Design), 392

polymorphism, 392

pop() method, arrays, 138

POS (point-of-sale) system, 178. (*see also* health club example)

pound sign (#), preceding comments, 95, 205

print() function, 4, 35, 387

program. (*see* code)

programming idioms, 386

protocol events, 321–322

protocol() method, apps, 322

pseudo-code, 127

.py file extension, 7

pygame library, 219–223, 229, 255
  downloading and installing, 220
  importing, 221, 226
  mixer object for, 221, 226
  platforms supported by, 219
  setting volume, 339

Python, 9
  books about, 386
  command-line execution of, 391
  compared to Java and C#, 9
  integrated into other languages, 388
  programming idioms for, 386
  systems supporting, 9
  version 2 of, 387
  versions of, 9

Python IDE. (*see* IDLE)

Python Shell, 5
  errors displayed in, 295
  running code in, 8

.pyw file extension, 237

Q

queues, 152

R

RadioButton() widget, 272–273, 275–280, 292

randint() function, 33, 35

raw_input() function, 387

read() method, 49

reading from files, 116–118

record, 179. (*see also* database)

recursion, 394

regex, 394

Regional Surfing Association (RSA) example, 160–167

regular expressions, 394

remove() method, arrays, 138

repeating pieces of code. (*see* loops)

replace() method, strings, 56

reserved words, 341, 348

return() statement, 87–88, 111

return values for functions, 87–88, 111

reusing code. (*see also* functions)
    with functions, 81–82, 351–360
    with modules, 192–199, 200–202, 205–211, 214

reverse() method, arrays, 138, 140, 144

right angle bracket (>), greater than operator, 62, 75

RSA (Regional Surfing Association) example, 160–167

Run Module option, Run menu, 7

S

Save option, File menu, 7

Scale() widget, 336–338, 340–345, 348

scope of variables, 104–108, 111

searching
    arrays, 138
    strings, 52–58

self variable, 369–370, 377, 383

set() method
data entry widgets, 278, 280

IntVar() variable, 249

set_volume() method, pygame, 339

sets, 152

sharing code. (*see* reusing code)

Shell. (*see* Python Shell)

showerror message boxes, 306, 308

showinfo message boxes, 304, 306

showwarning message boxes, 306

Sierra, Kathy (Head First Java), 388

sleep() function, time library, 70, 72–73

slider on a scale. (*see* Scale() widget)

sort() method, arrays, 138, 144

sorted() function, 158, 175

sorting data, 128–129
    algorithms for, 393
    in any data structure, 158, 175
    in arrays, 136–140, 144

sound
    pausing between playing, 221, 223
    playing, 221, 226–227
    pygame library for, 219–223, 229

starting and stopping, 316–317

volume, adjusting, 336–345

WAV files for, 221, 223

source code. (*see* code)

spaces, (*see* white space)

split() method, strings, 121–124, 144, 161–162, 175

SQL, 170. (*see also* database)

square brackets ([])

 creating arrays, 132, 134

 enclosing index of array, 132

 enclosing index of string, 42

 enclosing key for hash, 153

stack, 104

stack frame, 105, 111

Starbuzz Coffee example, 38–74, 78–110

 coffee supplies, maintaining, 78–91

 discount price, finding in HTML, 50–59

 health club discounts, calculating, 204–213

 low price, checking for, 60–74

 order messages, sending to Twitter, 92–110

 price, extracting from HTML, 38–49

startswith() method, strings, 56

Stellman, Andrew (Head First C#), 388

storage of data, 129–130

storeroom example, 294–310

strings, 41–42, 48, 75

 ending substring, checking, 56

 formatting, 180–184, 186, 214

 lowercase, converting to, 56

 methods for, 55–56

 offset value (index) of, 42

 removing white space from, 56

 replacing substrings in, 56

 searching for substrings in, 52–58

 splitting at spaces, 121–124

 splitting at specified character, 161–162

starting substring, checking, 56

substrings of, 43–46, 48, 49

uppercase, converting to, 54, 56

web pages as, 49

StringVar() variable, 278, 280, 292

strip() method, strings, 56

substrings, 48

 length of, 49

 searching for, in strings, 52–58

 specifying, 43–46, 49

Surf-A-Thon example, 114–143, 146–174

 highest score, calculating, 114–125

 names, matching to scores, 142–143, 146–157

 score data, extracting from database, 169–174

 score data, extracting from formatted file, 160–167

 scores, sorting, 136–141, 158–159

 three highest scores, calculating, 126–135

T

tabs in code, 22

testing, automated, 389

text. (*see* strings)

text boxes, 248

Text() widget, 261, 269, 292

 creating, 266–267

 methods for, 263

third-party libraries (packages), 220, 223

threads, 394

time() function, time library, 70

time library, 68–73

timezone() function, time library, 70

Tk() app, 234, 255

tkinter library, 233–236, 238, 255, 341

toggle switch. (*see* Checkbutton() widget)

transaction file, 179–184, 188–191

true value, 14

try statement, 298–300, 311

TVN example, 169–174. (*see also* game show example)

Twitter, sending messages to, 93–98, 101

TypeError message, 63–64

types. (*see* datatypes)

U

Unicode character encoding system, 394

unittest module, 389

upper() method, strings, 54, 56

uppercase, converting strings to, 54

urllib.request library, 69

urlopen() function, 49

V

ValueError message, 119–120

variables, 4, 35

    collections of. (*see* data structures)

    control variables, 278

    global variables, 108–109, 244

    local variables, 105, 106, 111

    scope of, 104–108, 111

vi editor, 395

view, 277. (*see also* widgets)

visual toggle. (*see* Checkbutton() widget)

volume, adjusting, 336–345

W

wait_finish() function, 221, 223

WAV files, 221, 223

web pages, as strings, 49

West, Dave (Head First Object-Oriented Analysis & Design), 392

while loop, 29–33, 61–65

white space

    in code, 22

    removing from strings, 56

    specifying in format strings, 182

    splitting strings at, 121–124

widgets

    Button() widget, 234–236, 239–244, 245, 255

    choosing, 341

    compared to objects, 368

    for data entry. (*see* data entry widgets)

    event loop for, 255

    Frame() widget, 364, 373, 383

    grouping, 363–364

    Label() widget, 248–253, 255

    list of, 248

    positioning, 235–238

Window Manager, 348

Window Manager events, 319–324, 326–327

WM_DELETE_WINDOW message, 322

WM_SAVE_YOURSELF message, 322

WM_TAKE_FOCUS message, 322

Get even more for your money.

Join the O'Reilly Community, and register the O'Reilly books you own. It's free, and you'll get:

- 40% upgrade offer on O'Reilly books
- Membership discounts on books and events
- Free lifetime updates to electronic formats of books
- Multiple ebook formats, DRM FREE
- Participation in the O'Reilly community
- Newsletters
- Account management
- 100% Satisfaction Guarantee

Signing up is easy:

1. **Go to: oreilly.com/go/register**
2. **Create an O'Reilly login.**
3. **Provide your address.**
4. **Register your books.**

Note: English-language books only

To order books online:

oreilly.com/order_new

For questions about products or an order:

orders@oreilly.com

To sign up to get topic-specific email announcements and/or news about upcoming books, conferences, special offers, and new technologies:

elists@oreilly.com

For technical questions about book content:

booktech@oreilly.com

To submit new book proposals to our editors:

proposals@oreilly.com

Many O'Reilly books are available in PDF and several ebook formats. For more information:

oreilly.com/ebooks

Spreading the knowledge of innovators   www.oreilly.com

Buy this book and get access to the online edition for 45 days—for free!

Head First Programming
By David Griffiths
November 2009, $49.99
ISBN 9780596802370

With Safari Books Online, you can:

Access the contents of thousands of technology and business books

- Quickly search over 7000 books and certification guides
- Download whole books or chapters in PDF format, at no extra cost, to print or read on the go
- Copy and paste code
- Save up to 35% on O'Reilly print books
- **New!** Access mobile-friendly books directly from cell phones and mobile devices

Stay up-to-date on emerging topics before the books are published

- Get on-demand access to evolving manuscripts.
- Interact directly with authors of upcoming books

Explore thousands of hours of video on technology and design topics

- Learn from expert video tutorials
- Watch and replay recorded conference sessions

To try out Safari and the online edition of this book FREE for 45 days, go to **www.oreilly.com/go/safarienabled** and enter the coupon code OYROJFH. To see the complete Safari Library, visit safari.oreilly.com.

O'REILLY®

Spreading the knowledge of innovators

safari.oreilly.com